"Like One Family"

"Like One Family"
The Armenians of Syracuse

Arpena S. Mesrobian

Gomidas Institute
Ann Arbor, Michigan

Published by Taderon Press, P. O. Box 2735, Reading RG4 8GF, England, by arrangement with the Gomidas Institute

Printed in the United States of America
06 05 04 03 02 01 00   5 4 3 2 1

ISBN 0-9535191-1-2

For inquiries please contact:
Gomidas Institute Books
PO Box 208
Princeton, NJ 08542-0208
USA

E-mail: books@gomidas.org

To my cherished Mom and Hairig
and to my beloved Billy
who left us too soon.

Contents

Illustrations

Foreword

During a panel discussion on the state of Armenian studies in the United States, Marc Nichanian deplored the fact that the Armenian diaspora is studied so little. The diaspora should study itself, he concluded, for its own sake, as a living and self-reflexive entity.[1] Although organized Armenian communities have existed in North America for over a century, there is a dearth of knowledge about them. A few books and articles in English deal with the North American diaspora in a systematic manner.[2] However, none provide a comprehensive historical study of one specific community through which the diasporic experience of Armenians in America can be examined in a "self-reflexive" manner. The current publication does just that.

Mesrobian's account of the Syracuse Armenians is a biography of one such community—its birth, growth, and decline. It is written by a member of that community, as a participant observer. Hence, her story is intertwined with personal and family biographies. In fact, she extensively uses family archives, along with other sources, to weave her narrative. Moreover, Mesrobian examines Syracuse in the context of wider developments in Armenian life and their impact on the small community. She outlines, for example, how the Genocide affected Syracuse Armenians and what the latter did to help their kin in the Ottoman Empire. Another example is the division of the Church after

---

1. As reported in "The Next 1.5 Million," *Armenian Forum* 1, no. 1 (Spring 1998), pp. 95–97.
2. Some of the more notable (academic) sources are: Anny Bakalian, *Armenian-Americans: From Being to Feeling Armenian* (New Brunswick, N.J.: Transaction, 1993); Robert Mirak, *Torn Between Two Lands: Armenians in America, 1890 to World War I* (Cambridge, Mass.: Harvard University Press, 1983); Jenny Phillips, *Symbol, Myth, and Rhetoric: The Politics of Culture in an Armenian-American Population* (New York: AMS Press, 1989); Sarkis Atamian, *The Armenian Community: The Historical Development of a Social and Ideological Conflict* (New York: Philosophical Library, 1955). There are also more general sources on the Armenian diaspora such as: Ulf Bjorklund, "Armenia Remembered and Remade: Evolving Issues in a Diaspora" *Ethnos* 58:3-4 (1993); Khachig Tölölyan, "Exile Governments in the Armenian Polity" in *Governments-in-Exile in Contemporary World Politics,* ed. Yossi Shain (New York: Routledge, 1991). More recently, the Gomidas Institute has published memoirs of individuals who recount their experiences as immigrants in the American diaspora. See Souren Aprahamian, *From Van to Detroit: Surviving the Armenian Genocide,* (Ann Arbor, 1993); Sarkis Narzakian, *Memoirs of Sarkis Narzakian* (Ann Arbor, 1995).

Archbishop Tourian's murder in New York in 1933. It is fascinating to read about the impact this event had at the community level; how it tore friends apart and gave concrete expression to nascent tensions. Developments in Syracuse, in many ways, paralleled or were indicative of dynamics in many other small Armenian communities throughout the United States and Canada. In Mesrobian's book we also see the extent to which other debates, issues, practices, organizational matters, and habits have changed or remained the same in the past three or four generations.

Some interesting themes emerge from this study. I will mention three of the more notable ones. First, there is a strong sense of deja vu. Mesrobian describes various community events such as lectures, party meetings, fundraisers, dances, etc. But in her detailed accounts of such occasions from the 1920s to the 1940s we see a mirror reflection of community life today. It is as if she is describing activities that have taken place not three-quarters of a century ago but last week. Some of the antics and mentality of the organizers have not changed at all. Furthermore, certain issues have been constant points of debate and tension within the North American diaspora for the past century. These include the generational divide between the young and the old, the use of the Armenian language, interactions between established immigrants and latecomers, as well as their relationship with the host society. Such continuity, however, is one side of the equation.

Second, despite such consistent characteristics, there is also a significant process of change and evolution. This is the other side of the equation of diaspora existence. Change has especially affected social and family dynamics and habits: the preparation and type of food, domestic chores, marriage, and so forth. Mesrobian has some wonderful passages about the household work of Armenian women in the "old days" which one rarely sees in the present. Curiously such evolution seems to be confined to the social realm, bypassing the essential dynamics of community politics.

Finally, the experience of postwar-generation Armenians consists entirely of life in divided communities. Mesrobian's history of Syracuse reminds us of the period (before the 1930s) when the various political parties and associated organizations were more willing to cooperate with one another. They supported each other's activities, and at times collaborated on various common projects, despite ideological and practical disagreements. The modern North American diaspora no longer retains the collective memory of a more harmonious existence, with a united church. And yet, through publications like this, we are reminded that such deep divisions have not always existed, that they do not have to be the given norm. There was a time, after all, when an Iron Curtain did not exist within Armenian communities.

In many ways, the Syracuse community is a microcosm of the Armenian diaspora in North America. However, given the decline of the former, the future of the latter—of the Western diaspora—seems to be bleak. But such does not need to be the case if diaspora Armenians are willing to learn from the experiences of Syracuse. In this respect, Mesrobian has done us a great service. While her book contains a wealth of detailed information about the Syracuse community, it is also illustrative of the more general traits of the Armenian experience in North America (as well as of wider issues related to diaspora existence and ethnic minorities). Is Syracuse indicative of the future of Watertown, Massachusetts? What about Fresno or Southern Ontario? There are many lessons to be drawn here, and it is up to the reader to come up with his or her own conclusions.

RAZMIK PANOSSIAN

London School of Economics and Political Science

Preface

This account of the one-hundred-year old Armenian community in Syracuse, a city of moderate size in central New York State, does not claim any exceptional attributes for the little group that numbered no more than three hundred at the largest. Whether or not it was special and if so in what manner can perhaps be better assessed in the future, when additional community studies have emerged with which to make comparisons.

One feature has become strikingly clear, however. As the story developed, it became evident to me that the community did not live and grow in isolation. On the contrary, it was constantly under the influence of events originating in far distant areas. Even while the recently arrived immigrants sought to establish themselves in a new land, their minds and hearts remained with the families and compatriots they had left behind in a homeland which most of them would never see again. Their personal interests and organizational affairs seemed to be constantly responsive to developments affecting the Armenian people.

As I sought to tell the story of the Syracuse Armenians, I found it necessary from time to time to provide a broader historical framework for the events to become understandable. As a result, this account tells a story on more than one level. Even as it traces the growth, tragic near-destruction, and painful rebuilding of the community, it sketches the major episodes affecting the Armenian homeland—increasing Turkish oppression from which so many sought to escape, the false promise of the changed regime of 1908 followed by the 1909 massacres, the devastation of the 1915 deportations and ultimate genocide of the Armenian people, the short-lived miracle of the first Armenian Republic, Armenia's fall to Soviet rule and the capture of the Armenian church, leading to a tragic schism in the Armenian communities that has lasted to this day. There was a renewal of hope with the reemergence of Armenian independence and with the liberation of the Armenian church from Soviet control, but old problems have simply been replaced by new ones. All of these events and more have been reflected in the efforts and concerns of the small group gathered in upstate New York.

The history of the peripatetic Armenian people, constantly in search of a more hospitable environment than a homeland in the grip of foreign invaders, may be found as much in the many communities they have established throughout the globe as on Armenia's historic lands. At present, the number of Armenians living outside the Armenian Republic equals or perhaps even exceeds the three million or so that are estimated to be resident within the country's boundaries.

Wherever the wandering Armenians found peace and prosperity, they proceeded to form families and to establish their most revered institutions—church and school. Toward the end of the nineteenth century, the emerging political parties, which were created to fight oppression in the homeland, began to take an important role in the direction of Armenian diasporan community life. Cultural and benevolent organizations also came into existence.

Migrations to the New World began in the late nineteenth century with concentrations in northeastern United States, California, eastern Canada and South America. Today's settlements extend to southern and southwestern United States, western Canada and Australia. More than one million Armenians currently live in the United States according to some estimates.

It has been my view that these diasporan communities merit study not only for their own sake, but also for an understanding of the considerable influence they have exercised on events within the Armenian homeland itself. They have affected the course of Armenian history in ways that have not been adequately recognized. For example, it was from the diaspora that Armenian printing and journalism emerged. The most important Armenian periodicals were published in places far from the Armenian homeland. Western ideas of reform and liberation first took hold in the minds of expatriates and students in Russian and European universities, whose vision of a better future for the Armenian people in Turkey fueled the fires of freedom that were soon kindled in the homeland.

Conversely, as the story of the Syracuse community illustrates, events in the homeland continually resonated within the diasporan communities as well, giving direction and impetus to their efforts on behalf of a fatherland that few expected to see ever again. The eyes of the immigrant communities were turned always to the east, seeking news of the homes and loved ones left behind and always ready to respond to the continual calls for help, even while they attempted to build the institutions intended to sustain their national and religious identities in the new world they now inhabited.

It is not enough that it has been Armenia's destiny to suffer war and invasion. There also exists a dark tradition of disunity and interior conflict that persists to this day. This unfortunate trait emerged to disrupt repeated efforts to establish national structures to deal with the needs facing the Armenian people during its times of trouble. Originating at the organizational level, these conflicts penetrated the separate communities, creating attitudes that doomed successive efforts for unified action.

The Armenians of Syracuse, described at first as being "like one family," were unable to insulate themselves from such sentiments, the first hints of which are revealed in a 1915 news account. Thus it is that in the story of this little community we see reflected a generosity of spirit that extends—without question—to any fellow Armenian, as well as an unreasoning hostility resulting in a schism lasting for more than sixty-five years.

A work such as this depends heavily on information gathered in interviews. Not surprisingly, memories differ resulting in inconsistencies and contradictions, not all of which could be fully resolved. Whenever possible, I tried to confirm names, places, dates by consulting city records and other documents available to me. Among major informants were Mianzara Zahrajian Eckhoff, Leah B. Armen, Antaram Desteian, Robert Koolakian, members of St. Paul's and St. John the Baptist Church communities. Most of the interviews took place during 1983–85 and 1992–93. Sadly, many of those interviewed are with us no longer.

In addition to informants, several collections helped immeasurably. The collection of Harutun B. Azadian, which has not yet been fully assessed or catalogued, is a treasure trove of material concerning the career of a remarkable inventor, factory owner and long-time Syracuse resident. The collection is in the safe hands of Azadian's biographer, Robert Koolakian, who generously took time from his own concerns to bring many precious documents and photographs from the Azadian and Koolakian collections to my attention. I cannot adequately express my appreciation for his valued help.

Major assistance was provided by Mianzara Zahrajian Eckhoff, both through her carefully preserved collection of newspaper clippings, printed programs, and photographs on the pre- and early post-World War I period which I was privileged to receive, as well as with her many letters and observations on community and organizational life. My profound thanks to her and to her younger sister, Rose Benjamin, who supplied a few pieces belonging to her sister Aghavni Boyadjian, as well as photographs, documents and comments that were very useful to me.

The Aramtagh Book provides details on fifty male immigrants from Divrig, Turkey. It is a rare source of biographical information and I am grateful to Khachig Minasian for contributing to the record and to his son, Agishe, for entrusting this remarkable document to me.

My own collections and those of my parents, Aaron H. and Eliza Sachaklian, supplied much material on Armenian community life in Syracuse, especially from the 1930s to the present. Aaron H. Sachaklian's papers provided valuable insights on the activities of the Armenian Revolutionary Federation, of which he was a prominent and dedicated member. I thank my mother and father for the many precious letters, speeches, documents and photographs they retained. Because of the schism in the community that took place in 1933, my holdings on the two communities that came into existence are not of equal depth. As a consequence of the beliefs espoused by my family, we (and others like us) and the institutions we were associated with were shunned during the hateful early days of the split. Things have calmed somewhat now although the break still exists. Nevertheless, individuals belonging to the "other" church responded generously and without reserve to my questions and I have tried to quote them fairly and accurately. To those who provided information and useful photographs, books, and occasional pieces, I express my deep appreciation.

Finally, to Syracuse University's Professor Stephen Webb, I express my enduring gratitude. This book owes much to his friendly guidance and encouragement.

Transliteration posed special problems which could not be neatly resolved. Scholarly usage gives preference to the eastern Armenian pronunciation, but that system seemed inappropriate for this work. The great majority of the Syracuse Armenians use the western dialects. They rendered their names into English in what presumably seemed to them to be equivalent sounds, but individuals often differed in the spellings of their names in English, even for names that are the same in Armenian. Variant spellings of the family name sometimes occurred as well.

A word about my own background: American-born, I have resided in Syracuse almost without interruption since coming to the city as an infant in 1920. In 1937–38 I spent a year as a student at the Armenian College of Beirut in Lebanon, the "Jemaran," at a time when Armenian community life there was in full flower. Here I was privileged to meet the giants in education and literature, Levon Shant and Nigol Aghpalian, legendary leaders of the Armenian Republic such as the last premier, Simon Vratzian, and others as well as the first few Armenian intellectuals arising from the new generation. This experience made an impact that has remained with me all of my life.

Beirut as it was in those exciting days epitomizes for me the ideal authentic Armenian community whose dynamism and rich cultural, intellectual and organizational achievements lay infinitely beyond the reach of the modest Syracuse Armenians, very few of whom had been educated beyond elementary school level. Yet, I recognize the aspirations exhibited by the Syracusans in their many public and organizational meetings, speeches, songs, plays and rudimentary efforts to establish schools for the teaching of Armenian language and history. What they lacked in polish and sophistication was offset by their earnestness and dedication. As the story shows, however, the early intensity of commitment has become diluted in today's community members, whose numbers are decreasing. This is a time that calls for rededication and renewal, if a Syracuse Armenian community is to continue to exist. Perhaps a look at the past will show us the way to the future.

"Like One Family"

I

To World War I:
Coming to a New Land

Beginnings

The first Armenian known to have come to the New World was called "Martin the Armenian." He was a member of the Virginia colony in 1618 or 1619. When he returned to England with some tobacco he had grown in the colony, customs officials imposed double the usual duties because of his foreign birth. Claiming to be a free man of Virginia, Martin successfully petitioned the London Company for relief. In 1653, two Armenians, expert silkworm cultivators, were brought to Virginia to develop sericulture. Other than these few historic figures, practically no Armenians appeared on the American scene prior to the 1830s.[1]

In the nineteenth century the American missionary movement in Turkey awakened the interest of Armenians in the prospect of studying in the United States. It is estimated that before 1890 from sixty to seventy-five individuals emigrated for that purpose. They probably knew English, having learned the language at the American Mission Board schools in Turkey, and it is likely that many of them were Protestants, rather than members of the Armenian Apostolic Church. They liked their new country so well that few of them returned.[2]

Some who made America their home made notable contributions to their new country. For example, Khachadour Osganyan, the first immigrant to come to America (1834) as result of missionary activity, became a feature writer for the *New York Herald-Tribune* and was elected president of the New York Press Club. Christopher Der Seropian, who arrived in 1843 to enter Yale

1. M. Vartan Malcom, *The Armenians in America* (Boston, Chicago: The Pilgrim Press, 1919), pp. 51–57.
2. Robert Mirak, *Torn Between Two Lands: Armenians in America 1890 to World War I* (Cambridge, Mass.: The Department of Near Eastern Languages and Civilizations, Harvard University, 1983), p. 37.

University, became a physician. He created the green ink that is used on American paper currency.[3]

Little by little, additional Armenians, mostly young males, sought opportunity in that fabled land to the west. Until the late 1880s, fifteen hundred Armenians are estimated to have migrated to the United States. Their numbers continued to increase until mid-1892 when the Turkish government abruptly curtailed travel permits for the Armenians. The reason for this action soon became clear with the beginning of massacres of Armenians in the interior provinces. The terror lasted from 1894 to 1896. One hundred thousand Armenians were killed and half a million had become homeless and robbed of all their belongings.[4]

Not surprisingly, the flight to America was spurred by these events. During the 1890s more than twelve thousand Armenians left Turkey. Everyone from business people and professionals to artisans and peasants joined the movement. Unlike those coming to America from many European countries, who were firmly turning their backs on their homelands, the early Armenian immigrants at first intended to work and send money to their families, expecting eventually to return to their homes with their savings. As conditions worsened in Turkey, however, the Armenians' objectives changed. They now planned to remain in America.[5]

Oppression, poverty, and the desire to escape the Turkish military draft were among the reasons for a great increase in migrations through the period 1900–1914. By 1914 more than sixty thousand Armenians had arrived in the new land.[6] Even the new Turkish regime of 1908 which permitted exit as well as entry to Turkey and promised a more democratic atmosphere was not to be believed, as the 1909 massacres in Adana soon revealed. Armenian community life in Syracuse began to flower during this period.

John Bayerian, from Marash, is generally considered to be the first Armenian in Syracuse, although at least two other Armenian young men are known to have been in the city at almost the same time. His daughter, Leah Armen, told me his story. To avoid conscription in the Turkish army, he sought to escape on a ship, but was apprehended and put in prison. After a brief imprisonment, he succeeded in his efforts to leave the country and eventually reached the port of Philadelphia in 1893, arriving with only a few cents in his pocket. From there he went to Waltham, Massachusetts, where he learned watchmaking. He came to Syracuse soon after and worked for Solvay Process

---

3. Malcom, p. 57; p. 98.
4. Mirak, p. 44; p. 46.
5. Ibid., p. 44; pp. 48ff.
6. Ibid., p. 59.

Company.[7] By 1895, he was a Syracuse resident, as shown in a photograph taken with another early arrival, Nazareth Rejebian.

John H. Bayerian appears in the Syracuse City Directory of 1896–97. He is identified as a laborer and a boarder at 951 Emerson Avenue. He was probably a bachelor when the information was secured, and by the time the directory appeared in print he had probably resided in Syracuse for at least a year or two.

Four years after his arrival in the United States. Bayerian wrote to his boyhood friends in Marash to ask for their sister's hand in marriage. They agreed, as did their sister, Mariam Yeranian, and the young bride-to-be, with money sent by her fiance and with the aid of American missionaries, set forth on the long journey to Syracuse.

Mary had suffered greatly from seasickness and upon arrival was immediately befriended by the Gifford sisters, Frances and Helen. The Giffords were the last survivors of a family closely associated with the city's earlier history. They lived together in the old family home, built by their father in 1835, at 501 West Genesee Street. Their father was the founder of the First Presbyterian Church in Syracuse, to which the two sisters were devoted.[8]

The Gifford sisters took Mary under their care. First, they oversaw her recovery to health, then they sponsored an elaborate wedding ceremony, which took place in 1897. According to Bayerian's daughter, the marriage took place in the West Genesee Presbyterian Church, with Rev. Edward Winshurst officiating. The city directory for 1896–97 lists a West End Presbyterian Church at 1207 Milton Avenue, Rev. E. Winshurst, pastor. This is probably where the ceremony took place. The West End Presbyterian Church does not appear in the 1904 directory. Four ministers who had been missionaries in Turkey assisted, and the witnesses were Mr. and Mrs. N. B. Tice and Frances B. Gifford.[9]

The young couple enjoyed a good education. Both were Protestants. Bayerian had studied at the St. Paul Institute in Tarsus, a school operated by

7. At that time, Syracuse apparently offered good employment opportunities. The city had been growing rapidly, soaring from 44,769 in 1870 to 100,179 in 1892, according to the Syracuse City Directory for 1892–93. From 1891 to 1892 alone, there was an increase of 4,306.

8. *Obituaries and Biographical Clippings of Residents of Syracuse; Onondaga County; and Adjacent Areas of Central New York from about 1860 to 1926,* vol. 9G, Collected and Compiled by the Local History Department, Syracuse Public Library, Syracuse, New York, pp. 136–37.

9. The 1896–97 Syracuse City Directory lists Norman Tice, engineer, whose home was on Caroline Street, near Milton Avenue, Solvay. Mrs. Armen stated that her parents boarded for a short time at that address.

the American Mission Board, and knew several languages, including English, Armenian, and Turkish. His wife attended boarding school in Marash, where she learned English, and acquired a diploma in 1895 in Froebel's System of Education in Kindergarten. This remarkable accomplishment merits brief attention. Friedrich Froebel was a German educator, born in 1782, who developed an educational system called kindergarten for young children. Considered by the Prussian government to be "breeding grounds for budding revolutionaries," the kindergartens were ordered closed in 1851. The kindergarten teachers whom Froebel had trained left Germany and started their own kindergartens abroad.[10]

Apparently, the movement had spread as far as Marash, Turkey, where Mariam Yeranian received her training. Leah Armen has stated that at the time her mother received Bayerian's proposal, Mariam was tutor to Mustafa Kemal Ataturk's child. Mariam may have tutored the child of a high-ranking Turk, but it probably was not that of Mustafa Kemal, who was born in 1881.

John Bayerian, laborer, is listed in the 1902–3 Syracuse city directory as living at 704 West Belden Avenue. In the 1904 directory he is identified as a machinist. He was employed for a time as superintendent by the Standard Gauge Manufacturing Company. The company transferred him to Foxboro, Massachusetts, where the family lived for five and one-half years, then he resigned to return to Syracuse, where he found employment in the Azadian Gauge Manufacturing Company.

The Bayerians had four children. The eldest, Grant, born in 1898, was the first Armenian born in Syracuse. His sister, Leah, born in 1900, was the second.

According to Leah Armen, her parents conversed with each other in Turkish, but changed to English to address their children. For a while their mother attempted to teach her children Armenian, but eventually abandoned her efforts.

Bayerian and his wife were devoted to their Presbyterian church. Several people have mentioned that he always carried a Bible in his pocket and was always in church on Sunday.[11] There is no evidence that they ever attended the occasional Armenian Apostolic services held in Syracuse by itinerant priests.

Religious affiliation has significance in understanding the Armenian community. Under the Turkish *millet* system, the ethnic groups in Turkey were

---

10. Diploma in Armen collection; *1782–1982: Friedrich Froebel,* bicentenary booklet; letter, H. P. J. Liebschner to Arpena Mesrobian, March 2, 1983. At the time, Liebschner was seeking a publisher for his biography of Froebel.
11. Mianzara Zahrajian Eckhoff.

divided into "religious rather than national and racial units."[12] It was the Armenian Apostolic patriarch who governed the Armenian people in Turkey. Thus, in Turkey Protestant Armenians were excluded from identification as Armenian nationals by the Ottoman authorities. Moreover, the American Mission Board schools tended to teach in Turkish language, rather than Armenian. Their graduates, especially those from western Turkey where the government sometimes prohibited the use of Armenian language, felt more comfortable in Turkish, rather than in Armenian. It was not uncommon for Armenian Protestants to use Turkish, rather than Armenian, even for familiar prayers such as the Lord's Prayer or grace before meals. In America, English often supplanted both Turkish and Armenian in the Protestant services. The Armenian ministers (called *badveli* in Armenian) "rarely urged their parishioners to speak the ancestral language at home."[13] On the other hand, Apostolic Armenians, especially the products of the church schools or academies, usually placed great value on the preservation of the Armenian language. The exhortation to their American-born children to "speak Armenian" was commonly made in many immigrant households.

The Bayerians were not closely involved in the affairs of the Armenian community. They are pictured in a group photograph identified by Mrs. Armen as having been taken in 1914 in Onondaga Park, but are absent from later group pictures.[14] They do not appear to have taken part in organizational affairs. According to an informant, Mianzara Zahrajian Eckhoff, they never attended programs of the Armenian political parties. Their daughter recalled that some Armenian family would come to visit every Sunday, obliging their hosts to serve them dinner, but that her parents never returned the visits.

So customary are linkages among Armenians that I was pleased but not surprised to learn many years later that Mrs. Bayerian's brother, by that time a minister, had attended my parents' engagement party in 1910 in Dort Yol, Turkey. Even this tie, however, did not establish a special relationship between the two families. Formal evening visits by both of my parents did not take place and my mother's daytime calls in the company of her small children were not reciprocated.

---

12. Mirak, p. 6.
13. Mirak, "On New Soil: The Armenian Orthodox and Armenian Protestant Churches in the New World to 1915," in *Immigrants and Religion in Urban America,* ed. Randall M. Miller and Thomas D. Marzik (Philadelphia: Temple University Press, 1988), p. 152. Note that Armenians often prefer to call their church "Apostolic," rather than "Orthodox."
14. Photograph in Armen collection.

Picnic in Onondaga Park, 1914. One of the earliest known pictures of the Syracuse Armenian community.

Leah Armen as well as the daughter of Nazareth Rejebian said that Rejebian was one of the earliest Armenians in Syracuse to make himself known to John Bayerian. Like Bayerian, Rejebian was also the product of a Protestant mission school. He had come from Hadjin, Turkey, to study in the United States. Rejebian's daughter, Vesta, did not know where he went to school, but stated that he studied chemistry and pharmacy and worked for Solvay Process Company. His name does not appear in any of the city directories for that period. Rejebian returned to Turkey and married there in 1903. He fathered several children, then was taken into the Turkish army where he died. His wife and children came to Syracuse in 1934.

Nazareth Rejebian's brother, Vahram, also lived in Syracuse at one time. He worked for Azadian Gauge Manufacturing Company and appears in a photo of the machine shop taken in 1912.[15] According to Robert Koolakian, Vahram left Syracuse to work for Stephen Philibosian, a former Syracusan, in Georgia and eventually moved west.

Like John Bayerian, Harutun Bab Azadian, who came to Syracuse in 1899, was a watchmaker. He was an inventor and precision instrument maker as well. The firm he established in Syracuse, the Azadian Gauge Manufacturing Company, was to employ numerous Armenians—among them John Bayerian—and bring Azadian to national attention as one of the country's outstanding instrument makers.[16]

---

15. Identified by Robert Koolakian.

Azadian came from a wealthy, illustrious family in Constantinople. His technical skills became evident at an early age and he was sent to Geneva, Switzerland for apprenticeship in watchmaking and to study mathematics and astronomy. He continued his education in Paris, where he studied art and engraving, and at the Polytechnicum in Stuttgart, Germany.

While in Germany, he was a frequent visitor at the home of a German family in Leipzig, who had given refuge to his fiancee, Akabi Kechebashian, after her father and brother were killed in a Turkish attack, probably during the 1895–96 massacres. Akabi came from an Evangelical family in Cesarea. They also owned a summer home in Smyrna. She had been educated in Vienna and knew several languages, including English. While teaching at the Armenian Girls School in Scutari, Constantinople at the American Bible House, she developed a close friendship with a woman from Leipzig named Johanna Zimmer, who was a member of the same staff.

It was Johanna Zimmer who had urged Akabi to leave Turkey with her and move to Leipzig, and Zimmer again who suggested that Akabi accompany her on a trip to the United States, where she had a relative. Akabi, as well as Azadian, agreed to the trip, and on October 1, 1899, all three set out for the United States. On arrival, the travelers were greeted by Mr. and Mrs. George Hine of Syracuse, with whom they stayed until finding quarters for themselves. Hine was a lawyer. His wife, Julia, Johanna Zimmer's cousin, was Professor of German at Syracuse University.

The two women soon settled in. Johanna Zimmer became a German teacher and Akabi enrolled in the Women's and Children's Hospital for nursing training. Mr. Azadian had intended to remain for only a short time, but within a few weeks his fiancee informed him that she would not return to Constantinople. For about a year he attempted to support himself doing engraving, lithography, and etching for book illustrations. In the spring of 1901 he went to work at the Syracuse Improved Gauge Company. Soon afterwards he and Akabi were married. At one time their household also included Akabi's mother and two sisters.

Azadian's technical skills very quickly became evident. His adjustable rack-and-pinion mechanism was granted a patent in 1902. This was followed by many inventions and improvements. His association with Brown Company Industries in 1899 led eventually to his doing all the die gauge work for Brown Company Industries which in turn was supplying parts for Henry Ford's

---

16. Robert George Koolakian, "Mr. Azadian Came to America," Master's thesis, State University of New York College at Oneonta, 1967; Mr. Koolakian's oral comments and materials from the Azadian collection provided much of the information concerning the Azadians that appears in this work.

Model T automobile. Ford supervised the work personally and visited the Syracuse plant more than once, as indicated by a telegram from Ford to Azadian dated May 17, 1908, in the Azadian collection.

In addition to these activities, Azadian apparently also sought to develop another business from his home at 410½ Burnet Avenue. A name card in the Azadian collection identifies him as a "Specialist" in oriental rug repair and cleaning. Oriental rug sales and repair were familiar occupations for many Armenians, but there is no evidence that Azadian himself had any of the necessary skills. Some individual from the small Armenian community may have been available for this service.

In 1909, at the age of thirty-four, Mr. Azadian embarked on his own enterprise, the Azadian Gauge Manufacturing Company, located on the sixth floor of the Syracuse Industrial Building at 107 North Franklin Street. None of the six initial employees were Armenian. Before the first World War came to an end, the firm employed more than sixty workers.[17] The Azadian factory provided employment opportunities for numerous immigrants, including Armenians, as indicated by its payrolls.[18]

According to payroll records in the Azadian collection, the first Armenian whom Azadian employed was Yeprem Saxenian, listed on the payroll for December 11–18, 1909. During 1910, others followed: Khachadour (Harry) Aghaian, Mr. Medigian, Setrak Kalebdjian, Ghougas Zahrajian. During 1911 there were still more: Mr. Kevorkian, Mr. Ruzian, Khachig Minasian, Mr. Deverian. By 1912, three of the Babikian children were also working for Azadian. By the end of 1910, the firm had seventeen employees. To the end of 1912, Azadian even employed a Turk, Mr. Durmush, which evoked Mrs. Azadian's displeasure, according to Robert Koolakian. The Azadian factory also employed many women, but none of them were Armenian.

While studying mechanical engineering in Germany, Azadian became acquainted with Charles Proteus Steinmetz, later associated with General Electric Company, who became recognized as one of the outstanding electrical geniuses of the United States. They became good friends and maintained close contacts long after both became established in the United States.[19] According to Azadian's biographer, Robert Koolakian, Azadian and Steinmetz shared an involvement in the development of ballistics and firearms. Steinmetz frequently visited the Azadians and often took Azadian with him on trips for

---

17. Koolakian, p. 92.
18. Ibid., p. 155.
19. Ibid., p. 133. A photograph in the Azadian collection shows Azadian and Steinmetz with a group of young men in Germany. The Azadian collection includes other photographs of Steinmetz.

business and pleasure to Schenectady and Niagara Falls. It may have been this association that led to Azadian's appointment to the consortium of technical advisors who served the United States War Industries Board headed by Bernard Baruch under President Woodrow Wilson's administration. This Board included Charles Steinmetz, Thomas Edison, George Eastman, Henry Ford, and other notable inventors and industrialists of the day.[20]

Business was good and Azadian was very skilled, but also "eccentric," according to Setrak Kalebdjian, his general manager for the period 1910–13. "He often spent more money on the development of instruments than he made."[21]

The Azadians' social contacts among non-Armenians and knowledge of English probably facilitated their early entry into Syracuse civic life. In 1908 or 1909, Azadian joined the Masonic order and Mrs. Azadian became a member of Eastern Star. Both were active in Masonic affairs for the remainder of their lives. Azadian was a charter member of Rotary and his wife was in the Women of Rotary. Husband and wife helped to establish the Americanization League in 1916 and worked actively to engage Armenians in its affairs. In 1919 they became founding supporting members of the Syracuse Symphony Orchestra.

Both Mr. and Mrs. Azadian took a keen interest, as well, in the welfare of the early Armenian community in Syracuse. Mianzara Zahrajian Eckhoff, who came to Syracuse in 1912 as a young girl, recalled that Mrs. Azadian was a "most wonderful person. In the early days when Armenians came here most of them could not speak English. They all called her for doctor or other things. She would be right there to help. In those days people did not have cars like today. She had to go on the trolly car, always helped them."[22]

For his part, Mr. Azadian appears to have entered into Armenian community life and especially the affairs of the Armenian Apostolic church, particularly during the second decade when the size of the community was growing rapidly. Some of those activities will be described later.

At first the Azadians attended the public meetings and programs sponsored by the organizations and political parties. The Azadians are included in the 1914 picnic photograph along with the Bayerians. Mr. Azadian presided at a 1916 memorial program for Armenians massacred in Turkey,[23] and Mrs. Azadian opened a program that was held to encourage Armenian women to

---

20. Arshalouis Azadian Randall, Foreword, p. 2 in "Mr. Azadian Came to America."
21. Koolakian, p. 136.
22. Letter, Eckhoff to Mesrobian, October 3, 1985. Mrs. Eckhoff also said of Mrs. Azadian, "She was the brains."
23. Printed notice in Eckhoff collection.

form an Armenian Red Cross unit.[24] Later, however, they did not appear at events of the Armenian Revolutionary Federation (ARF). Most of the men working for Azadian were "Tashnag" (members of the Armenian Revolutionary Federation), but Mrs. Azadian "was against the Tashnags."[25] It has been noted that Mrs. Azadian came from a wealthy urban family. Well-to-do Armenian urbanites tended to view the Armenian Revolutionary Federation, a radical party, with distaste, blaming its provocations for Turkish attacks against the Armenian minority populations.[26]

In 1919 Mr. Azadian moved his factory to 241 West Adams Street, merging it with the Strandell & Metzger Machine Company which was at the site. He incorporated the firm under the name Azadian Instrument Corporation and continued there until his death in 1965.[27]

Another pioneer, Harry Panos Philibosian, may have arrived in Syracuse almost as early as Bayerian and Nazareth Rejebian. Philibosian left his native Hadjin to come to the United States in 1894 and apparently came to Syracuse soon afterwards. He was probably the first Armenian to open his own firm in Syracuse. His oriental rug store, the Persian Palace Rug Company, was established in 1898, and was followed by branches in Columbus, Ohio and Rochester, New York, as well as a summer store in Richfield Springs, New York.[28]

The Syracuse City Directory of 1904 carries the listing: Philibosian, H. P. (Philibosian & Seferian) 414 S. Salina St., h. 409 Midland Ave. E. H. Seferian is listed at the same business and home addresses. The street directory gives an additional name as living at 409 Midland Avenue, so it may have been a boarding house. The listing in the 1905 directory is identical, except that Mr. Seferian's home is listed as Columbus, Ohio.

Philibosian apparently later branched into real estate. He owned the block on the corner of Onondaga and Salina Streets from the Strand Theater to the end of the block (where a parking garage stands today). There were two-family houses in the back. Philibosian, who lived on Salt Springs Road, later sold his properties and moved to California.[29]

24. *Hairenik,* October 23, 1915. Clipping in Eckhoff collection.
25. Letter, Eckhoff to Mesrobian, February 6, 1983.
26. Sarkis Atamian, *The Armenian Community* (New York: Philosophical Library, 1955), p. 118.
27. Koolakian, p. 170.
28. Name of firm and date of founding appear on letterhead, in Koolakian collection. Biographical information is from *Armenian/American Outlook,* vol. VIII, no. 1, Spring 1972, p. 4.
29. Letter, Eckhoff to Mesrobian, February 6, 1983. According to Koolakian, Philibosian left Syracuse in 1924.

Although Philibosian's name does not appear in the Armenian newspaper accounts of the various public meetings, he may have been an important presence in the Armenian community. Mrs. Eckhoff remarked that "Azadian and Philibosian tried to outdo each other."[30] According to Robert Koolakian, Azadian and Philibosian were close friends but friendly rivals when it came to buying new automobiles. Azadian bought Cadillacs and Philibosian favored Hudsons.

Harry Philibosian's young nephew, Stephen, also lived in Syracuse for a few years. In 1908, taking advantage of a new regime in Turkey that would allow expatriates to return without fear of retribution, Harry returned to Turkey to visit his family. They were now living in Tarsus, near Adana. On his return to America, Harry took Stephen with him. While still on the journey, in France, they heard about the massacres that broke out in April of 1909 in the district of Adana. After months of anguish, they learned that Stephen's family—his parents, two sisters, and a younger brother—had been spared, having taken refuge in St. Paul's American College in Tarsus. Six months later, at Stephen's insistence, they arrived in Syracuse.[31]

Stephen first went to work at W. S. Peck of Syracuse, a men's clothing factory, at a salary of one dollar a day for a ten-hour work day, six days a week. After one week, his uncle removed him, announcing that Stephen would now work in Philibosian's oriental rug store at 414 South Salina Street, directly across from Dey Brothers Department Store. He promised to pay three dollars a week plus room and board.

After Stephen's family arrived, he felt greatly pressured to make enough money so his fifty-year-old father would not have to work. After several attempts to sell oriental rugs in the nearby cities of Cortland and Auburn, he became a buyer for the oriental rug department in the H. R. Wait Furniture Store in Auburn. Stephen then took a position in a department store in Atlanta, Georgia, after which he went into business for himself. His subsequent great success enabled him to become involved in many charitable and benevolent activities.

John Philibosian, another nephew of Harry Philibosian, came to Syracuse in 1912. He worked for his uncle in the oriental rug business until the war started, when he enlisted. After the war ended, aided by the Red Cross, he was able to bring his family to this country. John went into the rug business for himself and eventually settled in California.[32]

---

30. Letter, Eckhoff to Mesrobian, February 6, 1983.
31. *Armenian/American Outlook,* Spring 1972. The entire issue is devoted to Stephen Philibosian.
32. *AMAA News,* vol. XX, no. 6, December 1986, p. 22

The Babikian brothers, Mihran and Nishan, arrived in the United States "around 1900 or 1903," according to Nishan's grandson, Leon Vetzikian. From New York they traveled to Pennsylvania and to Watervliet, then to Syracuse where both brothers found work at the M. L. Oberdorfer Company. According to another source, however, the two brothers came to America in late 1895. They lived in New York, Providence, Milford, and other communities, settling eventually in Syracuse in 1908.[33]

Within a few weeks they sent for their wives and families—fifteen people. For a short time the two brothers were employed in the Azadian factory. Their names appear in the payroll lists for 1910. Soon, however, the two families settled on a rented farm (located on Thompson Road approximately where Carrier Corporation stands today), which they eventually purchased, and started farming. They appear to have been very hospitable—"all the bachelors used to go there." "Mihran got jobs for them at Oberdorfer."[34]

The Babikian farm of about one hundred acres[35] became a gathering place for the entire Armenian community, which held picnics there every summer. Even today many recall taking the trolley to the corner of James Street and Thompson Road, and setting out for the long walk up Thompson Road, hoping to be rescued by the Babikians' horse and wagon and later by one of the few automobiles owned by the young members of the community. The house was not large enough to accommodate the large crowds that used to gather. I recall taking refuge in the henhouse during a sudden rainstorm and deciding that getting wet was preferable to enduring the stench of the coop.

Another early Syracusan was George Koolakian from Banderma. Like so many others he sought to avoid conscription in the Turkish army. Slipping quietly away from his home in 1905 without attempting to sell his family property to avoid signaling his intentions, he left his wife and young son behind, intending to send for them later.[36] An expert tailor, he found employment in New York City with the Schantz Clothing Company. Soon he developed a friendship with Harry Philibosian from Syracuse who came periodically to New York on business. At the invitation of his new friend, Koolakian visited Syracuse and liked the city so well he decided to remain and open his own business in custom and merchant tailoring.

---

33. *Hunchagian Darekirk Amerigayi Shrchani, Arachin Dari [Hunchagian Yearbook, American Region, First Year]*, (Providence: Social Democrat Hunchagian Party American Region, 1931), p. 276.

34. Leon Vetzikian.

35. Agishe Minasian.

36. Koolakian, Introduction, p. 1 in "Mr. Azadian Came to America."

The two Babikian brothers and their wives and children in front of their farm-house where they all lived together, approximately 1915. Also in the photo are some of the many friends who came frequently to visit.

Before long he was able to send for his wife and son both of whom arrived in Syracuse in the fall of 1908. Arrangements for their passage from Constantinople were made under auspices of William Peet at the American Bible House in Constantinople, according to a telegram Koolakian received from Julia Ward Howe dated June 30, 1908.[37] Koolakian was unable to travel to New York to greet them on arrival, so his friend Philibosian met the family at Ellis Island, brought them to Syracuse, and provided housing for the family until they were able to find quarters for themselves.[38] Philibosian maintained his interest in Koolakian, lending him the money to purchase his first home, and later encouraging him to purchase a farm on Beattie Hill in the Salt Springs district of Syracuse in June, 1916 within walking distance of the Philibosian farm. Both farms became gathering places for the Armenians of that time.

---

37. Telegram in Koolakian collection. W. W. Peet was treasurer of the American Missions in Turkey.
38. Koolakian.

The city offered attractive prospects for those with tailoring skills. For many decades through the nineteenth century, the manufacture of men's clothing had been a leading industry in Syracuse. When a fire in the eighteen eighties destroyed the manufacturing lofts in James and Salina streets, manufacturers were forced to farm out the business to local tailors, who mostly lived in the Second Ward. Contracting the business proved to be so satisfactory that the plant was never reopened.[39] The Syracuse City Directory for 1894–95 lists no fewer than one hundred eighty-one individuals and establishments under the heading "Clothiers and Merchant Tailors."

Practically upon his arrival in Syracuse, Koolakian formed a fast friendship with Azadian, who regarded him as his best friend.[40] At Azadian's invitation, Koolakian accompanied him on several business trips to Schenectady and Niagara Falls in company with Steinmetz and a Steinmetz associate, Ernst J. Berg. He made a suit of clothes for Berg in 1906 and again in 1914. Koolakian was a good amateur photographer and, according to Robert Koolakian, the Koolakian collection contains his many portraits and outdoor photos documenting the Armenians in Syracuse as early as 1906 as well as Syracuse buildings and scenes.

Koolakian was generous toward newcomers, as others have been. "Mr. Koolakian opened his tailor shop to those who were tailors and taught those who could hold a needle," said Mrs. Eckhoff.[41] Onnig Enfiejian, the three Apikian brothers (Minas, Krikor, and Harry), possibly John Hanessian, and numerous others all started tailoring with "High Fashion Koolakian Tailors."[42]

The eldest of the three Apikian brothers, Minas, was the first to come to Syracuse, arriving in 1910. He and Koolakian had been friends in Banderma. His brother Harry as well as his parents came with a compatriot, Peter Roomian, in 1913.[43] Roomian, also a tailor, was a distant relative of Koolakian's wife. Both Roomian and Y. Ayanian also worked for Koolakian following their arrival.

Among others who arrived during the first decade were Khachadour Aghaian, Mr. and Mrs. Dickran Desteian, and Ghougas Zahrajian. Aghaian, who came from Palou, probably in 1907, became founder and owner of several Midstate grocery stores in Syracuse. The Desteians came from Sepastia

39. Franklin H. Chase, *Syracuse and Its Environs* (New York and Chicago: Lewis Historical Publishing Company, Inc., 1924), vol. 1, p. 461.
40. Randall, Foreword, p. 2 in Koolakian.
41. Letter, Rose Zahrajian Benjamin to Mesrobian, relaying information from Eckhoff, October 6, 1982.
42. Ibid.
43. Nevart Apikian.

with their three young daughters. Both the Desteian and Zahrajian families were drawn to Syracuse because of the Azadians.[44]

Desteian preferred Syracuse over the pressures of living in a city as large as New York. Moreover, his brother's marriage in 1904 in Syracuse to Mrs. Azadian's sister, Dziadzan, had established a kinship with a resident family. The brother, Avedis, had come to America in 1898, and in Syracuse had become acquainted with the Azadian family which included Mrs. Azadian's mother and two sisters. By the time of the Desteians' arrival, Avedis had moved to Grand Rapids, where Dziadzan died only a year after the marriage. Avedis came from Grand Rapids to greet his family and get them settled in an upper flat on Burnet Avenue, in a three-family building that housed the Azadians on the first floor. Dickran Desteian had been a shoemaker and found work in the Nettleton shoe factory, where he stayed until retirement.[45]

Zahrajian, an inventor as well as a skilled mechanic and draftsman, came to Troy in 1909 from Rodosto, near Constantinople. He then moved to Syracuse where he found employment in Azadian's factory. He had heard about Azadian from other people from Rodosto who were already in Syracuse.[46] Zahrajian, literate in Armenian, went to night school to learn English. Inventive by nature, he had learned his trade by working for others. A pressure gauge he invented was issued a patent.[47] Other inventions and improvements were put into use by the Azadian company.

As the number of Armenian immigrants began to increase, the newcomers turned to earlier arrivals, especially to those who had their own businesses, to help them find employment. In my interviews, not once was I told of anyone's refusal to help.

The Second Wave

The Armenian massacres in 1909 opened the floodgates of emigration from Turkey. "By 1907 nearly 3,000 Armenians were arriving annually in America and in 1913 nearly 10,000 Armenians entered the promised land."[48] Growth of the Syracuse Armenian community reflected the typical pattern of increase. The early immigrants, both bachelors as well as married men, began to send for their families, and families began to arrive together.

Among those arriving during this period were the Kalebdjian brothers, Setrak and Missak, with their mother, Elise. They arrived after the Adana

---

44. Koolakian; Antaram Desteian.
45. Desteian.
46. Letter, Eckhoff to Mesrobian, February 6, 1983.
47. Document is in Benjamin collection.
48. Mirak, *Torn Between Two Lands,* p. 49.

massacres of 1909. Setrak, a graduate of Robert College in Constantinople, found employment with the Azadian firm. Later, he and his brother opened a meat market.

Zahrajian's family—his wife and four daughters—arrived in 1912, escorted by Onnig Enfiejian. At that time there were around one hundred fifty Armenians in Syracuse, according to Mrs. Eckhoff. The community grew rapidly to mid-decade. Mr. Enfiejian's wife, who was related to Mr. Zahrajian, came about three or four years later.

The Zahrajian parents knew Turkish, like most of the Armenians from Turkey, but they spoke Armenian in the home. Mrs. Zahrajian was among the minority of Armenian immigrants who were not literate in Armenian. The daughters knew Armenian fluently and soon appeared on stage before the Armenian public. In the accounts appearing in *Hairenik,* the official newspaper of the Armenian Revolutionary Federation, a political party about which more will be said later, the eldest daughter, Mannig, was referred to as *unger,* "comrade," indicating that she was a member. This was unusual for a woman at that time. The next two daughters, Aghavni and Mianzara, performed frequently at public events and were often named in the *Hairenik* news reports of this period. Mianzara took flute and voice lessons. The youngest at the time, Zarouhi, who is distinguished in photographs by her long curls, also appeared in performances.

A private record book, here called "Aramtagh Book," provides brief, but useful profiles of fifty male immigrants from the village of Aramtagh near Divrig, a city not far from Sivas (Sepastia) in central Turkey. The biographical entries appear to have been recorded by Khachig Minasian.[49] According to this record, the fifty male immigrants profiled on pages 9 through 67 arrived in the United States as follows:

Year	Number of Arrivals
1903	1
1905	1
1906	2
1908	2
1909	2
1910	3

49. The book was entrusted to me by Agishe Minasian, Khachig's son. See Appendix for description.

Year	Number of Arrivals
1911	4
1912	23
1915	7
1918	2
1920	1
1927	2

Of the above fifty men, twenty-eight made Syracuse their home for at least part of their lives. Many of them came to Syracuse by way of Troy or Watervliet, where a colony of their compatriots had previously gathered to seek information and guidance from those who had arrived earlier. It is clear that they kept in close touch and assisted each other. The record notes that Minas Giragosian, who had arrived in 1905, was settled in Watervliet where he owned property. "For that reason,"[50] many compatriots, on arrival in this country, went to his address. Giragosian may not have had wealth, but presumably his property provided a stable address to which newcomers could direct their steps.

The young men from Aramtagh came from a rural environment and had no special skills or education which could be employed in their new country. Until coming to America, they were farmers.[51] Their education probably did not extend much beyond the elementary level, although they appear to have been sufficiently skilled in arithmetic and record-keeping to maintain successful businesses in later life. Most of them appear to have moved about until choosing a community that suited them. Several worked as laborers on the roads in Iowa, probably earning not more than one or two dollars a day.[52] Massis Arayan labored on the highways and then on the railroad until his death. Most of the laborers, however, returned to Syracuse where they went to work for the Solvay Process Company or L. C. Smith typewriter factory. Few remained in the factories for long, preferring to open their own businesses. At least seven of the Aramtagh men operated grocery stores, located well apart from each other in different sections of the city.

---

50. Aramtagh Book, p. 11
51. Ibid., p. 107.
52. "Immigration," *Humanities*, National Endowment for the Humanities, vol. 4, no. 3, August 1983, p. 12.

Khachig Minasian, the keeper of the Aramtagh Book, came to Watervliet in 1910 then to Syracuse in 1911 where he worked in Azadian's factory.[53] His wife and son arrived in 1913. Minasian's original family name had been Parghamian, but he changed it on arrival in Syracuse to avoid being confused with other unrelated Parghamians in the city. As his son, Azad, explained it, "There were too many families named Parghamian." Minasian and a compatriot, Hagop Dumanian, bought a farm "in Camillus,"[54] but sold it after two years.[55] Minasian operated his own barber shop for a number of years, then worked at L. C. Smith from where he retired.

Some of the married men remained separated from their wives and families for long years until their fortunes allowed them to send money for passage. Arakel Bedigian waited seventeen years, Khachig Parghamian fifteen years, and Abraham Nigolian fourteen years.[56] Several Aramtagh men returned to *yergir* ("country") to marry and return with their brides or to bring back wives and families. A hapless few did not live long enough to return to America.

Armenian immigrants to Syracuse from other areas in Turkey also took factory jobs at first, although many of those coming from urban environments already had or quickly learned special skills, such as tailoring, barbering, rug repair, photography, and machine work in the Azadian factory.

Through the first decade and into the second there appear to have been very few elderly people in the community. The senior members were barely past what would today be considered middle age. The photograph taken in 1914 in Onondaga Park shows a youthful group of forty-one men, eighteen women, and eighteen children. Only John Bayerian, estimated to be fifty-one years of age at this time, and Dickran Desteian, then fifty-five years of age, appear to be white-haired. According to family members, Desteian was eighty-five when he died in 1945. His wife was one hundred one at her death in 1971. Some of the women in the photograph were mothers of adult children, but it is likely that at least two—Elise Kalebdjian and Aghavni Apikian—were barely in their early fifties, as indicated by their dark hair. Furthermore, their children, as yet unmarried, were probably in their twenties, with the likely exception of Setrak Kalebdjian who may have been older. Other older members of the Syracuse community prior to World War I included Prapion Kasparian Koolakian (born in 1848) who came to Syracuse in 1913, Guilvart Kechebashian (mother of Akabi Azadian) who came in 1899, Sarkis

53. Agishe Minasian.
54. Sarah Minasian.
55. Aramtagh Book, pp. 21 and 29.
56. Ibid., pp. 47, 53, 57.

Manoogian, who came about 1906 and later moved to Detroit, Mr. and Mrs. Yeprem Philibosian (Stephen Philibosian's parents).

All of the newcomers appear to have been literate in Armenian, but learning the English language must have proved difficult. The Fourth Presbyterian Church offered classes in English "and Civics,"[57] and some of the men may have attended night school, as did Zahrajian. An article in the *Syracuse Post-Standard* of October 6, 1915, wrote approvingly of the peaceful atmosphere that prevailed among students who were studying English in a single room at Putnam School. There were "17 nationalities representing every one of the countries now at war except Japan." The headline pointed out that even Armenians and Turks were among those who studied harmoniously side by side.

Higher education was out of the reach of most newcomers, but a few Armenians managed to take advantage of Syracuse University's offerings. The first Armenian to become a Syracuse University student appears to have been Harutyun G. Terzian. A native of Syria, Terzian attended the American University at Beirut before coming to the United States in 1910. His name first appears in the Syracuse University Directory for 1910–11 as a second-year student. Registered in mechanical engineering in the Applied Science program, Terzian continued his studies without interruption, receiving a master's degree in 1913.[58] After graduation, Terzian went to work for the Syracuse Lighting Company's gas production department. He subsequently became an outstanding authority in his field. By the time of his premature death at age fifty-three, Terzian had become "one of the country's outstanding authorities on production of carburetted and blue water gas." He also developed "the Terzian factor used by gas engineers in controlling water gas production."[59]

Another early student was Yeranos Habeshian, first listed in the Syracuse University Directory of 1911–12 as a second-year science student. He received a bachelor's degree in 1913 and a master of science degree in 1914. His thesis was on "The Solubility of Aluminium Hydroxide in Ammonium Hydroxide."[60] In 1914, Habeshian was an employee of the Azadian Gauge Manufacturing Company.

Both Terzian and Habeshian were active participants in Syracuse's Armenian community affairs. Terzian was a leading member of the local committee of the Armenian Revolutionary Federation and director of an athletic

---

57. Booklet, Fourth Presbyterian Church, Eckhoff collection.
58. Alumni Directory for Syracuse University, 1835–1925; The Syracuse University Commencement Program for 1913.
59. *Syracuse Herald,* September 4, 1941; *Syracuse Post-Standard,* September 5, 1941.
60. Syracuse University Commencement Programs for 1913 and 1914.

program for the community's young men. Both he and Habeshian also participated in the affairs of the Armenian Apostolic Church.

H. B. Garabedian of Camillus is listed in the Syracuse University Directory
of 1911–12 as a special Liberal Arts student, but for that one year only. In
1913–14, Krikor H. Aigouni (*sic*) appears as a special music student in Fine
Arts. His name continues to appear in the annual directories for five more
years, to 1918–19.

Sarkis G. Sarkissian appears in the Syracuse University Directory for
1913–14 as a first-year civil engineering student. For the next three years he is
listed as a second-year student, finally achieving junior year status in the directory for 1917–18. By this time, Sarkissian must have become discouraged,
because his name appears no more, neither as a student nor as a graduate.

Enrolled in architecture in 1914–15, Sumpat Stephen Kaish transferred to
the College of Forestry, receiving a degree in 1918. Kaish remained in Syracuse where he opened an oriental rug store and became a leading figure in the
Syracuse Armenian community.

Vahe Balikdjian received a bachelor's degree in architecture in 1919. He
does not figure in Syracuse Armenian community life and may have been from
out of town. A New York City home address was given in the Alumni Directory.[61] The Syracuse University Commencement Program for 1918 lists
Bessie Z. Gertmenian as the recipient of a certificate for Oratory, Two Years.
It is not known whether she was related to the Gertmenian family, Syracuse
residents around that time.

Others attending Syracuse University during those years, but who did not
receive degrees, were Arshavir Der Arsenian, who studied agriculture in 1917–
18 and 1918–19, then transferred to law; Vivian H. Gozigian, who studied
agriculture as a special student in 1917–18; Mianzara Zahrajian, a special
student in music for 1918–19 and 1919–20; Lazarus Der Giragosian, who
studied classics as a special student in 1919–20 and 1920–21; Arshalouis J.
Azadian, a music student in 1920–21; Anahid Kurkjian, a student in classics
for 1920–21.[62]

In a survey done at the time, the Armenian Students Association (ASA)
found that in the year 1916 there were more than two hundred fifty Armenian
students enrolled in institutions of higher learning in the United States.[63] The
ASA recorded only one student at Syracuse University for that year, whereas
Syracuse University sources show a total of four students, one of whom was a
special student in music. Based on the Syracuse experience, it does not seem

---

61. Volume for period 1835–1925.

62. All information is from Syracuse University annual directories for the years listed.

63. Reported in Malcom, pp. 108–12.

unreasonable to conclude that actual enrollments of Armenian students in colleges and universities nationwide were probably larger than found in the ASA survey.

Building Institutions

Armenian activities in Syracuse started "very early."[64] By early in the second decade, members of the Syracuse Armenian community were enjoying an active social and organizational life among themselves. There were frequent picnics at the parks in the area, at the Babikians' farm, or at Khachig Minasian's farm. Friends came together in the homes for conversation or card playing.[65] No Armenian ghetto developed. Armenians appear to have lived in clusters, but these were "all over the city."[66]

Except for school, most of the newcomers tended to remain aloof from American associations at first. Gradually, some of the young men made use of the athletic facilities of the YMCA. Also, at the urging of Mrs. Azadian and under her direction members of the Armenian community began to participate in the programs of the Americanization League.

A report on the Armenians prepared under the auspices of the Episcopal Commission in 1913 and based in part on notes furnished by A. H. Sachaklian (then living in Boston and later a Syracuse resident) found that:

> The social life of Armenians in America is distinctively colonial; they do not enter into American society, due to various causes. Language has a great deal to do with it, and then the American society is not so warm in her reception of strangers (foreigners) as is expected.
>
> The home conditions, oppression in Armenia and the consequent thought of "how can we be relieved?" is the binding cord between Armenian colonies.[67]

In Syracuse, there were some exceptions to this observation, especially among those who were the products of the American mission schools in Turkey and had arrived in America already equipped with a knowledge of the English language. For example, the Bayerians had their American friends from the West Genesee Presbyterian Church, of which they were devoted members.

---

64. Letter, Eckhoff to Mesrobian, February 6, 1983.
65. Photographs in Eckhoff, Benjamin, and Sachaklian collections.
66. Desteian.
67. Rev. John Higginson Cabot, Boston, Mass., "Report on Armenians." Typescript in Sachaklian collection.

Mr. and Mrs. Azadian's many civic interests have already been mentioned. They were members of the South Presbyterian Church which they joined in 1906–7. Mr. Azadian was raised in the Apostolic faith and was, for many years, an active participant in affairs of the Armenian Apostolic church in Syracuse, but he also supported his wife's Protestant beliefs. Harry Philibosian was also a member of the South Presbyterian Church. He joined the Masonic order in 1909. As businessmen, both he and Azadian moved comfortably in American business circles. According to his grandson, Koolakian came from an Apostolic background, but at his marriage became a Protestant, like his wife. Mrs. Koolakian had been educated in the mission schools and knew English well. Koolakian joined the South Presbyterian Church in 1909, then moved to the First Baptist Church in 1912. In 1912 he, too, became a Mason.

Other Syracusans from the immigrant generation who joined the Masonic order were Setrak Kalebdjian and Aaron H. Sachaklian, both well-educated businessmen who were fluent in English. Kalebdjian attained the level of Knights Templar while Sachaklian achieved the thirty-second degree. S. S. Kaish, who operated an oriental rug store, was a Rotarian and a member of the American Legion. A Syracuse University graduate, he was active in the alumni association. His wife, who had learned English as a college student in Turkey, was active in Women of Rotary and in the Americanization League.

For the majority of Armenian immigrants, however, language and cultural barriers hampered easy entry into American life. Moreover, many of them sought to retain their native language, customs, and values for as long as possible. They hoped to do so by forming their accustomed political, philanthropic, social, and educational organizations. By 1911 an Armenian Apostolic parish had been formed followed quickly by a Protestant congregation. By 1913 and 1914 political parties had taken shape. Soon the Aramtagh society formed a chorus, a group of players called "Avarair" was organized, and in November 1914 a ladies' society presented a comedy. Their efforts may have been directed primarily toward education, because all three speakers, Messrs H. Bijian, H. Adjemian, and L. (N.) Mangouni, stressed the necessity of teaching the Armenian language to Armenian children.[68]

The intellectual development of adults was also a matter of concern. Contained in the Azadian papers is a four-page list in Armenian language bearing the heading: "List of Books in the Armenian National Library." The numbered entries, written in Azadian's precise hand, identify eighty-one books by title and author, ranging over a wide variety of topics. There are several novels by the popular author, Raffi (Hagop Melik-Hagopian), a copy of the Bible and some religious books by clergymen, Bishop Moushegh Seropian among

---

68. *Hairenik*, December 29, 1914. Clipping in Eckhoff collection.

them, volumes dealing with Armenia's woes at the hands of the Turks, titles on health, and a few books in English including one on wrestling. The list is undated, but it may have been prepared in 1912 or 1913.

It was undoubtedly this collection of books that was the subject of a public meeting called to discuss the founding of a library. A notice in the Azadian collection announces a public meeting for Sunday, October 26 (1913) at 2 p.m. at the Myers Block, corner of East Genesee and Warren streets. This location, to which the community became so accustomed that in subsequent notices it was sometimes referred to as "the usual meeting place," probably became the rented quarters for the club maintained by the political party, the Armenian Revolutionary Federation, into the early 1930s. A stamp on the flyleaf and title page of a book in the Sachaklian library gives evidence that it had been shelved in the Syracuse ARF club, even though a notation in Eliza Sachaklian's handwriting reads: "This book was given to me by Baidzar Parghamian." Club rooms in many Armenian communities often contained shelves of books that were customarily left unattended, subject to the honor system, to be borrowed for reading and returned.

Athletic activity was apparently very popular with the young men. The Yeprad Athletic Club "from which the community's youth benefits without discrimination" (without consideration to political or religious persuasion) "resumed" its instructional program on the first Monday in October 1915 under the direction of *unger* H. Terzian.[69] The use of the term *unger* (comrade) for Terzian and the language imply sponsorship of the club by the ARF.

The Syracuse branch of the Armenian General Benevolent Union (AGBU), an international charitable organization, was in existence by 1914. The Azadian collection contains a letter dated June 23, 1914 from Union headquarters acknowledging receipt of a check for $3.75 representing dues from the Syracuse chapter. The Union was created in 1906 by Boghos Nubar Pasha, a distinguished Armenian in Egypt.[70] During its early years, the AGBU directed attention to the needy Armenian communities overseas, particularly in the Middle East. It then developed an extensive educational program and remained an important charitable-social institution in the diaspora. Since the emergence of the Armenian Republic after the fall of the Soviet Union, it has dedicated considerable effort to the country's development.

The Armenian Students Association came into being in 1910.[71] By 1915 a Syracuse branch existed.[72] This nonpolitical and nonsectarian society sought to promote an awareness of the Armenian heritage among young Armenian-

69. *Hairenik,* October 23, 1915. Clipping in Eckhoff collection.
70. Atamian, p. 208.
71. Mirak, *Torn Between Two Lands,* p. 177.

Americans. Membership was not limited to students. After a few years the Syracuse group was transformed into the Young Ararat Club.

Compatriotic societies were important institutions in the early immigrant communities, in many cases taking the places of families that had perished. Ties between fellow countrymen were so close at one time that marriage with someone outside one's own village or town was sometimes referred to as marrying an *odar,* i.e. "foreigner." Such societies commonly sought to raise funds for their home school or church or for educational purposes. Later, after the home communities had been destroyed, the societies helped refugees. Some also sent aid to Soviet Armenia for use in constructing new communities in the names of destroyed cities and towns, such as "New Malatia" or "New Aintab," in establishing scholarships for the children of their countrymen, or for some other purpose. The young men from Ormutagh and Aramtagh villages in Divrig had come together as early as January 1917 in a society that appeared to be based in Watervliet, but with the greater number of members residing in Syracuse.[73] The reorganized Aramtagh village society was established in July 1, 1919, with its base in Syracuse. It had been founded in 1911.[74] But most of the community's organizational activities were centered on the church and on political organizations.

Church Affairs

As noted previously, many of the early Armenian immigrants to the United States were products of the American Mission Board schools in Turkey. Some came with the purpose of entering American seminaries to prepare themselves for careers as clergymen. With their training completed, they went where assigned, sometimes to serve Armenian congregations and sometimes finding themselves entirely apart from any Armenian community.

Probably one of the earliest Armenian ministers in the upper New York State region was Rev. Johannes B. Garabedian. A history of a town in the Tug Hill area identifies Garabedian as pastor from May 1908 to January 1911 for the Congregational Church. A photograph in the volume pictures him with his wife and six children. There is no information regarding his background, nor does the volume make any reference to the pastor's Armenian roots.[75]

---

72. The Armenian Students' Association, Inc., Leadership Seminar Handbook, Sept. 1992, The Harley Hotel, Enfield, Conn.

73. Aramtagh Book, p. 79.

74. Ibid., p. 109. The seal on the title page gives date of founding.

75. Lola Moore and Elizabeth Quinn, *Osceola, Jewel of Tug Hill: A Pictorial History of Osceola* (Blossvale, N.Y.: Compco Custom Print., 1985).

Another minister in the central New York area who had a non-Armenian parish was Rev. Arsene Schmavonian, who died in 1940 after serving as pastor of the Cazenovia Presbyterian Church for twenty-three years. A native of Kharpert in Turkey, he graduated in 1896 from Robert College in Constantinople and continued his religious training at Hartford Theological Seminary in Connecticut. While in Hartford, he was one of the three students who ran the Armenian Protestant mission in New Britain-Hartford-New Haven. In 1900 he married a non-Armenian woman in Falls Church, Virginia, where he served as pastor. In February 1904 he returned to Turkey to build and organize the Armenian Evangelical Church in Constantinople. Ten thousand Armenian children in orphanages were said to have been placed under his care. He returned to the United States in 1917, after witnessing the tragedy of the Armenian deportations and massacres.[76] While in Cazenovia, neither he nor his family mingled with the Armenian community in Syracuse, but a few Armenians made occasional formal calls. Many Armenians were present at funeral services conducted by Rev. Schmavonian in 1936 for Mrs. Hagop Topouzian, who had lived on a farm in the eastern suburbs.[77]

The national Armenian Apostolic Church has traditionally taken a central place in Armenian life, being a major source of national identity as well as providing spiritual solace to a leaderless people. Laymen take an active role in church affairs and have a voice in the selection of the parish priests and the primate, or regional bishop, who is democratically elected at the convention of the National Representative Assembly, composed of laymen and clergy.

The Armenian Apostolic Church in America traces its beginnings to Worcester, Massachusetts, where the first church was established in 1891. Thereafter, other communities formed parishes and, after making use of rented quarters for services, built their churches. The record of the Armenian Church in Syracuse is difficult to trace, because the community had no stable location for its services nor a regular priest. The Apostolic Armenians of Syracuse formed a parish in 1911.[78] They used local churches for occasional services conducted by itinerant priests.

In 1912 the Protestant Armenians also organized themselves. According to Robert Koolakian, some early members of the Armenian Protestant church in Syracuse were George Koolakian, president, Hagapoz Haigazian, secretary,

---

76. *Hayasdani Gotchnag,* August 24, 1940, no. 34, p. 833–35.

77. *Hairenik Weekly,* May 1, 1936.

78. Rev. Arden Ashjian, *Vijagatsouytz yev Badmoutiun Arachnortagan Temi Hayotz Amerigayi* [Directory and History of the Armenian Diocese of America] (New York: Diocese of the Armenian Church of America, 1949), p. 243.

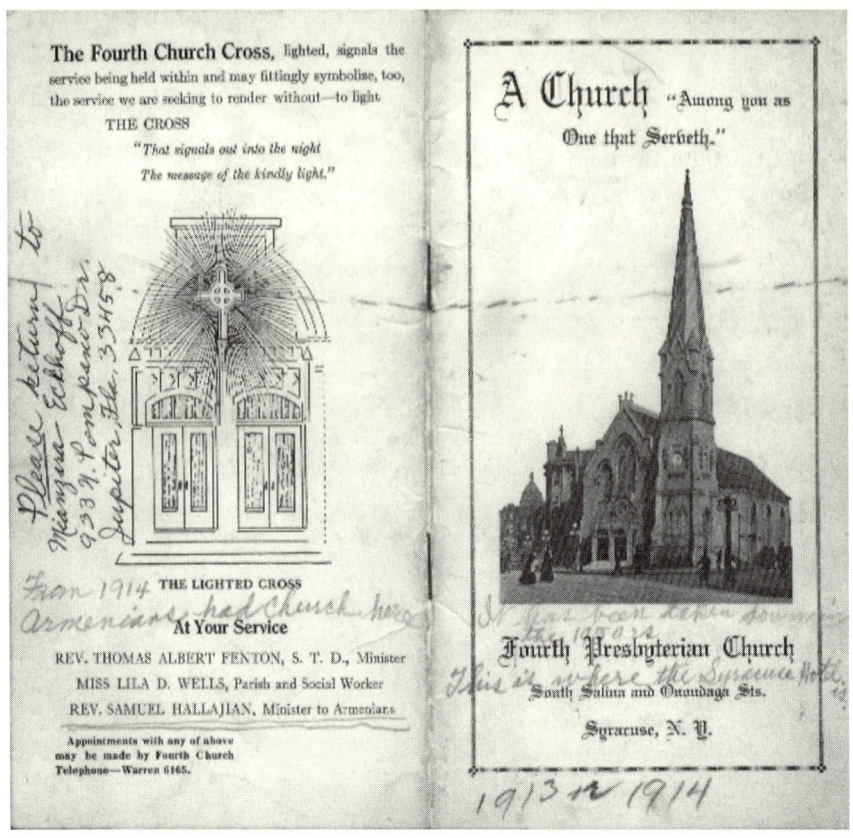

The Armenians who gathered at the Fourth Presbyterian Church were described by Mianzara Zahrajian Eckhoff as one big happy family. They began to make use of the facilities as early as 1913 or 1914 and continued until the mid-twenties, when the church was demolished.

Hagop and Krikor Yessaian, and Sarkis Manoogian. Except for Manoogian, all were from Banderma.

Both groups made the Fourth Presbyterian Church their earliest spiritual home where Protestant Armenian services were offered regularly and were also attended by the Apostolic Armenians. Mrs. Eckhoff supplied a printed booklet about the church with a notation: "It has been taken down. . . . This is where the Syracuse Hotel is." She dated the brochure 1913 or 1914. The printed piece describes the church's location as "The Five Points on Salina Street." A tiny photo of a group of at least one hundred twenty-five men, women, and children appears over the label, "The Fourth Church Armenian Branch." Below it is the following passage:

A well-organized work for Armenians is carried on in the Fourth Church with an Armenian minister in charge. Regular Sunday services are conducted in the Armenian language and during the week classes in English and in Civics. Social gatherings bring out as many as two hundred Armenians.

Mrs. Eckhoff's penciled notation at the back of the booklet tells us: "From 1914 Armenians had church here." Some informants recall well-attended Armenian suppers in the church basement. The church offered its facilities free of charge, but from time to time the Armenians would donate a ton of coal.[79]

Protestant services were provided by Rev. Samuel Haladjian, whom the booklet identifies as Minister to Armenians. Rev. Haladjian was not a resident pastor. He was assisted and succeeded by another visiting minister, Rev. Depoian.

Mr. Azadian appears to have been one of the leaders of the small Armenian Apostolic parish and his collection provides glimpses of its early activities. The earliest item is dated September 25, 1911. The handwritten letter lacks a letterhead and the signature was indecipherable to me—it could be Karekin. Verb usage suggests familiarity with the Caucasian Armenian dialect. It addresses Messrs H. Azadian, S. (probably Setrak) Kalebdjian, and Khosrov K. (Kyoomjian?) as "respected officeholders" (*bashdonagitzner*). The writer says he is sending the letter from the *hayr sourp* (celibate priest), suggesting that they should confer in order to determine when would be a suitable time for him to come. Apparently the Syracuse Armenians had requested that a priest be provided to conduct church services.

Satisfactory arrangements appear to have been made, because we next find a letter dated October 11, 1911, on the letterhead of the Rectory of the Armenian Apostolic Church, 139 East 29th Street, New York. Signed by the *vartabed* (doctor of divinity, celibate priest) Paul Kattanian, it is addressed to Harutun Azadian and expresses deep appreciation for the warm reception that was shown to him. He praises Azadian and his family as exemplars of Armenian hospitality and expresses the hope that there will be more such families in the future. The letter closes with warm greetings to Azadian's wife, mother, and sister, small children "and, especially, a kiss to little Eleanor."

The Syracuse community appears to have established a formal organization to oversee its church activities, but all did not go smoothly. We find a letter of complaint dated February 25, 1914, addressed to Mr. H. B. Azadian and signed Secretary, S. Kalebdjian. It acknowledged receipt of a notice signed by

---

79. Armen; Desteian.

Harutyun Terzian as president of the Syracuse Armenian board, inviting them to a meeting on February 26 at the Bastable Block in room 129. The letter observed that the notice did not bear the signature of the board's president, Mr. Azadian, and queries:

> If it has come from the board, why did it not bear your signature? Or perhaps a different new board has been elected? If that is the case, then what purpose would be served by our presence?

> We as members of the previous board, excepting for you, come to announce to you that in the near future we former members of the board will have a public meeting in which we will express our arguments.

> We refuse to come, not only because the notice does not bear your signature, but also we have other criticisms as well, which can be resolved only in a public meeting.

Whatever the difficulties, they appear to have been resolved within a matter of months, as suggested by a handwritten undated notice announcing the forthcoming meeting of the members of the city's Armenian Apostolic Church, to take place on Sunday, May 11 (1914) in the Myers Block. The meeting's purpose was to discuss church affairs. Members were urged to come and to bring non-members. The notice was signed simply: Syracuse Armenian Apostolic Church Board.

Further evidence of the existence of a viable organization is provided by a letter dated August 2, 1914, verifying that Nishan Babikian paid church dues for the year 1914. The letter closes with headings for signatures of co-chairmen, but bears only one signature: Y. Habeshian. The letter is in the same handwriting.

The salutation of a letter dated June 17, 1914, addressed Mr. Y. Habeshian at the office of his employer, the Azadian Gauge Manufacturing Company. Written in English on the letterhead of The Armenian Colonial Association of New York City, the letter is signed by Colonel Mesrob Nevton, identified in the printed heading "The Gotchnag." *Gotchnag* (The Church Bell) was a religious weekly supported by the American Missionary Association and the Armenian Protestant Church in America.

The writer expresses appreciation for "kindly and flattering invitations like yours." He comments, "The object of your organization is exceedingly meritorious, and I should have liked very much to come up and assist you in your patriotic undertaking." However, he expresses regret that he cannot visit

Syracuse on June 21, as requested. There is no information on the organization or its purpose.

Proceeding with its own concerns, the church board approached the Prelacy of the Armenian Church in Worcester, as indicated by a response dated
July 6, 1914, handwritten on the Prelacy letterhead and directed to the chairman and board of the church of Syracuse. After acknowledging the board's letter of July 2 requesting His Eminence Moushegh (Seropian) to come to
conduct church services, the writer (the signature appears to read Vahram
Vartabed Nazarian) says that he has forwarded the request directly to the
surpazan (term of respect) for response.

Moushegh Seropian was a controversial figure in Armenian Church affairs
at that time. He had been bishop of Adana in Turkey, which was under the
jurisdiction of the See of Cilicia. The Cilician See, with its Catholicos, had
been in existence for many centuries in order to govern church affairs of Cilician Armenia. The Catholicos of the Great House of Cilicia is coequal in rank
to the Catholicos at Etchmiadzin, but with a circumscribed region under his
jurisdiction.

Seropian escaped from the 1909 Adana massacres and arrived in the
United States in late 1910. Although he had come without invitation from
America and without the sanction of the Etchmiadzin See, under whose jurisdiction the American Diocese was governed, he waged a controversial, but
successful, campaign to be elected Prelate. After a turbulent period he vacated
the position and was succeeded by Arsen Vartabed Vehooni in late 1913.[80] At
the time he received the above invitation from Syracuse, he was no longer Prelate.

Seropian, who had known Azadian from Constantinople, responded
quickly to the invitation to visit Syracuse. A telegram to H. Azadian dated July
14, 1914 announces: "I will come Friday. I will be at Syracuse seven o'clock
p.m." It is signed "Mr. Serotian (*sic*) from Jamaica Plain."[81]

It is a surprise to discover that the Prelate Vehooni was also invited to the
Azadian home at almost the same time. Writing from the Plaza Hotel in Chicago on July 28, 1914, while returning from a trip to California, Vehooni
acknowledged the letter of July 2 from the "gracious Mrs. A. Azadian." He
accepted the invitation and announced his plan to arrive by train on Thursday
and leave on Saturday. This was not his first stay at the Azadian home in view
of the greetings he extended to the Azadian family, including mother, sister,
and children. That this was to be a social visit is suggested by the fact that the

---

80. Mirak, *Torn Between Two Lands,* p. 188.
81. Telegrams and letters discussed in the following paragraphs are all in the Azadian col-
    lection.

invitation was extended by Mrs. Azadian, who had no official standing as a member of the Armenian Church or of its board. Moreover, the Prelate would not be in Syracuse on a Sunday to conduct Church services.

The Vehooni visit was apparently a cordial one. The Azadian collection contains a photo of Vartabed Vehooni dated "31 July 1914" and inscribed in Armenian: *"Hishadag ee Syracuse"* (memento of Syracuse).

A few days following his return to Prelacy headquarters in Worcester, the Prelate wrote on August 4, 1914, addressing Azadian as chairman of the board of the Armenian Apostolic Church of Syracuse to acknowledge receipt of $11.00 in payment for travel expenses. According to Vehooni's letter dated August 22, 1914 addressed to Azadian as chairman, he was enclosing certificates of baptism for the children of Mihran Babikian and Kevork Saxenian. Was the christening of the two children the reason for the Prelate's visit to Syracuse in July?

Again addressing Azadian as chairman, the Prelate wrote on November 16, 1914 to acknowledge receipt of the board's letter of the fourteenth, its report, and $28.00 for prelacy dues. The Prelate also expressed the opinion that it would have been advisable for the Syracuse board to have designated a delegate to attend the church assembly. The letter provided no information as to the meeting date or place.

In a letter dated September 4 (1915), Vehooni sent a brief message in response to Mrs. Azadian's letter of September 3. Unlike the previous letter to Mrs. Azadian, it is entirely businesslike in tone. He announced his intention to arrive on September 9, Thursday evening at 7:35 and depart early the next morning. He requested that Mr. Azadian arrange for other members of the board to participate. Mrs. Azadian may have written in her husband's place in order to assist him during the busy war years when he was preoccupied at his factory.

Perhaps by the following year an inexperienced new church board had taken office, because they had apparently violated protocol in inviting the Rector of St. Illuminator's Armenian Apostolic Church at 221 East 27th Street in New York City to conduct Easter services on May 14. Writing on May 5, 1916, Rev. M. Maniguian, without giving specific names, acknowledged the board's invitation, but advised them to direct their request to the Prelacy office.

As for Seropian, his close association with Azadian is evident from correspondence and photographs in the Azadian collection. A telegram from L. Frankeian, Binghamton dated April 1, 1915 and addressed to Archbishop Seropian at Syracuse, New York, reads: "Binghamton meeting postponed until after Easter." Seropian also apparently was alert to business opportunities. Acting on information provided in Seropian's letter of February 4, 1916,

Azadian wrote to Mr. M. H. Johnson of Boston, Massachusetts, of whom nothing else is known, offering his factory's services for making shrapnel. Azadian's factory was by this time humming with activity producing arms for the war in Europe. Seropian's telegram to Azadian dated March 12, 1917, directs: "Please send me at once six hundred dollars." The reason for this peremptory request is not known.

Antaram Desteian remembered Seropian well. With Khachig Minasian as deacon, the Archbishop conducted services "many times" at the Episcopal Church Of The Saviour on James Street. She did not remember Vartabed Vehooni, but she stated that clergymen from out of town were always guests of the Azadians.

Seropian's story contains further adventures. An undated photograph in the Azadian collection shows him in military uniform, although he has inscribed it as "archbishop." Robert Koolakian has informed me that according to Antranig Chelebian, biographer of General Antranig, Seropian served as a volunteer in the Armenian army. Later photographs show Seropian in layman's dress and eventually with his wife and daughter. Sadly, Miss Desteian recalled that at his last visit to Syracuse, the dynamic former archbishop had lost his memory.

Parties and Politics

The Armenians were "like one family" during the early days.[82] The Apostolic Armenians attended Armenian Protestant services and the Protestant Armenians went to the occasional Apostolic rites. "Everyone" even attended activities sponsored by the two major political parties in Syracuse, the Armenian Revolutionary Federation and the Social Democratic Hunchagian party. This amity did not remain constant, however, as events were to show. Rivalry between the parties often provoked disputes, leading at times to open rifts between the groups, affecting community harmony.

Revolutionary and political parties emerged among Armenians in Turkey and in the Caucasus during the latter half of the nineteenth century, along with a literary and intellectual awakening. Armenian students at Russian and European universities were infected by the same radical fervor that fostered the Russian revolution. Encouraged by Europe's calls for reforms in Turkey, the new Armenian revolutionaries—especially those in Caucasian Armenia— began to demand a better life for the repressed Armenian peasants in Turkey. The long-suffering countrymen welcomed the prospect for relief from constant Turkish and Kurdish depredations, but not all Armenians favored

---

82. Letter, Eckhoff to Mesrobian, February 6, 1983.

change. Such destabilization was resisted by the wealthy and mostly urban-dwelling merchants and traders, officials who held influential posts in the government of Sultan Hamid, and the clergy whose power over the people was being challenged by the revolutionary parties. These conservative Armenians were especially repelled by the socialistic tenor of the new revolutionary organizations.[83]

The Marxist Social Democratic Hunchagian party, founded in Geneva in 1887, was the first permanent political party to defend Armenian rights and the first socialist party in Turkey and Persia.[84] Among its goals, as described in its constitution, were elimination of all despotic regimes, liberation of the Armenian people, freedom for the working class, and improved working conditions in order to create class consciousness. The party grew rapidly in the United States during the period 1890–96.[85]

The *Hunchagian Yearbook,* cited previously, devotes particular attention to Mihran Babikian, an early Syracusan, as an active and dedicated Hunchagian and provides some biographical details. Mihran was born on November 22, 1866 in the village of Chara, Sepastia. He became a Hunchagian very early and while in Constantinople in 1895 as an employe of the railroad, he took the opportunity to transport party publications and even guns. In America, before coming to Syracuse, he busied himself with party matters. In Syracuse, he joined with Setrak Barsamian, Khachadour Aghaian, and Philibos Mnoushian to establish a Hunchag party branch in Syracuse.[86] He enjoyed public speaking and was listed as a participant in the special memorial program held by the Syracuse community on November 12, 1916. In later years Mihran appears to have distanced himself from party activity. His grandson stated that the brothers were interested only in the church.

The *Yearbook*'s assertion that soon after its founding the membership of the Syracuse Hunchag branch reached 50 is without doubt a severe exaggeration. However, the claim that it preceded the ARF in Syracuse appears to be valid. A poster bearing the printed heading "S. D. Hunchagian party" dated July 20, 1913 announced a public meeting to take place on Sunday afternoon at 1:30 p.m. "in the usual meeting place."[87] Reference to a customary meeting

---

83. See Louise Nalbandian, *The Armenian Revolutionary Movement: The Development of Armenian Political Parties through the Nineteenth Century* (Berkeley and Los Angeles: University of California Press, 1963) for the development of the Armenian revolutionary movement. Atamian, *op. cit.,* discusses how political parties affected Armenian life.

84. Nalbandian, p. 104.

85. Garo Kevorkian, *Amenoon Darekirk 1963* [Everyone's Yearbook] (Beirut, Lebanon), p. 354.

86. *Hunchagian Yearbook,* p. 276.

place clearly indicates an earlier date of formation for the organization. The Syracuse branch occasionally co-sponsored programs with the Armenian Revolutionary Federation, although disputes also often occurred. The Syracuse Hunchag organization was still in existence in 1920, according to a telegram dated May 27, 1920 in the Azadian collection, but appears to have faltered thereafter.[88]

The Armenian Revolutionary Federation (*Hai Heghapoghagan Tashnagtsoutiun*) was founded in 1890, based on the merger of various Armenian groups, primarily in Russian Armenia.[89] ARF committees appeared in the United States in 1895. At first seeking reforms, the ARF eventually dedicated itself to the goal of a free, united, and independent Armenia. Its strong nationalism tended to overshadow the socialist plank in its platform. The party's focus on national unity distinguished it from the Hunchag party, which placed class interest above national interest. It became the most influential political party in Armenian life,[90] evoking a degree of antipathy from its opponents that fully matched the passion of its adherents. The oath-taking was a solemn ritual with the gravity of marriage vows. In 1937, to join one of the committees in Beirut, Lebanon, new members pledged their loyalty with one hand on a revolver, not a Bible.

The major objective of the ARF among the immigrant communities was to keep the Armenian cause alive in the new environment and to raise funds for the gaping needs that emerged continually. Funds were needed to support the press, to buy arms for self-defense in the homeland, for public relations and propaganda, to care for refugees, for the Armenian army during independence, and for a time even to buy the release of Armenian slaves from their Moslem owners. The fund drives in America started very early, while there was scarcely an Armenian community to which to address an appeal. The hint of an early Armenian community in Rochester appears in a list dated February 1911 indicating that the Rochester community contributed $24. Troy gave $800.[91] Syracuse does not appear in this list. The funds, to be sent to the Armenian Patriarch in Constantinople or to Mr. K. Zohrab, member of the Ottoman Parliament, were to be used to aid Armenians imprisoned by the Tsarist government in the Caucasus. An amazing $10,000 was raised in three months. It was Mr. Zohrab's fate to perish in the 1915 massacres.

---

87. Azadian collection.
88. *Hunchagian Yearbook,* p. 278.
89. Nalbandian, p. 151.
90. Mirak, *Torn Between Two Lands,* p. 233.
91. Kevorkian, p. 362.

Rapid growth of the central and upstate New York Armenian communities is reflected in the emergence of ARF committees in Troy, Niagara Falls, and Binghamton and, by 1915, in Massena, Syracuse, Rochester, Utica, and the small neighboring town of Herkimer.[92] The ARF convention which convened in Worcester, Massachusetts on December 24, 1913, did not include Syracuse in its list of committees entitled to representation, although Binghamton was present.[93] By the following year, however, the Syracuse ARF committee had fully blossomed, as indicated by the report of its gathering on December 2, 1914, appearing in the *Hairenik* of December 29, 1914 (to be described later). But a formal ARF committee in Syracuse appears to have taken shape well before the end of 1913. The Azadian papers contain two preprinted forms bearing the insignia of the ARF on which meeting notices have been posted by hand. One carried an announcement for a public meeting on Sunday, September 14 (1913), and another for Sunday, December 7, 1913, at 1:30 p.m. That the meeting in September was not the first one to which the public was invited is indicated by the reference to the meeting site: "at the usual meeting place." It is possible that the ARF and Hunchag parties shared the same quarters. The December meeting notice finally identified the location as "Myer's Block." Such public meetings regularly sought to entertain the audience as suggested by a line printed on the notice promising that songs and recitations would be offered. Printed at the very bottom of the notice, in large bold face letters, is the plea: "The public is requested to be present at the designated time."

The September ARF meeting notice was signed: "Comrade N. Mangouni." Nazareth Lazarus Mangouni was from Boston, where he was closely associated with the ARF. In 1909 he was elected to the Central Executive body and served as its executive secretary. In 1911 he was again elected to the Central Executive and was also designated "permanent" field worker. He may have used Syracuse as a base for visits to other Armenian communities for the purpose of organizing ARF committees. According to his son, through this period Mangouni traveled to Niagara Falls, Hamilton, Brantford, Chicago, Granite City, Detroit, and St. Louis. After a few years Mangouni moved to Highland Park, Michigan. In 1918 he entered the University of Michigan at Ann Arbor, graduating in June 1920.[94]

---

92. *Voroshoumner H. H. T. Amerigayi Shrchani 22rt Bdg. Joghovin, 1915 Kaghvadzkner.* [Selected Decisions of the 22nd Convention of the ARF American Region, 1915].
93. Kevork Donabedian, "H.H.T. Hiusisain Amerigayi," ["The ARF in North America"] in *Hairenik,* February 13, 1992, p. 10.
94. Letter, Norman Mangouni to Mesrobian, April 16, 1996.

During those days, fund-raising was a customary feature of the public meetings. The gathering on December 7 followed the usual pattern. A handwritten notice dated December 9, 1913 on formal ARF letterhead directs Azadian to pay the amount pledged (amount not stated) on December 7, 1913 to Comrade H. Kyoomjian. The stationery was that of *Droschak,* the party organ in Geneva, Switzerland, which also served as party headquarters. The letter closes with an expression of thanks. It is signed by the chairman, Krikor Hamamjian, and the secretary, Harutiun (last name undecipherable).

The Ramgavar (Democratic) party had a brief presence in Syracuse, but there does not seem to have been a strong organization. Antaram Desteian said that her father was an early member, but did not remain in the party very long. He was very active in the Armenian General Benevolent Union, especially in fund-raising for the Armenian refugees. Although she also identified Krikor and Khachadour Aghaian, first cousins from Palou, as being Ramgavar "around 1920 or before," other evidence associates them with the Hunchag party. Krikor had a grocery on Washington Street. Khachadour worked for Mr. Azadian then he, too, opened a grocery store. Khachadour was for many years in charge of the censer during church services.[95]

Much of the political fervor welling up within the small Armenian immigrant communities was fostered by the press of the political parties. The earliest immigrant newspapers, one-man efforts published from the late 1880s and early 1890s, lacked adequate resources or circulation. As Armenian political parties began to emerge in the United States, so did a strong and active political press whose influence extended into all of the new communities. It was largely the Armenian political press that kept the far-flung immigrant populations informed concerning matters affecting the Armenian people.[96]

In view of the activities and interests of the early Syracuse Armenians, as mentioned, it is reasonable to expect that they would have been familiar with the content of the Armenian immigrant press in America. But news also traveled in the other direction, as well. One wonders how H. Azadian's address fell into the hands of Mekertitch Portugalian, editor of the journal *Armenia* based in Marseilles, France. Addressing Azadian in Syracuse, in a letter dated October 8, 1913, Portugalian wrote (in Armenian):

> We are mailing you a package of 5 sample issues of the journal Armenia which we have been publishing in France for 29 years. It is the only Armenian-language weekly in Europe, outside of Constantinople. We hope that after becoming acquainted with this

---

95. Desteian.
96. See Mirak, *Torn Between Two Lands,* pp. 247–52 on the immigrant press.

paper you will become a subscriber. In order to form an opinion on any question, it is important to listen to all sides.[97]

Portugalian was an educator from Constantinople whom the Turkish government banished from Van because of his activities. He left Turkey for France in 1885, never to return to Armenia. The newspaper that he founded in Marseilles later became identified with the first, but short-lived revolutionary party, the Armenakan, which Portugalian helped to form.[98]

Aaron Sachaklian, who joined the Syracuse community in 1919, attributed his devotion to the Armenian cause to Portugalian's influence. He joined the ARF a few years after arriving in the United States and became one of its leaders throughout a lifetime of service. In 1895, while still a youth, traveling on his way to America from his native Malatia, young Aaron met Portugalian in Marseilles. Eliza Sachaklian, Aaron's wife, recorded the following in her biography of her husband:

> This individual, M. Portugalian, praised Aaron, encouraging him, and said, "I see that you have a bright future because you are well-behaved and intelligent. So, my son, go get your education. Those countries are melting-pots. Don't let that happen to you. Do not forget your nation and your religion. Go, may God be with you. Again I say, do not forget your language." In later years, Aaron would tell me, "This man's advice still rings in my ears. It was his advice that kept me Armenian."[99]

Central to the community effort of the political parties was the traveling field worker, the *kordzich*. He was the moving link in the great Armenian chain from its national heart in the Caucasus and in Turkey to the far-flung immigrant communities. Lacking a central government, the people depended on the network of the political party to keep them in touch, to establish national policy, and to give release and direction to the fears, frustrations, and anxieties of those who found themselves a huge ocean away from the families and friends who had been left behind in an increasingly dangerous environment. The arrival of the field worker in the community promised fresh news from the old country and information about conditions within the Armenian world. All parties and organizations sponsored traveling speakers from time to time, but in my recollection the appearances of ARF speakers were more

---

97. Letter in Azadian collection.
98. Nalbandian, pp. 90–95.
99. Unpublished biography in Sachaklian collection.

frequent and over a longer period of time than those of other political parties or groups.

From the moment of his arrival in the community, often tired and perhaps ill from the fatigue of traveling long miles by bus or train, the field worker became the center of attention. For two or three days, he had not only to endure but to perform throughout discussions with the membership, sessions with the executive members, public meetings, ceremonial meetings with Armenian or non-Armenian dignitaries, receptions, speeches, toasts, dinners.[100] Setting aside his personal needs, the field worker was expected to inform, guide, advise, uplift, and excite the far-flung immigrant communities, for whom this was the closest possible contact with the homes left so many thousands of miles away. He also served as arbiter in settling local disputes. It is no wonder that few field workers achieved old age.

Membership business meetings were, of course, closed to outsiders, but great visibility was given to the "public meeting," which was the showcase for the field worker. As noted earlier, "everyone" attended. A typical public meeting displayed the talents of the local community, offering entertainment, speeches, recitations, and performances prior to the main event. The centerpiece of the meeting was the speech given by the field worker, who would also respond to questions following his presentation. Usually, the meeting concluded with fund-raising, during which donors would call out the amounts of their gifts. Pledges in high amounts were usually greeted with applause.

Following is a shortened description of such a meeting in Syracuse on December 2, 1914, as reported in the Armenian-language ARF newspaper, *Hairenik*.[101] The chairman, *unger* (as the political newspapers always termed members of the party), S. Nigsarian opened the meeting and gave a concise biography of the deceased freedom fighter, Nigol Douman. To honor his memory, the audience stood up and sang "Mer Hairenik" ("Our Fatherland," a song which became the anthem of the 1918–20 Armenian Republic). Douman, an ARF leader, became a hero to the Armenians for his exploits in the Expedition of Khanasor against Kurdish attacks and during the Armenian-Tatar wars of 1904–5.

Next came a song by the choral group, a recitation by Miss A. Zahrajian, a solo by comrade M. Bedrosian. Comrade L. (N.) Mangouni gave an address in which he stressed the mission of the Armenian-American women. There followed a song by the choral group, a speech by comrade B. Marzbanian, a song by the young women, a solo and encore by comrade A. Hovhannesian, and then a dramatic presentation by the young women.

---

100. Kevorkian, p. 384.
101. December 29, 1914.

The stage was decorated with pictures of ARF heroes, noted Armenian authors, and national leaders, with the ARF emblem in the center. Misses Aghavni Zahrajian, Antaram Desteian, and Siranoush Kupelian entered, dressed as Armenian Red Cross nurses.[102] Miss Zahrajian spoke, urging the formation of an ARF-affiliated Red Cross chapter in Syracuse.

Armenian women's auxiliary groups emerged when conflicts broke out in Turkey and in the Caucasus. The tradition made the transition to the New World. Although the role changed from nursing physical wounds to aiding distant compatriots, the auxiliary was still thought of as composing a nurses' corps. In 1910, the Armenian Red Cross was formally organized in the United States and by 1911 there were fifteen chapters. Early photographs of members show women wearing white nurses' uniforms or white arm bands bearing a red cross.[103]

Continuing the presentation, the sisters Mianzara and Zarouhi Zahrajian entered, dressed as soldiers[104] and singing "Menk Yenk Azad Hai Badanik" ("We Are Free Armenian Youth"). Miss A. Zahrajian concluded with the stirring marching song, "Loosin Chigar" ("There Was No Moon"), to the intense delight of the audience.

With the audience now in a mood of heightened anticipation, the field worker, Arsen Mikaelian, began his address. First, he described the desperate political and economic situation prevailing in the mother country. He condemned Germany's despicable actions in Turkey, the disarming of Armenian soldiers, and the persecution of the ARF. He stressed the desperate need for self-sacrifice and self-defense at a time that was full of promise. At the conclusion he responded to two questions from the audience. Another song by the choral group brought the meeting to a close. There followed a short social period during which several new people came forward to join the party.

The featured speaker, Arsen Mikaelian was a tall, handsome youth of twenty-eight, on his first tour of the United States. He had been schooled in several noted Armenian academies in the Caucasus and only a few months earlier had received a degree in law from the university at St. Petersburg. From 1919 to 1921 he devoted himself to the affairs of the Armenian Republic. After its fall, he returned to the United States. Mikaelian's entire life was dedicated to the Armenian cause. He died in South America in 1941 at the age of fifty-three, while on a tour of the Armenian communities there.[105]

---

102. Photographs in the Eckhoff collection.
103. *Hairenik,* July 16, 1992; see photos in *Album Hai Garmir Khach ir Ksanamyagin Artiv 1910–1930* [Album of the Armenian Red Cross on Its Twentieth Anniversary] (Boston: Hairenik, 1930).
104. Photographs in Eckhoff collection.

Siranoush (Lulu) Kupelian, Aghavni Zahrajian, and Antaram Desteian as Armenian Red Cross nurses and Zarouhi and Mianzara Zahrajian as Armenian soldiers in a performance at an ARF public meeting on December 2, 1914.

Mikaelian's charismatic personality and commanding speaking ability made him a favorite wherever he traveled. His visit to Syracuse in 1914 was the first of several.

The Syracuse ARF committee had intended to raise funds at the December 2 meeting, but they canceled such plans in accordance with a directive from headquarters. The ARF, in turn, was acceding to a decision of the "Interpolitical Committee," composed of representatives of the four Armenian political parties in America which sought to coordinate fund-raising efforts in all the

Armenian communities. Negotiations met constant road blocks and eventually the ARF decided to proceed without waiting for universally-acceptable arrangements to be made.[106]

The fund-raising that was suspended at the meeting of December 2, 1914, became the purpose for a meeting held on January 26, 1915. In a news report of the event, there is also a hint of the disunity that seemed always to exist within the Armenian communities. The reliable Zahrajian sisters opened the meeting with a song, "Hairenyats Siroun" ("For the Love of Fatherland"). After a few words of welcome by comrade chairman, comrade A. Hovhannesian sang two songs. Next Aghavni Zahrajian spoke extolling the Armenian fighter. The choral group sang "Menk Bedk e Gurvink Yev Voch Lats Unink" ("We Must Fight and Not Weep"). Comrade L. (N.) Mangouni gave an absorbing speech in which he compared Armenian fighting preparedness of today with that of twenty-five years ago. Kh. Papazian sang "Lretz Amberu" ("The Clouds Were Silenced"), comrade O. Tavitian recited Agnouni's "Tebi Yergir" ("Toward Our Country"), Miss M. Zahrajian urged Armenian women to form a Red Cross group. The exhortation was received with applause. After the song "Govgasi Kacher" ("Caucasia's Braves") came the main address by the visiting speaker, comrade S. Chitjian. Chitjian became the editor of the *Hairenik* for the period 1918–22.[107]

The speaker noted that the Armenian people were living through momentous days and explained the reasons for disunity in Armenian life. The news article does not provide the speaker's explanation, but it probably dealt with the continuing strain of opposition to the ARF. There was generous response to the fund drive that followed and within a short time $600 was raised. This was a staggering sum, considering the low wages earned at that time and the likelihood that the audience did not number more than one hundred fifty or two hundred, counting men, women, and children.[108] After the meeting, four people came forward to join the ARF ranks. The article concludes, "And thus the people with their actions gave a slap to those gentlemen who tried to confuse their minds." This may have referred to comments in the opposition press that were critical of the ARF.

---

106. See *Hamerashkhagan Panagtsoutiunner* [*Negotiations for Agreement*], 1914–1916 (Boston: Hairenik Press, 1916).

107. *Hairenik*, February 11, 1915. Clipping in Eckhoff collection.

108. "To live adequately in 1910 a family of five required an income of $900 a year but only one in seven foreign-born persons earned that much." From "Immigration," p. 13. The same article reports that although at $750 the annual income for Armenians was below the minimum, it was nevertheless the highest of a group which included Jews, Greeks, and Serbs.

Adherents to the various political parties differed widely in cultural, philosophical, and social outlook. Believing passionately in the cause they espoused, they believed with equal passion that those taking a differing position were in error. The conflicting objectives and interests of these various groups contributed to the development of deep and long-lasting antipathies that survived the change of generations, revealing themselves many years later in the Armenian communities in America.

Thus, even as the Armenians began to develop their own visions of a future for their people, not all entertained the same vision. Their divergent views made it difficult, if not impossible, to band their meager forces together in the common good. Armenia's desperate needs through these fateful years occasionally forced the political parties to seek some common ground, but attempts to establish national agencies to deal with disasters such as the plight of the refugees after the 1915 deportations and massacres and similar calamities encountered controversy, leading to collapse. Old antipathies and suspicions refused to die, rising up time and again to disrupt coalition attempts.

The Murder of a Nation

By late spring of 1915, news was beginning to arrive concerning the terrible fate of the Armenian populations in Turkey, although details were not known until later. The American missionaries, caught themselves as unwilling eye-witnesses to the horrendous events and in some cases sharing in the suffering, sent a succession of reports to the home office. These, in turn, were compiled and relayed to concerned individuals and groups in the United States. The Azadian collection contains extensive data and photographs from the American Board of Commissioners for Foreign Missions. Presumably, this information was shared with the Armenian community.

The Sachaklian collection contains carbon copies of typewritten reports signed by James L. Barton, identified on the letterhead as secretary of the Foreign Department of the American Board of Commissioners for Foreign Missions, located in Boston, Massachusetts. There are five variously dated reports for 1915[109] and three issued in 1916.[110] The chief focus of these reports is the welfare of the missionaries trapped in Turkey after the outbreak of the deportations and massacres. According to the report dated October 22, 1915, all missionaries were "given authority by the Board to leave the country whenever in their judgment it is wise for them so to do." Many did indeed find their way

---

109. April 3, May 20, July 6, August 31, October 22.
110. February 14, May 17, and June 30.

to safety, but others preferred to remain and to do "everything possible for the refugee Armenians" as did Rev. Francis A. Leslie at Oorfa.[111]

The report of August 31, 1915 tells us that "Miss Graffam of Sivas," in a heroic gesture of self-sacrifice, obtained permission from the Governor-general to go "with a party of exiled women and children from Sivas to some point unknown." She was allowed to travel with the group as far as Malatia, but was turned back from there by the government. The report offers the following brief description of the deportations: "Throughout Eastern and Western and parts of Central Turkey, nearly all of the Armenians—men, women and children—are taken from their homes and sent, under guard, to remote sections of the country inhabited by Moslems. Little preparation is made for the journey. Hardship and suffering among them are beyond description. Many executions of men have occurred in all of these places."

It is clear from these reports that the Turkish government placed strict controls on the American missionaries, in many cases prohibiting them from helping the Armenians. The May 17, 1916, report reveals that Mr. Peet, treasurer of the American Missions in Turkey, was "forbidden altogether" from paying money to individual Armenians, "the Government being suspicious of him as a partner in revolutionary movements." The report concludes, "Turkish hopes for help from America are still strong. Turkey would like American money and influence minus the American missionary." The Sachaklian file also contains responses from the American Board to Aaron Sachaklian's efforts to send money to his mother in Dort Yol and to secure news concerning events in Malatia, his home region.

Even more comprehensive information was supplied by news reports appearing in the European and American press as Turkey proceeded to carry out its plan to rid itself forever of the Armenian Question. A dispatch to *The London Morning Post,* reprinted in *The New York Times* of January 13, 1915, quoted a statement by Talaat Bey, Minister of the Interior, to the Councillor of the Greek Patriarchate that "in Turkey henceforth there will be room only for Turks."[112] Soon reports of pillage and murder of Armenians increased to such a degree that *The New York Times* reported on May 15, 1915, that the United States State Department had received "a flood of communications from various parts of the country urging that steps be taken to protect native Christians in Armenia and in regions under Turkish control."[113]

---

111. Leslie A. Davis, *The Slaughterhouse Province: An American Diplomat's Report on the Armenian Genocide, 1915–1917,* edited with an introduction and notes by Susan K. Blair (New Rochelle, NY,: Aristide D. Caratzas, Publisher, 1989), p. 15.

112. Richard D. Kloian, *The Armenian Genocide: News Accounts from the American Press: 1915–1922* (Berkeley, Calif., 1988), p. 3.

Unlike the Jewish Holocaust, the full horror of which was not revealed until the war's end, the sufferings of the Armenians at the hands of the Turks did not remain a secret from the outside world while they were taking place. One of the earliest observers to raise the alarm was United States Ambassador to Turkey, Henry Morgenthau. The Koolakian collection contains the following telegram (punctuation mine) sent on September 7, 1915 by R. Chambers of the American Board of Commissioners at Boston, Massachusetts to George Koolakian and H. Haigazian, president and secretary respectively of the Armenian Presbyterian Mission in Syracuse:

> K G Koolakian Pres. Armenian Presbyterian Mission Syracuse NY
> H Haigazian Secty
> Notify content of Ambassador Morgenthau cable as follows:
>
> To Secretary of State Washington 1005 Sept 3, 1915, 9 a.m. Minister of War has promised to permit departure of such Armenians to the United States whose emigration I vouch as bona fide. Destruction of Armenian race in Turkey is progressing rapidly. Massacre reported at Angora and Broussa. Will you suggest to Cleveland Dodge, Charles Crane, John R. Mott, Stephen Wise and others to form committee to raise funds and provide means to save some of the Armenians and assist the poorer ones to emigrate and perhaps enlist California, Oregon, and Washington to transport some of these people direct to their shores via Panama Canal.
>
> Morgenthau American Ambassador Constantinople
> R. Chambers, American Board of Commissioners
> Rcd Syracuse, N.Y. Sept. 8, 1915
> 10 a.m.

Koolakian apparently acted promptly upon receipt of the telegram from Chambers, as indicated by the following wire he received from President Woodrow Wilson on September 12:

> Your letter has been handed to me of September ninth and I must give myself the pleasure of telling you how much Mrs. Wilson and I appreciate the gift of the Armenian cross made by your mother's own hands knowing she has recently come to the United States. We shall keep her treasured gift as a very acceptable momento [sic] of your kind thought. I am shocked and dismayed at the recent turn

---

113.Ibid, 13.

of events toward the Armenians in Turkey. I beg to assure you this international problem is receiving our undivided attention and hope to meet with Ambassador Morgenthau and others soon in the matter of a proper and just resolution.[114]

While some tried to determine how to provide relief for the survivors, others sought to put an end to the outrages. The front page of the *Syracuse Post-Standard* carried an article reporting the plea of Viscount Bryce, formerly British Ambassador to the United States, that "America try to stop the slaughter of the Armenians." Stating that accounts from different sources agree that the Christian population is being deliberately exterminated, he pleaded:

if anything can stop the destroying hand of the Turkish government it will be an expression of the opinion of neutral nations, chiefly the judgment of humane America.[115]

Then he acknowledged that:

Only one power can take action. It is Germany. Would not the expression of American public opinion, voicing the conscience of neutral nations, lead Germany to check the Turkish government?[116]

It may have provided some small measure of comfort to the Syracuse Armenians to learn that Washington had finally informed Turkey that the American people were disturbed over the Armenian massacres. The news item read as follows:

Washington, Oct. 4.—Ambassador Morgenthau at Constantinople was instructed by cable to-day to inform the Turkish minister of foreign affairs that public sentiment in the United States was so stirred by the reports of the Armenian atrocities that unless the massacres ceased friendly relations between the American people and the people of Turkey would be threatened.[117]

The next paragraph revealed the lack of any teeth in this supposed warning:

Officials made it clear that this message did not threaten a break in diplomatic relations. Turkey already has let it be known that she

---

114.Koolakian collection.
115.*Syracuse Post-Standard,* September 21, 1915, p. 1.
116.Ibid.
117.Ibid., October 5, 1915, p. 2.

will not permit interference by any foreign power with her so-called "Armenian policy." As American life or property has not been affected, the United States government, without submitting an official protest, merely informs Turkey of the effect continued Armenian atrocities would have upon the American people.[118]

The public does not appear to have fostered unrealistic hopes that Germany would intervene to stay Turkey's hand. A *Syracuse Post-Standard* editorial remarked that Count Johann Bernstorff, the German ambassador, made the "thin" explanation that "the stories of Armenian massacres come from Russian sources and are therefore false." The stories are not false, asserted the editorial. Rather, they come from unimpeachable sources. The writer then makes reference to the mass meeting on October 3, 1915, being planned by the Syracuse Armenians to protest the massacres.[119]

Meanwhile, the bad news continued. A front-page article in the *Syracuse Post-Standard* on October 4, 1915, was headlined: "Helpless Armenians Massacred by Turks in Unparalleled Orgy." The article reported the work undertaken by Charles R. Crane, Cleveland H. Dodge and others who had formed a committee to investigate the facts of the Armenian massacres and to aid sufferers.

The trauma of the deportations and massacres of this period left its mark forever on the Armenian people. "Not one family remained unaffected" by this national calamity. "They lost not just friends, but close family members." Many years later the few survivors still felt the terror of those days. Karekin Chengerian was nine years old when armed men took away his three sisters and older brother and killed them. Almost seventy years later, he still dreaded the memories of those experiences. "It just shakes me to remember."[120]

Every Armenian's concern was focused on securing reliable news from the home country. Meanwhile a stream of refugees was beginning to straggle into safe havens in bordering countries, starving, ill, stunned by deprivation and brutality. Armenian communities everywhere sought to respond.

The Armenians in Syracuse prepared for a mass meeting on October 3, 1915, to protest the massacres. A news article in the *Syracuse Post- Standard,* long and prominently displayed, reported:

More than 250 Armenian residents of Syracuse plan to hold a mass meeting Sunday evening in the auditorium of the Fourth Presbyterian Church to voice through Americans as well as themselves an

---

118. Ibid.
119. Ibid., September 30, 1915, p. 4
120. Desteian; *Syracuse Herald American,* April 24, 1983.

unofficial appeal to Kaiser Wilhelm of Germany to halt the deportation and slaughter of their compatriots by the Turkish government.

Rev. S. H. Haladjian, the new pastor of the Armenian Protestants
in this city, said last evening that several prominent Syracuse men
have been invited to address the gathering, which has the sanction
of the Ministers Association.

Among the speakers is Charles Andrews, former chief judge of the
Court of Appeals. A reply is expected to-day from Judge Andrews,
who is in Baltimore for the consecration of Rev. Dr. Charles Fiske,
recently appointed bishop-coadjutor of the diocese of Central New
York.[121]

The article reports that the Syracuse mass meeting "is in line with the
nationwide movement to organize a relief fund and commission to send and
distribute food and clothing" to the starving refugees. It also reported the estimate of the noted missionary leader, Dr. Robert Chambers, that "there are
only 750,000 Armenians living out of a total population of 1,500,000."[122]

Neither the printed program for October 3, 1915, nor a report of the event
appearing in *Hairenik* mentioned non-Armenian speakers. The elaborate
three-part program promised an extensive array of speeches and musical performances, while the article described an earnest, but otherwise conventional,
if excessive, Armenian public meeting. The program listed no fewer than eight
musical performances, four recitations, a dramatic presentation by the
Zahrajian sisters, and three speakers in addition to the chairman's opening
remarks.[123]

Akabi Azadian, overcoming her antipathy toward the Tashnags, lent her
presence, opening the meeting and inviting the public to stand and join the
children's choral group in singing the American national anthem. Thereafter,
H. Terzian chaired the meeting.[124]

The highlight of the program was the introduction of the Syracuse chapter
of the Armenian Red Cross. By the fall of 1915, the women of Syracuse, in
response to the calls of the Zahrajian sisters, had moved to form a chapter
under the auspices of the ARF. Elise Kalebdjian (mother of Setrak and Missak)
invited others to join the newly formed chapter of twenty-one members and

121. *Syracuse Post-Standard,* September 29, 1915.
122. Ibid.
123. Printed program in Eckhoff collection.
124. *Hairenik,* October 23, 1915.

eight associate members.[125] Despite a fine start, the chapter faltered and remained inactive until 1920, when it was revived.

The *Hairenik* account of the event devotes far more attention to the details of the program than to the fund-raising. The amount raised to be used on behalf of the wounded was not even mentioned. The October 3 gathering offered opportunities to showcase the children of the community. In addition to the children's choral group that opened the meeting, there were violin performances by "Professor" K. Aiqouni's two pupils, "little" D. Philibosian (most likely the son of Harry Philibosian) and H. Koolakian (son of George Koolakian), there was a recitation by "little" A. (Agishe) Minasian, and presentations by the young Zahrajian sisters and S. Kupelian. The adults also contributed to the entertainment: there were songs by an adult choral group, a solo by Kh. Papazian, and two violin performances by Syracuse's resident musician, Aiqouni.[126]

After speakers comrade S. Nigsarian and Rev. Haladjian of the Fourth Presbyterian Church made their presentations, the spotlight fell on Arsen Mikaelian, the ARF field worker making what was probably his second trip to Syracuse. He stressed Armenian determination to withstand the sufferings of centuries. He spoke again at a public meeting on October 5, providing more details on Armenia's struggles to survive and responding to questions. In a meeting on October 7, Mikaelian explained Armenia's relations with Russia. On this occasion five new members joined the Syracuse ARF committee.[127]

A photograph, probably of the Syracuse ARF committee, taken at the time of Mikaelian's visit shows a group of forty men and a woman wearing a large hat peering between two heads at the back. The woman appears to be Mannig Zahrajian, who has been referred to as a "comrade." At the center in front are Mikaelian and Terzian, who had chaired the October 3 meeting. Two young girls (one of them Zarouhi Zahrajian), seated on their laps, are holding a framed photograph of the Armenian hero, General Antranig, while a small boy (probably Agishe Minasian) sits nearby on the grass. Autumn leaves scattered in the foreground help to confirm the dating of the photograph.[128]

In the fall of 1915, an extensive plan to raise funds for the refugees was created. The American Committee for Armenian and Syrian Relief, established under the auspices of the American Board of Commissioners for Foreign Missions, later incorporated as the Near East Relief, conducted national drives for funds, food, and clothing. In Syracuse, a Committee for

---

125. Ibid.
126. Ibid.
127. Ibid.
128. Photograph in Eckhoff collection.

ARF members and sympathizers photographed with Arsen Mikaelian at the time of his second visit to Syracuse on October 3, 1915. At the center in front are Mikaelian and Harutiun Terzian holding a photo of General Antranig. The lone woman in the photo is Mannig Zahrajian seen at the back.

Relief in Armenia was formed, most likely spearheaded by the Armenians who were among the members of the distinguished executive committee. It included: Bishop Charles Fiske, D.D., Rev. Dr. James Empringham (chairman), L.R.C. Whittaker (vice-chairman), H. P. Philibosian (treasurer), Rev. Dr. A. C. Fulton, Chancellor James R. Day of Syracuse University, A. W. Hedden, M.D., Rev. J. Applebee, Rev. S. H. Haladjian, Mrs. Donald Dey, Mrs. G. L. Barnard, Mrs. H. B. Azadian. Almus Olver was executive secretary with headquarters in the YMCA building. The committee set up an orderly method for receiving contributions in cash, food, and clothing[129] and maintained close communication with headquarters in New York City, as indicated by correspondence in the Azadian archives. A benefit violin concert in July 1918 performed by Haig Gudenian (from Albany) produced a profit of $83.60 which was quickly forwarded to headquarters of the American Committee for Armenian and Syrian Relief in New York City. [130]

More modest efforts within the Armenian community were carried out as well. Proceeds from a four-act play, presented on March 5, 1916, in Ramion Hall, at the corner of Seymour and Oswego Streets, were to benefit the needy

---

129. Printed notice in Azadian collection.
130. Official receipt and letter of acknowledgment in Azadian collection.

of the Caucasus. Mrs. Eckhoff has noted on the printed program, "The very first play the Armenians had in Syracuse."[131] The program identifies the players as the newly formed ARF Avarair group.[132]

An ARF picnic on July 4, 1916, also sought to raise funds for the refugees in the Caucasus. A photograph of the Armenian hero Keri was auctioned off for $30 and a total of $80 was realized from the event. An Armenian priest, Vagharshag Vartabed Arshagouni, from Providence, was the featured speaker. Although the news account does not mention it, he was probably in Syracuse to perform Armenian services, held occasionally when a priest became available. He spoke with passion, extolling Armenia's revolutionary heroes, rejecting the tears of slavery and demanding revenge.[133]

Gradually, as reliable accounts began to arrive, the stunned Armenians began to comprehend the full scope of the cataclysm that had overtaken their people. For years, broken families sought news about the loved ones from whom they had become separated. Most of those left behind had died or disappeared. Many agencies participated for years in the work of resettling refugees and caring for orphan children. Members of the Zonta Club of Syracuse were evidently moved by a talk given by "Lady" Anne Azgapitian on "Work of Americans in Asia Minor." Following the talk, a motion was made, seconded, and carried that the Zonta Club adopt two of the Armenian children. Later minutes made no further mention of the children.[134]

The emergence of quota restrictions and bureaucratic rules added to the woes of a suffering people. Sarah Minasian recounted one such instance to me. An Armenian in America finally accumulated the money to pay for passage to America of two sons he had left in France, who had by now become adults. At New York they were turned back because in response to inquiry they said they intended to work. Apparently, they were coming as tourists, not as immigrants under the quota.

There would be many a scholarly argument as to the number of Armenians who were massacred versus how many were displaced and deported. But the fact remains that today the six Armenian provinces in eastern Turkey and the territories of Cilicia, where an Armenian kingdom reigned during the Crusades, have been emptied of their Armenian populations. Their homes, properties, and even bank accounts were confiscated. Approximately three-quarters

---

131. A comedy had been presented two years earlier, according to a *Hairenik* report dated December 29, 1914.
132. Printed program in Eckhoff collection.
133. *Hairenik,* July 26, 1916. Clipping in Eckhoff collection.
134. Zonta Club of Syracuse, minutes of March 3, 1924. In Zonta archives at the Onondaga Historical Association.

of the seventy thousand Armenians yet remaining in Turkey live in Istanbul, where they maintain a very low profile.[135]

In 1916, the wounds were very fresh. What could be done in the face of such horror? First it was necessary to mourn. On November 12, 1916, at the Department of Public Instruction, the Armenians of Syracuse came together in a solemn memorial service. The printed notice indicates that H. Azadian presided and the able S. Nigsarian chaired the meeting. Speakers included N. Mangouni, M. Babikian, H. Ouzounian, and D. Gozigian. There were declamations by Mr. Kh. (Khachadour) Aghaian and Miss M. Zahrajian, recitations by Misses N. Babikian (Nishan's daughter) and A. Desteian, and solos by Messrs Gh. Tufenkjian and H. Babikian. Professor K. Aiqouni played violin. A paragraph at the bottom exhorts the public to turn away from tears and mourning and instead to dedicate itself to rebuilding mother Armenia.[136]

A second printed notice for the same event contains much of the same information, but adds certain details. The sponsors are identified as the trustees of Syracuse's Armenian Apostolic and Evangelical churches, the local Hunchagian branch, and the ARF committee. In a message of several paragraphs, the notice directs attention to the recently inaugurated publication, *The New Armenia,* which was intended to acquaint non-Armenians with Armenia's history, culture, and present plight. The message notes that the new English-language monthly was praised by the Armenian Prelate in America, Bishop Arsen Vehooni, and that American readers of the publication had already donated more than $100,000 to the American Committee for Armenian and Syrian Relief. Yet, funds were lacking to underwrite the publication. The public was urged to respond. *The New Armenia* was a private enterprise, although it had individual and organizational supporters.

Fighting Back

It was not only their hard-won dollars that the immigrant youth willingly sacrificed to relieve the sufferings of unknown compatriots. They offered their lives as well. As early as the late 1890s, and especially in the early 1900s, young immigrants, moved by patriotism, left their safe havens in America to join the self-defense efforts in Turkey and the Armenian forces engaged in conflict with the Tatars in 1905.[137]

The response was even greater after hostilities broke out between Russia and Turkey in 1914. The ARF in the United States not only recruited

---

135.*Armenian Weekly,* July 19, 1980, p. 3.
136.Printed notice in Eckhoff collection.
137.Kevorkian, p. 361.

volunteers, but sometimes sought to train them as well. The Hrair military training group of the Providence ARF committee sent more than one hundred fifty volunteers to fight in the Armenian Legion (to be discussed later) or in the Caucasus.[138]

With Russian approval and support, four Armenian volunteer units were formed to fight on the Caucasian front, each under the command of a popular Armenian hero: Antranig, Dro, Hamazasp, and Keri. The Armenians fought valiantly. By October 1915, five hundred of them had given their lives and there were more than twelve hundred wounded or missing. Soon, however, Tsarist sentiment reverted to the standard Russification policies and the Armenian units were ordered to be dismantled. The volunteer contingents, who had fought so bravely under their beloved Armenian commanders, were to be absorbed into the Russian army. For the Armenians, Russia's war was not necessarily their war. During the first three months of 1916 more than three thousand Armenian volunteers withdrew from the army. The remaining Armenian volunteers were reformed into six Armenian rifle battalions under Russian officers.[139]

Some of these forces remained to fight in the Armenian army after the withdrawal of Russian military units in 1917–18. Among them was one of the earliest volunteers from Syracuse, Vagharshag Shahinian. A native of Van in central Turkey, he had come to Syracuse in 1910 and worked in the Oberdorfer Foundry. When war broke out in 1914, he went to Armenia and participated in the decisive battle of Sardarabad in 1918, after which Armenia declared its independence. In 1917 in Erevan, Armenia, he married the sister of Zarmair Taft, later a Syracuse resident, and after Armenia's independence he returned to the United States with his wife.[140]

B. Marzbanian, who had spoken at the ARF public meeting on December 2, 1914, was another early volunteer. He appears in several photographs in the Eckhoff collection. On the back of one photo, in Mrs. Eckhoff's handwriting, appears the notation: "Bedros M. went back to Armenia to fight under Gen. Antranig to face [save?] Armenia from the Turks." He is shown in military uniform with two other soldiers. A photograph of Marzbanian in civilian dress, dated December 6, 1924, carries a notation indicating that it had been sent from Armenia.[141]

138.*Armenian Weekly,* March 9, 1972, p. 1.

139.Richard G. Hovannisian, *Armenia on the Road to Independence 1918* (Berkeley and Los Angeles: University of California Press, 1967), p. 44; p. 62.

140.Zarmair Taft.

141.*Hairenik,* December 29, 1914; photographs in Eckhoff collection.

ՀԱՄԱԶԳԱՅԻՆ ՍԳԱՀԱՆԴԷՍ

ՆՈՒԻՐՈՒԱԾ ՀԱՅԱՍՏԱՆԻ ԱՆԹԱՌ ՆԱՀԱՏԱԿՆԵՐՈՒ ՅԻՇԱՏԱԿԻՆ

եւ

ՀԱՄԱԿՐԱԿԱՆ ՄԵԾ ԺՈՂՈՎ

ՀԱՑ ԴԱՏԻ ՊԱՇՏՊԱՆ **THE NEW ARMENIA** ՊԱՐԲԵՐԱԹԵՐԹԻՆ

ՆԱԽԱՁԵՌՆՈՒԹԵԱՄԲ

ՀԱՅԿԱԿԱՆ ՆՊԱՍՏՈՐԻ ՏԵՂԱՅԻՆ ՕԺԱՆԴԱԿ ՑԱՆՑՆԱԿՄՐԻՆ

եւ ՀԱՄԱԳՈՐԾԱԿՑՈՒԹԵԱՄԲ

ՍԻՐԱԿԻՒՁԻ ՀԱՅ ԱՌԱՔ. եւ ԱԻԵՇ. ԵԿԵՂԵՑԻՈՑ ՀՈԳԱԲԱՐՋՈՒԹԵԱՆՑ,

Ս. Դ. ՀՆՉԱԿԵԱՆ ՄԱՍՆԱՃԻՒՂԻՆ եւ Հ. Յ. ԴԱՇՆԱԿՑՈՒԹԵԱՆ ԿՈՄԻՏԷԻՆ:

ՏԵՂԻ ՊԻՏԻ ՈՒՆԵՆԱՑ

ՅԱՌԱՋԻԿԱՑ ԿԻՐԱԿԻ, 12 ՆՈՅ. 1916

DEPARTMENT OF PUBLIC INSTRUCTION ԺՈՂՈՎԱՍՐԱՀԻՆ ՄԷՋ

ԿԷՍ ՕՐԷ ՎԵՐՋ ԺԱՄԸ ՁԻՇՏ 2ԻՆ

Նախագահ՝ Տիար Բ. Ազատեան   Ատենապետ՝ Տիար Ս. Նրկսար

Ատենապաստութիւնբ՝ Տեարք Հ. Մանկունրի, Ս. Պապիկեանբ, Հ. Ուզունեանր
                              եւ Տ. Կոզիկեանի կողմէ:

Արտասանութիւններ՝ Օրդ. Ս. Ձահրէնան, Ն. Պապիկեան եւ Տիար Խ. Ազայեան:
                              Տեարք Հ. ԹրիֆէնկՇեան եւ Հ. Պապիկեան պիտի ճնելրգեն:
                              Երգեր Երգեցիկ Խումբի կողմէ:
                              Հայկական երգերու Քառաքաշարութիւններ ԲՐՈՋ. Դ. ԱՑԳՈՒՆԻԻ կողմէ:

Հայրենակիցներ,

Հայաստանի աղէտը գիտնած է բոլորս ալ: Չայ ողբալու լատացող կերան է, սակայն, գո-
տեպնդուելլ եւ աշխատել Մար Հայաստանին վերաբանմունին համար: Հայ նահատակներու ոսկորները
պիտի ցնծան, եթէ անոնց վրալ, փոխանակ ողբ ու կոծի, սատանեն մեր ստեղծացործ շունչը:

Ահա ատոր համար այս սգահանդէսին կը միացինին գ ջացմանց քաղսամական ժողով կը համելդ The New
Armeniա, որ նոր Հայաստանին մը լոյսդ կը Հեծիցեց մեր ակտաքներուն:

Եթէ ներրացացկը ու Ամնեթիկացկը ըստ արժանուի ծանօրացած բլլայն Հայ Ազգին քաղաքա-
կրբՔից դերից, Ըերեսս ջարդի ու քաղդումի վերջին աշատեր պատուճանդ չի պալլքնք մեր գլխսն:
    The New Armenia, աճս, լայնաշորցն կը կատարէ Հացց ծանօրացնելու անխատաքեթ եւ կն-
սական պարատկանությիւնը, զոր խառրատնաորէն դնաշատեր են ձ՚լմ Պրոբք նման ակստաւ Հա-
լւատբներ, եւ Ամերիկեան ու ներ ոպեն կարեր որաԹերեթ:

Ջան աներկնել The New Armeniա քազագման ծառայութիւնը Հայկական Ինֆոպրխության ակ-
սացկող, որուն ժամին տո ադֆ պատարեկ ձի խոստ, The New Armenia գլխատոր ազգակ եղակ երաս,
Հայկական Նպատորի լածղութեան, ծուռակ կը լարաոպատո Դեր. Արբե Ս. Վ. ՎեՀևնֆ, Ամերի-
կասլ ԱռաՁոճրբ:

    Բաց ատտ, The New Armenia Ամերիկեան ընքերցողնեզ տեզեդ ըման 100,000 տոլար նպատ
դրբեր են American Committee for Armenian and Syrian Relief:

Սակայն գինա՞նե ապղեռզ, բէ The New Armenia իր ոպապրունեան ծակած բակ չի կրնար
ՀայաՔէք: Ի՞ն պիտի խորֆին ձր ստար բակկնավճ երբ իժանան The New Armeniա ներԹական
ոնձկունքՔիզ:

    Լոֆքե, Ամբերիկան ԾեոդայնունՔիա տարքորդուն տո Թէ, կր գրե:

    ՀեզթնֆիրԸնե ձէ արձակնում չեղակիչ արձապանֆ ամրող աշարֆ լոտրֆ լուեցոստ:
Հալրենակիցներ, աշխավմուր գնատատոսծԹիս ճ գուհ ատտ The New Armeniա համալէ, որ ծեր
ծեսնարֆ արձաանֆ դոՇֆ բորր Ամերիկունֆ գոզոPերոտ ձէֆ, եւ խրբեուֆ զանուֆ՝ ստար
Հատնֆստնա այ ազգանֆր պարբերակսնֆ:

«Հայկ Ֆզարոսծ»
HAIG PUBLISHING CO., 136 E. 26TH ST., NEW YORK

Memorial program for Armenia's martyrs, November 1916.

B. Marzbanian, in center, one of the volunteers from Syracuse, as an Armenian
soldier, about 1916.

A photograph in the Vartkas and Zephyr Minasian collection shows fifteen
young men and a boy (Agishe Minasian) in which a sign appears with the legend:

We are leaving the U. S
as volunteers for the
Armenian Army

Aug. 1915

Karekin M. Magarian
Garabed M. Giragosian

All those that it has been possible to identify were from Divrig and most of
them were living in Syracuse in 1915, so it may be presumed that the photo
showed members of the Divrig compatriotic society and may have been taken
in Syracuse. Magarian and Giragosian were both from Aramtagh and are listed
in the Aramtagh book, but neither lived in Syracuse. The Aramtagh book
notes that Giragosian left to volunteer for the Armenian army, but does not

Two volunteers for the Armenian army are shown surrounded by their compatriots, 1915. All are from Divrig.

give that information for Magarian. By January 1917, Giragosian was back in the United States, as indicated by his signature under the minutes of five sessions of the Educational Society of Ormutagh village of Divrig which took place in Watervliet, New York from January to July 1917. Apparently volunteering at another time was Setrak Yeghigian, a member of the Aramtagh society of Syracuse, whose name in the book's membership list is marked with the notation "went as volunteer."[142]

Another photograph from about the same period shows a group of thirty young men with an unidentified uniformed youth in the center. All of those who have been identified are known to have been members of the ARF, so this is presumed to be a photograph of the Syracuse committee.[143] Several other photos of ARF members exist, some of which have been marked ARF, but without dates.[144]

Some young men joined the American war effort. Peter Roomian, who came to Syracuse in 1913, served as an instructor with the United States

142. Aramtagh Book, p. 23; p. 43; pp. 3–8; p. 79.
143. Photograph in Zephyr and Vartkas Minasian collection.
144. Photographs in Benjamin collection.

army.[145] Other young men from Syracuse had been called to active duty with the United States Army. Setrak Jigarjian, Souren Hovnanian, and Harry Terzian were on another front, part of a military expedition into Mexico, ordered by President Woodrow Wilson, in pursuit of the revolutionary general, Francisco "Pancho" Villa, to punish him for his cross-border attacks on Americans.[146] However, not everyone was eager to go off to war. The Eckhoff collection includes a photo of two men, one of whom, according to the inscription on the back, went to Canada to avoid the draft.

After the outbreak of World War I, an effort was made to unify the fund-raising activities within the Armenian communities. It was hoped that a collective drive would ensure greater efficiency in reaching the community and more effective distribution of the funds raised. The four major Armenian political factions, with the mediation and participation of the Armenian Apostolic Church and the cooperation of the Armenian Evangelical Church, formed the National Interests Defense Union of America. It was intended to forward the Union's resources to the National Plenipotentiary Delegation headed by Boghos Nubar, called "Pasha" in recognition of his distinguished status.

Nubar was a polished, urbane gentleman, son of the noted finance and foreign minister of Egypt and himself once the director of the Egyptian State Railways. He was appointed in 1912 by Catholicos Kevork V to seek European backing to ensure reforms for the Armenians of Turkey.[147] When war swept away the issue of reforms, he modified his own mission, directing his efforts toward the liberation of the Armenian provinces.

Fund-raising coalition efforts soon broke down because of disputes over the distribution of the funds. The ARF, which had already been engaged in raising money for the Armenian volunteers in the Caucasus,

> insisted that 50 percent of all the funds be sent to the National Bureau of Tiflis for the assistance of the Armenian volunteer forces in the Russian army. The remaining members insisted that the money be sent to a committee that would operate under the Catholicos of all Armenians and be used only for those volunteers who were willing to go and fight in Turkish Armenia.[148]

---

145. *Syracuse Herald Journal,* February 4, 1987.

146. *Hairenik,* July 26, 1916. Clipping in Eckhoff collection. This is mentioned at the end of an article about a community picnic organized to raise funds for Armenian refugees in the Caucasus by the ARF.

147. Richard G. Hovannisian, *The Republic of Armenia: The First Year, 1918–1919,* vol. I (Berkeley, Los Angeles, London: University of California Press, 1971), p. 257.

In 1917, through an initiative originating in Egypt, a new group called Armenian National Union of America was formed to take the place of the defunct National Interests Defense Union. The organizing committee consisted of three individuals representing the three major parties: ARF, Hunchag, Ramgavar. The new union soon formed chapters in the American communities.

There was generous response from everywhere to the call for funds. A million-dollar fund-raising campaign raised $931,982 in four years.[149] The immigrant Armenians dug down deep into their pockets, probably depriving themselves of many personal needs in order to reach the ambitious goal that had been set. From April to December 31, 1917 the Syracuse chapter collected $3,500. An additional $3,235 was collected from April 1 through December 31, 1918, a total of $6,735 from a small community.[150] The funds were used for the volunteers, for the Armenian National Bureau in Tiflis, for Nubar's National Delegation in Paris, for the National Union in Egypt, for the Armenian prisoners of war in Germany, for the families of volunteers, and other needs.[151]

Under the auspices of the Armenian National Union, Nubar arranged with French authorities for the establishment of a volunteer unit to be composed of Armenians and Syrians of Ottoman origin to serve in Cilicia under French command.[152] Although the roots of ancient Armenia were in the Caucasus, the Armenians also had a strong historical presence in Cilicia. This was the locale of the last Armenian kingdom, which ended in 1375. The recent deportations had uprooted hundreds of thousands of Armenians from the Cilician cities and rich farmlands where they had previously flourished. It was presumably the hope of liberating Cilician Armenia that prompted the proposal to form an Armenian volunteer legion to fight in this area.

Enthusiastic response greeted the proposal to form an Armenian legion. Among the 1,172 volunteers responding from America, there were seven from Syracuse. In the listing they are numbered and identified by name, home city, and city of residence in the United States. They are as follows: 48, George Aintablian, Kesab; 56, Karnig Andonian, Ekrek; 57, Karnig Andonian, Sepastia; 618, Bedros Mikaelian, Sepastia; 706, Khachadour Nigoghosian,

---

148. *Documents on the Schism in the Armenian Church of America* (New York: Diocese of the Armenian Church of America, 1993), p. 7.

149. Kevorkian, p. 365.

150. *Deghegakir Hai Azkayin Miutyan Amerigayi 1917–1921* [Report of the Armenian National Union of America 1917–1921], p. 71.

151. Kevorkian, p. 365.

152. Hovannisian, *Armenia on the Road*, p. 66.

ARF members with a volunteer, about 1915.

Sepastia; 840, Bhevot (Ghevont?) Vartabed Bekyarian, Rodosto; 940, Sarkis Soghomonian, Hadjin. The list also includes number 434, Norair Garabedian, Divrig, from Troy, who later came to Syracuse to live.[153] Number 840, Vartabed Bekyarian, a clergyman, is a surprise. He appears as a volunteer from Syracuse, but there is no evidence to show that Syracuse had been his parish. Another surprise: number 86 identifies the fiery Vagharshag Vartabed Arshagouni of Rodosto, from Providence, who had spoken in such a heated manner at the Syracuse picnic on July 4, 1916.

It is difficult to envision that such activities could have been carried out in secrecy, without publicity and propaganda, as requested by the administrative leaders of the Armenian National Union, "in order not to invite the attention of our enemies or to provoke retaliation against the Armenians and Syrians remaining in Turkey."[154]

The Legion d'Orient, later called the Armenian Legion, was composed almost entirely of Armenians. The volunteers fought with distinction in several major campaigns in Palestine and Syria, and at the end of the war occupied strategic sites in Cilicia over which France had taken a mandate.[155]

153. *Deghegakir,* pp. 89–99.
154. Ibid., p. 28, col. 2.
155. Hovannisian, *The Republic of Armenia,* vol. I, p. 258; Atamian, p. 100.

Not all the volunteers returned and the search for information about lost, deceased, or displaced relatives now included legionnaires as well. In his efforts to secure news about his nephew who had served in the Legion d'Orient, Aaron Sachaklian of Syracuse wrote on March 10, 1920, to the British and French Consulates in New York City, the American Consul General in Paris, and the United States Department of State in Washington. An earlier inquiry July 1, 1919) sent to the British Red Cross with headquarters in Alexandria, Egypt, had been forwarded to the Chief of the French Medical Service in Palestine. Responses were courteous, but not helpful.[156]

Despite some successes, the Armenian National Union began to dissolve as disputes and disagreements emerged between the coalition parties and it met the same fate as previous efforts for unity. Over the years the Armenian people have been aware of the need to come together in some kind of united manner to govern their affairs and to present a common face to the outside world, but they have not been able to overcome severe cultural and ideological differences. They lacked the tradition of a central government and had lived for centuries in widely separated communities under the domination of empires that differed from them and from each other in their culture and traditions. A prayer in the Armenian liturgy beseeching love and unity among the Armenian people reflects the nation's factionalism from ancient times.

Life Goes On

While momentous events continued to unfold in Armenia, life in Syracuse went on as before. The program for the ARF public meeting on February 8, 1917, adhered to the usual formula. Comrade K. Borchanian opened the meeting. The choral group sang "Azadn Asdvatz." Miss Aghavni Zahrajian recited K. Vartanian's "Jampa Patsek." An agricultural student at the "local" university, as the *Hairenik* article reported, Comrade A. Der Arsenian, spoke on ways to relieve Armenia's distress. Comrade Kh. Papazian sang "Tsain Door, Ov Sovag." Comrade Kh. Minasian recited Aharonian's "Harkank Kez." The visiting speaker, Shahan Natalie, explained the reasons for Armenia's troubles over the centuries, the struggle for independence, and the reasons for disunity within the Armenian-American community for the past two years. The audience apparently was attentive, because they raised many questions following the talk. Regrettably, the article fails to provide Natalie's explanations for the community's lack of harmony.[157]

---

156. Sachaklian collection.
157. *Hairenik,* March 21, 1917. Clipping in Eckhoff collection.

The musical benefit program given in Syracuse in 1917 by the noted singers A. Shah Mouradian, tenor, and Mrs. Zabelle Panosian, soprano, was one of the highlights in Syracuse community history. Seated left to right are Zabelle Panosian, Mannig Zahrajian Bedrosian, Satenig Apikian. Standing are S. Nigsarian, Krikor Aiqouni, A. Shah Mouradian, and Jasper Abajian.

Family celebrations also often became public events in the small community. The engagement of comrade K. Bedrosian (from Constantinople) to comrade Mannig Zahrajian (from Rodosto) had been announced in July 1916. The community joyfully witnessed their wedding on February 11, 1917. A photograph shows a cluster of slightly dazed-looking men and Mannig, grouped around a festive table. A note on the back of the photograph, probably written by Mrs. Eckhoff, reads: "Five o'clock in the morning. This picture was taken at the wedding."[158]

Only two and one-half years later, the *Hairenik* announced the death of one of the community's "best and most respected members, comrade Mannig Bedrosian." She had fought illness, but in vain. An inscription on the back of a photo of a group of women, including Mannig, notes that it was taken at the Khachig Minasian farm "where sister stayed," presumably to recover her health. The entire community attended the funeral. Eulogies were spoken by Rev. Markarian, K. Gozigian, representing the Hunchag party, and A. Shavarshouni, on behalf of her fellow ARF comrades.[159]

One of the community's most lavish programs was presented under joint sponsorship of the ARF and Hunchag committees. The widely acclaimed Armenian singers, A. Shah Mouradian, tenor, and Mrs. Zabelle Panosian, soprano, were brought to Syracuse for a special benefit performance. The program also included K. Aiqouni, violin, and John Elbert Chadwick, pianist.

158.Ibid., July 26, 1916; March 21, 1917; photograph in Eckhoff collection.
159.*Hairenik,* December 23, 1919; photograph in Eckhoff collection.

The large printed notice announced the event would take place on April 8, 1917, at Cooper Hall, 817 South State Street, Syracuse, as a benefit concert for the Armenians who had escaped from Turkey to take refuge in the Caucasus. Members of both sponsoring parties were on the committee.[160] The committee's stirring message to the community exhorted action in the face of tragedy: "During these unspeakable days of mourning and grief it is not enough to pour tears over the unforgettable memory of our unburied martyrs. We must keep in mind the resurrection of Armenia in the future and heartily greet its rebirth."[161]

The Republic of Armenia

Scarcely a year later Armenia was indeed reborn, but the grim circumstances allowed no joy. Since the beginning of the war, the region had had no respite from conflict and strife. Russian advances into eastern Turkey, in which the Armenian volunteer forces participated with enthusiasm, gave the Armenians hope that their territories would be reclaimed, but the Russian advances then turned to retreat. The outbreak of the Russian Revolution in March 1917 had severe consequences in the Caucasus, destroying whatever security that had been provided by Tsarist rule. Insisting on ending the war, the Bolsheviks (who had come to power in November 1917) moved quickly to sign a humiliating peace with Germany and Turkey. The March 1918 Treaty of Brest-Litovsk was especially disastrous for the Armenians, requiring the evacuation of Russian forces from Turkish Armenia, Kars, Ardahan, and Batum.[162]

Midst chaos, a Transcaucasian Federation composed of Georgia, Azerbaijan, and Armenia was formed, but their differing interests soon led to the collapse of the unstable union. One by one, each declared independence. Georgia sought to preserve itself by welcoming German occupation, while the Azerbaijanis, a Turkic people, cemented an alliance with the Turks. This meant only more complications for the Armenians, who were left to invent a governing structure while dealing with a Turkish army that was encroaching on Erevan, the last city in Armenia remaining in Armenian hands. To this day, the heroic and historic battles at Karakilisa, Bash-Abaran, and Sardarabad, which stopped the Turkish advance, are commemorated as the pivotal engagements that preserved Armenia from extinction.[163]

---

160. O. Enfiejian, chairman, K. Tufenkjian, secretary, K. Apikian, treasurer, S. Nigsarian, K. Aghayan, K. Borchanian, K. Gozigian, Mrs. S. Apikian, Mrs. M. Bedrosian, Misses A. Desteian, S. Kupelian, A. Zahrajian, M. Zahrajian. All except Aghayan, Borchanian, Gozigian, and the Desteian sisters were affiliated with the ARF.
161. Poster in Eckhoff collection.
162. Hovannisian, *Armenia on the Road*, p. 104.

Thus was born the Republic of Armenia on May 28, 1918, the first Armenian state to exist since the fall of the Cilician kingdom in 1375. It remained in existence for two and one-half tumultuous, war-torn years. Throughout that period, the goal of its leaders was survival—survival not only of the pitiful new state, but also the physical survival of the hundreds of thousands of refugees who crowded into the tiny territory seeking precarious sanctuary. During the first few months of the Republic, more than two hundred thousand of them died of disease and deprivation. Hostilities had interrupted farming for several seasons and starvation loomed. Desperately, Armenia's leaders sought help of any kind from any source.[164]

Finally, in November 1918 the terrible war that had brought misery and death to so many millions came to an end. Was the fall of 1918 to bring Armenia's spring, at long last? All eyes were now directed toward Paris, where the peace conference, starting in January 1919, was to negotiate a settlement. Surely, it was thought by Armenians, the Allies, who had all made many warm expressions of sympathy and support for Armenia, would finally reward their "Little Ally" for its many sacrifices in the war effort.[165]

With hopes high, the delegation representing the Armenian Republic, headed by Avedis Aharonian, a distinguished author and public figure, made its way to Paris, only to discover that the Republic of Armenia was not included on the list of delegations to the peace conference. The major powers were troubled by the role of Russia and had determined that neither Russia nor any of its nationalities which had attempted to set up national governments would participate in the deliberations to take place.[166]

A further problem for Aharonian and his delegation was the presence of Boghos Nubar's National Delegation, which also sought to represent the interests of the Armenian people. Thus, even in these life-and-death circumstances, the Armenians were divided. The presence of two Armenian delegations undermined the effectiveness of Armenian claims and created an atmosphere of indecision and confusion.

Although they tried desperately to form a common front, the leaders of the two delegations at the Paris Peace Conference could not have differed more widely in temperament, outlook, and even in their goals and values. For some Armenians, the existence of the Republic of Armenia was nothing less than a heaven-sent miracle, but others—Boghos Nubar among them—had no

---

163. Hovannisian, *The Republic of Armenia,* vol. I, pp. 30–35.
164. Ibid. 126–55.
165. See Appendix, pp.147–54 in Hovannisian, *Armenia on the Road* for British, French, Italian, and American expressions of support.
166. Hovannisian, *The Republic of Armenia,* vol. I, p. 255.

commitment to a state which had reclaimed only part of historic Armenia, leaving the now depopulated six Armenian vilayets of eastern Turkey and Cilicia still in Turkish hands. Even worse, the Armenian Republic was the creation of the Armenian Revolutionary Federation, a radical and socialist party—anathema to the conservative Ramgavar Nubar and his followers.[167] In any case, their orientation was not to the Caucasus, but rather to the Armenian vilayets and the territories of the fourteenth century Armenian kingdom in Cilicia.

The question of the boundaries for Armenia not only provided an additional topic for argument among the Armenian people, but confused Armenia's friends as well. There was general agreement that a viable Armenian state required additional lands, but even if the eastern vilayets were to be awarded to Armenia, how could the exhausted nation expect to govern a territory in which it had no inhabitants? The euphoria of great expectations overcame all obstacles. Taking its cues from the good will expressed toward Armenia on all sides, the American Committee for the Independence of Armenia, a support group with many influential Americans in its ranks, demanded an expanded state encompassing Russian Armenia, Turkish Armenia, and Cilicia extending from sea to sea.[168]

It was expected that the peace conference would provide the help that would be needed. Or perhaps the United States would undertake to protect Armenia for a period of time, until the country was able to stand on its own feet. But, weary of war and foreign entanglements, America was ready to turn inward and it was clear that the idea of an Armenian mandate, while much discussed, was not likely to be adopted. For the Armenians, however, this appeared to be the best—perhaps the only—opportunity to press for the realization of their dreams.

Different views regarding the boundaries and the protection for the Armenian Republic were to engage the various diasporan communities, leading to disputes and disagreements that widened already existing fractures. But during the heady days of 1918 and 1919, the future still offered promise.

The American Committee for the Independence of Armenia

Throughout this period, warm and widespread sympathy for the Armenians had welled up among the American people. Now that the war in Europe was over, how could that sympathy be channeled into providing an effective voice to rally support for the Armenian cause in the peace treaties being formulated

---

167. Atamian, p. 210.
168. Hovannisian, *Armenia on the Road*, p. 253.

at Paris? The American Committee for the Independence of Armenia (ACIA) became that voice. The organization came into being largely through the efforts of Vahan Cardashian, a lawyer and director of the Press Bureau of the Armenian National Union. It was formed in December 1918 under the presidency of James G. Gerard, former ambassador to Germany. Within a short time, the ACIA recruited some of the most prominent individuals in the nation. Members included Congressional leaders of both parties, twenty or more state governors, and other distinguished national leaders, industrialists, and philanthropists.[169]

Telegrams in the Azadian collection provide evidence that Azadian and Koolakian became engaged in the activities of the ACIA from the early weeks of its formation. Probably through Charles Proteus Steinmetz, as well as through his own business contacts, Azadian had become acquainted with the leaders of American industry, such as Bernard Baruch, Thomas Edison, George Eastman, Henry Ford, and many other inventors and industrialists. Now their good will was shown in expressions of sympathy and support for the Armenian people, as they responded to an invitation to meet at the Hotel Plaza in New York on February 8, 1919.

One of the first messages of support came from former United States President Theodore Roosevelt in a telegram dated January 5, 1919, sent from Oyster Bay, Long Island, to H. B. Azadian and G. G. Koolakian, addressed at Near East Relief, McCarthy Bldg., Syracuse, N.Y. Roosevelt wrote (I have supplied punctuation):

> Received Elihu Root's directive for Armenian independence assembly New York February eighth. Roosevelt family will attend. Number unconfirmed. One of the earliest nations and the first Christians Armenia has been a proud bulwark of western civilization demonstrating long ago her inalienable right to democratic self government. Her awaited hour of liberation is upon us. It is our requited duty to see that justice and freedom be opportuned to all who seek its hallowed ground. None are more deserving than the Armenians.

Sadly, this may have been the last message sent by the former President. He died in his sleep on January 6. His family, however, kept the promise he had made. A photograph of the event in the Azadian collection shows Roosevelt's widow, Edith, and his two daughters Alice Roosevelt Longworth and Ethel Roosevelt seated at a table next to Azadian and Koolakian.

169.See Gregory L. Aftandilian, *Armenia, Vision of a Republic: The Independence Lobby in America 1918–1927* (Boston: Charles River Books, 1981) for a discussion of ACIA.

Azadian and Koolakian also heard from Josephus Daniels, whose telegram dated January 11 was signed simply "Naval Secretary." His message read:

> Members of naval consulting board expected at American Committee Armenian Independence meeting Hotel Plaza. Have met with key congressional representatives on independence. Expect to convene with President Wilson preparing for Paris Conference. Advise constituents attendance confirmed February eighth.

Another message of support came in a telegram dated January 15, 1919, from Thomas A. Edison to H. B. Azadian at the Azadian Gauge Manufacturing Company in Syracuse. It read:

> Baruch requests my opinion on the Armenian Question. I have employed Armenians from my early days in the telegraph instrument business. I attest to their strong application in technology and the arts. They serve business with enterprising distinction and resource. Friends Ford and Steinmetz agree we have no better examples than in domestic industry. Acts of barbarism should be condemned to our distant past. You may draft a public statement and put my name to it. I endorse the democratic liberation of these denizens of civilization by every humanitarian means.

George Eastman, Azadian's close friend, sent an equally warm message from Rochester on January 19, 1919:

> Accepted Ambassador Gerard's invitation for Presidential gathering at Hotel Plaza, New York February eighth. Members of War Board honored to support independence of Armenia. Regarded as positive step for lasting peace. Expect to see you at delegation and dinner meetings. Arrive on the seventh. Firm pleasure to attend with good friends.

James Gerard, head of the executive committee of ACIA, sent the following message to Azadian and Koolakian on February 4, 1919:

> Expecting you at executive dinner American Committee Hotel Plaza February seventh six thirty sharp. Will advise about banquet arrangements and last minute changes for the eighth. Confirm with office as soon as possible.

The ACIA launched its public campaign with a dinner at the Hotel Plaza in New York City on February 8, 1919. A feature of the program was a pageant depicting three thousand years of Armenian history. It showed some of the trials that Armenia has endured in the cause of civilization and Christianity.

A photograph in the Azadian collection shows some of the five hundred Armenians and friends in attendance, many coming from distant parts of the United States.[170] Among them were luminaries such as former ambassador to Turkey Henry Morgenthau, noted authors F. Scott Fitzgerald and Willa Cather, past and future United States presidents, members of the Edison family, the industrialist from Rochester George Eastman, translator of Armenian poems Alice Stone Blackwell, labor leader Samuel Gompers, the composer Irving Berlin and his wife, and many others whose names are known to us today. James Gerard presided. Others at the head table included Joseph P. Tumulty, President Wilson's secretary (perhaps representing the President, who was in Paris at the time), Andrew Mellon, Secretary of the Treasury, Senator Henry Cabot Lodge, and others of equal distinction.[171]

Seated at a center table bearing the number 24, surrounded by the nation's notables and close to the head table, are the two friends from Syracuse, H. Azadian and G. Koolakian and Mrs. Azadian. Among those sharing the table are the future President Calvin Coolidge and his wife and Secretary of the Navy Josephus Daniels, head of the Naval War Consulting Board. The Syracuse rug dealer and real estate entrepreneur and Azadian's friendly rival, Harry Philibosian, is seated at table 23 nearby. Another Syracusan, Krikor Aghaian, also attended the banquet.

Three additional telegrams in the Azadian collection, all dated February 7, 1919, demonstrate that sympathy for the Armenian people was felt at the highest levels of American public and industrial life. A wire sent from Washington, D.C. from President Wilson, dated February 7, 1919, and addressed to H. B. Azadian and G. G. Koolakian, American Committee for Armenian Independence, Hotel Plaza, New York, New York, reads as follows:

> Industrious the Armenians have demonstrated unfailing aptitude for freedom and deserve long wanted democracy. Much is planned for free Armenia. Stability is needed in the Near East. Including Armenia in our Fourteen Points will insure achievement of this important goal. An example for all peoples we need to put to rest forever the injustices and sufferings of your nation for all of humankind lest they be repeated. I am confident the American

---

170. *New York News,* February 9, 1919. According to Aftandilian (p. 28), four hundred attended.

171. All identifications are by Robert Koolakian.

delegation will vote on this resolution tomorrow. Congratulations. Your work is well done.

Admirably,
Woodrow Wilson

A second telegram dated February 7, 1919, is from Azadian's old friend, Charles Steinmetz, at Schenectady. Addressing Azadian and Koolakian as "American Delegation" at the Hotel Plaza, the telegram reads:

> Express regret cannot attend American Committee meeting at Hotel Plaza, New York tomorrow. With best of wishes to Messrs. Baruch, Hughes, and Bryan for successful resolution at Paris Peace Conference. Armenians deserve freedom and democracy. Lend my name. Count me among loyal supporters for Armenian independence. I consider your people among the most progressive of civilized races throughout the world.

Faithfully,
Charles Steinmetz

A third telegram on the same date, also addressed to Azadian and Koolakian at the Hotel Plaza, is signed simply "Baruch." In 1919 Bernard Baruch became a member of the Supreme Economic Council of the Peace Conference in Paris. He later served as financial advisor to several presidents. The Baruch message reads:

> We have strong backing for American Delegation decision tomorrow. Gerard and Kardashian are ready. Bryan Hughes to voice imminent plea for Armenian independence. Balfour and Pichon expected to follow. Steinmetz will wire everything in order for Paris Peace Conference. Proceed.

Baruch
3:30 p.m. Official Priority
Dispatch American Delegation

A long article in the *New York News* on February 9, 1919, described the Hotel Plaza event in considerable detail. Among the speakers were Charles Evans Hughes, later to become Chief Justice of the United States Supreme Court, and William Jennings Bryan, famed Democratic leader, who "pleaded for a free Armenia." With James Gerard presiding, "a resolution was passed asking the peace conference to help Armenia to establish an independent state."[172]

The meeting also sent a cable to President Woodrow Wilson in Paris where he was seeking to persuade the peace conference to accept the principle of the League of Nations as the basis of the peace. Wilson responded sympathetically to this and other messages from the ACIA. The presence at the dinner of his wife and his secretary, Joseph P. Tumulty, who was seated prominently at one end of the head table, may be viewed as a further expression of Wilson's support and sympathy for the Armenian cause. The meeting heard messages from Foreign Minister Balfour of England and Foreign Minister Pichon of France promising support for Armenian independence. There was also "an expression of thanks for America's interest in Armenian freedom" from the Armenian National Delegation at Paris.[173]

Azadian and Koolakian must have been deeply gratified to receive a second personally addressed communication from President Wilson, expressing his sympathy for the Armenian cause. From Washington, and dated February 26, 1919, the telegram read:

> Ambassador Gerard has kept me informed of your invaluable work on behalf of the American Committee. Let me say that I am deeply touched by the sobriety of your dedication. As the prospects of a democratically independent Armenia come increasingly into focus we must be aware of important negotiations awaiting at the Paris conference which I am sure your efforts will assist in the months ahead. Mrs. Wilson informed me of her meeting with you in New York and I am gratified. We will not forget your many kindnesses.[174]

During the four years of its existence, the ACIA worked tirelessly, largely under Cardashian's direction, sending out letters, telegrams, and circulars on Armenia's behalf. There is no information concerning the further involvement of the Syracuse Armenians with the work of the ACIA.

From Euphoria to Despair

Against all odds, the frail Armenian Republic was still alive one year after its surprising birth. It was an occasion for celebration. In Syracuse, an enthusiastic audience (most of whom were probably ARF supporters) assembled on June 1, 1919, to observe the first anniversary of the Armenian Republic and

---

172. Clipping in Azadian collection.
173. Ibid.
174. Azadian collection.

the twentieth anniversary of the founding of the ARF's *Hairenik* newspaper.[175]

With S. Nigsarian as chairman, the program proceeded in conventional fashion: a recitation by Drtad Drtadian from Utica, a song by the Aramtagh choral group, a speech by S. Kafafian on the significance of the occasion. Mianzara Zahrajian played the flute and later sang, to the intense delight of the audience. She was accompanied by S. Kupelian on the piano. Comrade S. Ajemian, one of Professor Aiqouni's pupils, played violin.[176] The visiting speaker, Vahe Ardzrouni, discussed the significance of the event being celebrated and stressed the role and responsibilities of the communities. The ARF Avarair group presented a play, after which a fund drive for the *Hairenik* took place. Ardzrouni spoke again briefly, pointing out the public's responsibility toward the publication which for twenty years had helped to link together the scattered Armenian communities in this country. In a short time $400 was raised. All those contributing to the program appear to have been ARF members or supporters.

A long article in *Hairenik* on December 23, 1919, provided a comprehensive report of events sponsored by the Syracuse ARF during the autumn months that followed the June program, omitting the exact dates on which they had taken place.

Aram Proodian, a visiting speaker, lectured in a meeting open only to ARF members. At another event, this time open to the public, a visitor, A. Der Manuelian, discussed political issues facing the nation. The speaker was probably the same individual who wrote to Aaron Sachaklian eight months later, signing the letter as secretary of the Legation of the Republic of Armenia in Washington, D. C. The meeting offered the typical program: speeches by Misses Zahrajian and Kupelian, songs, and performances on the violin by Aiqouni, and his pupil, Haig Koolakian.

A month later, the ARF sponsored another program which took place "as usual" in the YMCA hall. Chairman S. Nigsarian opened with a few words, Khachig Minasian and A. Sarkisian gave recitations, A. Shavarshouni spoke, the choral group sang, and S. Rushdouni (probably the visiting speaker) discussed Armenia's external and internal enemies and the role of the Republic in Armenian history. Following this "intensely interesting meeting," there was

---

175. *Hairenik,* July 17, 1919. Clipping in Eckhoff collection.

176. Steve Ajemian (known in later years as "Archie"), then a youth of sixteen, had arrived in Syracuse in 1913 at the age of ten in the company of an adult relative, to join his father. After the death of his mother and sister in the 1915 deportations, his father remarried.

another meeting, attended by most of the community, at which time Rushdouni discussed "The essence of socialism."

In addition to their other efforts on behalf of Armenian causes, Syracuse Armenians also participated in fund-raising for the Near East Relief. By a special act of Congress, the American Committee for Relief in the Near East was granted a national charter in August 1919 to provide relief and to assist in the resettlement of the refugees of the Near East. It was also to care for orphans, widows, and to promote the welfare of "those who have been rendered destitute or dependent directly or indirectly, by the vicissitudes of war, the cruelties of men, and other causes beyond their control."[177] Armenian ladies bravely toured the downtown area of Syracuse soliciting donations. Miss Desteian recalled that Satenik Apikian met with great success by visiting the bars.

Armenians everywhere were heartened by the arrival in New York on October 9, 1919, of an Armenian civil mission headed by Hovhannes Kachaznouni, who had been the first premier of the Armenian Republic. From America the mission sought economic and political assistance, but it also sought to bring together the divided Armenian-American community in order to enlist the manpower and technical skills so desperately needed for the fledgling independent state.[178]

Arriving on the heels of Kachaznouni's mission were Professor Abraham Ter-Hakobian, representing Boghos Nubar and the National Delegation, and a military mission sent by the Armenian Republic's Paris delegation. General Hakob Bagratouni, who headed the military mission, was accompanied by the highly popular General Antranig at the request of Boghos Nubar. The objective of the military mission was to solicit American military aid, seek volunteers for the Armenian army, if permitted, and recruit instructors and technicians.[179]

After a tumultuous reception in New York, Kachaznouni's mission made its way to Washington, where Kachaznouni, Dr. Garegin Pasdermadjian (Armen Garo), and Vahan Cardashian, who represented James Gerard, spoke before Senator Warren Harding's subcommittee regarding conditions in Armenia and to appeal for economic and political assistance. Discussions regarding a possible American mandate for Armenia were also going forward at that time, but the mission avoided the subject, emphasizing Armenia's worthiness to receive military and financial assistance.[180]

---

177. Hovannisian, *The Republic of Armenia: From Versailles to London, 1919–1920,* vol. II
    (Berkeley, Los Angeles, London: University of California Press, 1982), p. 398.
178. Ibid., p. 383.
179. Ibid., p. 385.
180. Ibid., p. 383.

Banquet at Copley-Plaza Hotel in Boston on December 14, 1919 given in honor of Armenian premier Hovhannes Kachaznouni and his mission. Eliza Sachaklian is seated at table 34.

The delegation then visited the White House where they were received by Vice President Thomas R. Marshall, Senate majority and minority leaders Lodge and Hitchcock, Senator King, and Secretary of State Lansing. The President's secretary, Joseph P. Tumulty, expressed Wilson's sympathy and regret that his health did not allow a personal interview.[181]

Armenians in general looked with favor upon President Woodrow Wilson, who had made numerous statements that they found gratifying. They regarded him as a friend and hopes were high that America would rally behind the Armenian Republic offering recognition, protection, and material aid.

The missions may not have achieved all that they would have wished in Washington, but they were supremely successful in their impact on the Armenian communities. Their welcome was wildly enthusiastic and without reserve. Celebrations and rallies greeted the missions on their visits to the Armenian communities. Eliza Sachaklian cherished a photograph and a menu card of the gala banquet at the Copley-Plaza Hotel in Boston on December 14, 1919, given in honor of Kachaznouni and his mission. She regretted that her husband, who had come to Syracuse about a month earlier, was unable to attend.[182] Apparently Sachaklian was able subsequently to meet the Armenian

---

181.Ibid., p. 384.

premier, because the Sachaklian collection contains Kachaznouni's photograph inscribed to him and dated 1920.

Sachaklian's collection also contains a printed notice announcing that at his departure from the United States, Kachaznouni had left behind one million Armenian rubles, which were to be offered for purchase at the rate of ten cents per ruble, with the intention of raising $100,000 for the Armenian Republic. Unfortunately, there is no information concerning the success of the campaign in Syracuse, but two crisp bills—a 250 and a 50 ruble note—in the Sachaklian collection would indicate that Sachaklian had made a purchase.

In Syracuse, the visit to the United States of the missions was celebrated in a community-wide meeting on November 16, 1919, in the YMCA hall. Arranged at the initiative of the ARF, the gathering included representatives from all elements of the community. The reporter who recorded the event reflected the excitement felt by the participants: "For our community this day was a festive one. This day everyone in the community from the oldest to the youngest forgot all doubts and opposition. All had come with clear objectives and emotions to offer their respect toward the Republic and to express their desire and intent to become its citizens."[183]

With the Armenian Tricolor and the American Stars and Stripes on display, the program proceeded. The chairman, V. Sheperdigian, invited the audience to open the meeting with the Armenian national anthem, "Mer Hairenik." There were recitations by Khachadour Aghaian and Miss A. Desteian, songs by Ghazaros Tufenkjian and Haig Babikian, speeches by comrades S. Kupelian and M. Zahrajian, as well as by K. Gozigian, A. Shavarshouni, and Vartabed Markarian. At the conclusion, the secretary of the organizing committee read letters directed to the Armenian delegations in Paris and the missions in the United States, asserting the community's recognition of the Armenian Republic and declaring the desire to be considered its citizens.

The printed notice for this event calls on everyone in the community to express the wish to become Armenian citizens.[184] A directive in the Sachaklian collection dated September 13, 1920, sets forth the conditions and procedures for becoming a citizen of the Armenian Republic. The directive was issued for the guidance of representatives of the Legation who had been designated for each community. Sachaklian was the Syracuse representative.

Through these turbulent months, the Republic's indefatigable minister plenipotentiary, Pasdermadjian, made plans for the future. In a letter dated

---

182. Sachaklian collection; Eliza Sachaklian memoir.
183. *Hairenik,* December 23, 1919. Clipping in Eckhoff collection.
184. Eckhoff collection.

May 24, 1920, in his own handwriting from New York, on the letterhead of Republic of Armenia, Economic Mission to the United States, he offered Aaron Sachaklian of Syracuse the position of vice consul in New York at a salary of $250 a month. Sachaklian would find a building whose first two floors would be for the offices, while Sachaklian and his family would live on the upper floors, rent free. Pastermadjian wrote that he proposed to name as general consul a non-Tashnagtsagan, "someone like Krikor Chibook," but the position would be essentially a formality, as the real work would be done by the vice consul.[185] Sachaklian did not accept the post.

A few months later, Sachaklian received a handwritten letter dated August 14, 1920, on the letterhead of the Legation of the Republic of Armenia from A. Manuelian, secretary, requesting *unger* (comrade) A. Sachaklian's help. Manuelian asked Sachaklian to designate individuals in Syracuse and Binghamton who could collect the names of Armenians who wished to be registered as Armenian citizens. He also asked when Sachaklian expected to visit Washington.[186]

The Washington legation evidently did not wait to hear from Sachaklian. A typewritten letter dated August 20, 1920, from the Armenian embassy, signed G. Pasdermadjian, ambassador, Armenian Republic, and addressed impersonally "Dear Sir," notified the receiver that he has been designated to act on behalf of the embassy to collect names of those who are not American citizens, who wish to become Armenian citizens. A packet of application forms bears no date but may have accompanied a notice dated September 13, 1920, from the Armenian Legation to the Representatives.[187]

The missions whose presence in Washington had engendered so much hope among Armenians evoked a good deal of sympathy and many friendly speeches at the highest level among American legislators and dignitaries, but little practical aid was forthcoming, except for refugee relief. Over the many months of the Senate's deliberations, the questions of military assistance and an Armenian mandate had become hopelessly entangled in a variety of counterproposals and domestic political issues. The Senate was further confused and dismayed by the proposal that the United States take a mandate over Turkey as well as Armenia. Recoiling from the prospect of a long-term and widespread commitment in the region, the Senate stalled until it was too late for effective action.[188] The signs were there for those who could recognize them.

---

185. Sachaklian collection.
186. Ibid.
187. Ibid.
188. Hovannisian, *The Republic of Armenia*, vol. II, p. 397; James B. Gidney, *A Mandate for Armenia* (Kent, Ohio: The Kent State University Press, 1967), pp. 240ff.

Announcement offering the sale of one million Armenian rubles at the rate of ten cents per ruble, 1919.

Receipt dated July 25, 1920 for Aaron Sachaklian's donation of $30.00 in support of the Armenian army.

The doubts of the US administration itself are clearly indicated in a "strictly secret" letter dated August 2, 1919, from Robert Lansing, Secretary of State, to James Gerard reporting the following: "In the opinion of military experts among the Allies, who are acquainted with events in that region, only military intervention from the Allies or from America will bring about sufficient and influential protection for Armenia." Lansing stressed that this information is only for Gerard and his committee.[189]

One of the few Armenians who was able to foresee the direction of Washington's sentiment was Vahan Cardashian, an astute political observer. As director of the Press Bureau of the Armenian National Union and the individual most closely involved with the inner workings of the American Committee for the Independence of Armenia, Cardashian had his finger constantly on Washington's political pulse. As early as November 1919, even while Armenians were reveling in seeing Armenian dignitaries being received at the

---

189. Copy of letter in Sachaklian collection.

highest levels of Washington political power, Cardashian advised Pastermadjian, Armenia's minister plenipotentiary in Washington, that

> should Wilson request authority for the mandate, the Senate would refuse and the Armenian cause would be forgotten. If, on the other hand, the president recognized the Erevan government and Congress sanctioned military, technical, and financial aid, Armenia would gain all the benefits of a mandate as well as those of a sovereign state holding membership in the League of Nations. The fate of Armenia would thereby be separated from that of the Versailles treaty.[190]

Cardashian had read the signs correctly. It became evident by May 1920 that America would not agree to take a mandate over Armenia.[191]

Such political sensitivities were not widely understood within the Armenian community, where disagreements resurfaced. When it became known that the official position of those associated with the Armenian Republic (the Armenian Revolutionary Federation) was to discourage efforts for an American mandate over Armenia, the outraged Hunchagian party declared its withdrawal from the coalition. This was announced to the Hunchag members in Syracuse (and elsewhere, presumably) as follows:

Boston, Mass
May 27, 1920
G. A. Aghaian
735 East Washington St., Syracuse, N.Y.

It is recently disclosed in Washington that according to authoritative statement Pasdermajian Bishop Muratbegian and Kardashian have jointly appealed to Lodge Spencer Harding and other influential senators expressing opposition to American mandate of Armenia. This is the hardest blow our national cause has ever suffered. Owing to and in protest of this treacherous action on the part of Pasdermajian clic [sic] we decided withdrawal from participation in the mass meeting.

Central Committee of Armenian National Democratic Party
Dikijian Ana [destroyed] May 28[192]

---

190. Hovannisian, *The Republic of Armenia*, vol. II, p. 394.
191. Gidney, p. 240.
192. Telegram in Azadian collection.

The mass meeting the telegram refers to is the second anniversary celebration in observance of the founding of the Armenian Republic. Its government was regarded by opponents to the ARF as a "Tashnag" administration. No doubt, the Syracuse Hunchagian members dutifully obeyed the directive. Revolutionary parties do not tolerate rebellion in the ranks.

Just a few months earlier, ARF and Hunchag party leaders had been carrying out a series of negotiations in hopes of launching a cooperative fund drive on behalf of the sadly underequipped army of the Armenian Republic. The Hunchag spokesmen insisted on a formula that would provide for 50 to 30 percent of the funds to be sent to areas in Cilicia where self-defense efforts were being carried out. Both sides remained adamant and negotiations broke down. Deciding to carry on alone, the ARF Central Executive called on its membership in a circular dated March 31, 1920, for yet another act of sacrifice in support of a desperate fatherland. The response was immediate. In its issue of April 22, the *Hairenik* announced that $77,000 had already been donated. In the 1920s the average annual income was not much more than $1000, so the $400,000 ultimately raised represented considerable sacrifice on the part of the new immigrants.[193]

It is not known how much was given by Syracusans, but receipt number 24 acknowledges Aaron Sachaklian's donation of $30. The receipt depicts a soldier carrying the Armenian Tricolor of red, blue, and orange. It is dated July 25, 1920, and bears the stamp of the "A.R.F. Central Committee for Funding the Armenian Army, 1920."[194]

While funds were being collected in support of the Republic, the situation in Armenia was becoming increasingly desperate. The United States continued to refuse direct involvement in the region, and peace negotiations in Europe dragged on. The Treaty of Sevres, August 10, 1920, provided for the creation of an Armenian state, but it was clear that Turkey had no intention of complying with its terms.[195]

In November 1920, even while President Wilson was defining the proposed boundaries for the doomed Republic, Armenia finally collapsed in the face of Soviet-Turkish pressure. An uprising in February 1921 briefly reinstated the government of the ARF, which fell again in April when Soviet troops crushed all resistance. Armenian independence had come to an end, as the country was socialized, eventually becoming part of the USSR. Armenian

---

193.Kevorkian, p. 365 reports that $400,000 was raised, but in Kevork Donabedian, *H. H.Tashnagstoutiune Hiusisain Amerigayi Mech [The ARF in North America]*, vol. II (Boston: Hairenik Press, 1995), p. 518, the total of $500,000 is given.
194.Sachaklian collection.
195.Gidney, p. 241.

hopes were dashed. Was it all to end like this? Was there to be no justice or recompense for the years of suffering?

Seeking Justice

The news that jolted the entire nation came suddenly. On March 15, 1921 in Berlin, an Armenian youth, Solomon Tehlerian, had assassinated the hated Talaat Pasha, the Turkish Interior Minister considered one of the leaders responsible for planning and ordering the genocide of the Armenian population of Turkey in 1915. Tehlerian had been arrested and was held in a German prison, awaiting trial.[196]

Some condemned this act of terror, but many others—especially those who had witnessed and experienced those dreadful days or who had lost their loved ones—rejoiced that at last Armenians had secured vengeance with their own hands. Support for Tehlerian poured from communities everywhere. In Syracuse, Armenians gathered in a mass meeting to voice their sentiments. A draft message, probably intended to be sent as a telegram, prepared by Aaron Sachaklian and addressed to the "Honorable Secretary of State, Washington, D.C." reads:

> Armenian residents of Syracuse—many of them citizens of the United States—each having suffered the loss of a father, mother, brothers, sisters or other close relative during the late war due to the atrocities perpetrated upon the Armenians by Talaat as the head of the Turkish Government at that time, assembled at a mass meeting held in the Y.M.C.A. hall, Sunday, April 10, 1921, respectfully pray you to use your good offices to obtain the release of the young student, Solomon Tillerian, who is now imprisoned in Berlin, Germany accused of the murder of Talaat the Turk.[197]

A second draft, misdated April 10, 1917, addressed to the Honorable Minister of Justice, Berlin, Germany also pleads for release of the prisoner. Hinting that Germany—the ally of the Turkish government that ordered such horror—may itself be considered an accessory to the crimes committed in 1915, the message adds: "thereby offering to the world an evidence that the present German Government does not condone the atrocities perpetrated upon the Armenians by Talaat, as head of the Turkish Government."[198]

---

196. Lindy V. Avakian, *The Cross and the Crescent* (Los Angeles, Calif. 90015: DeVorss & Co., Inc., 1965), p. 132.
197. Sachaklian collection.
198. Ibid.

Shahan Natalie, who participated in the Secret plan to punish Turkish leaders responsible for the genocide of the Armenians, had visited Syracuse in 1917 as a speaker for an ARF public meeting.

The Syracuse community did not know at this point how closely it was associated with this act. It was not revealed until most of those participating in the 1921 meeting were dead that the assassination of Talaat was part of a secret plan initiated by the ARF to execute the Turkish leaders—especially the hated Talaat, Enver, and Djemal—responsible for issuing the orders to destroy the Armenian nation in 1915. One of the three men at the center of the group who devised and carried out the plan called *hadook kordz* (special mission) was the author of the telegram petition, a Syracuse resident, Aaron Sachaklian, "responsible for logistics, training, and above all, finance."[199]

---

199. Gerard Chaliand, Foreword, p. xiv in Jacques Derogy, *Resistance & Revenge: The Armenian Assassination of the Turkish Leaders Responsible for the 1915 Massacres and Deportations,* preface [foreword] by Gerard Chaliand; trans. by A. M. Berrett (New Brunswick and London: Transaction Publishers, 1990.

Sachaklian, a certified public accountant, had moved to Syracuse in 1919, coming from Boston where he had served as general manager of the *Hairenik* newspaper. For many years he continued as auditor for the *Hairenik* and for the ARF. A younger member of the planning group, serving as coordinator of operations, was Shahan Natalie, who had addressed the Syracuse community at the ARF public meeting on February 8, 1917. At the head of the project was Garegin Pasdermadjian, the dynamic national leader who served as the Armenian Republic's minister plenipotentiary in Washington. Having lost his entire family in the massacres, Pasdermadjian dedicated his life to the quest for justice for the Armenians. A commentator asserts: "Credit for this operation clearly belongs less to those who carried it out, determined young men in their twenties, than to the organizers who supplied the logistics, the intelligence, and the conditions for its execution."[200]

Tehlerian faced the death penalty. The defendant did not deny having shot the hated Turkish leader. He maintained that his was an act of justified retribution, performed at the command of his murdered mother. He was an epileptic, a condition brought on by the trauma he had suffered. The testimony revealed the horrors of the deportations and massacres for which Talaat bore responsibility. This was information previously unknown to the German public. The terrible scenes described by the witnesses evoked cries of condemnation of the Turkish leadership by the spectators, and brought tears to the eyes of the jurymen. German witnesses sought to absolve German military and diplomatic officials from complicity in planning or carrying out the murders of the Armenians.[201]

Before the trial, Shahan Natalie, one of the planners of the "special mission," wrote to his comrades in America about the likely outcome. He said that the German Minister of Justice had suggested the possibility of a pardon if Tehlerian should be convicted. He urged the American communities to donate funds for defense.[202]

After a dramatic trial lasting several days, the matter was placed in the hands of the jury, whose charge was to determine whether or not the killing was premeditated. In one hour came the decision: "No." Almost unheard in the sound of applause was the prosecutor's announcement that the decision would not be appealed. Tehlerian later came to live permanently in America, where he received a hero's welcome.[203]

---

200. Ibid.
201. See Chapter 6 in Derogy for a description of the trial.
202. Letter dated March 19, 1921 in Sachaklian collection.
203. Derogy, 103.

Syracuse Armenians had an opportunity to meet a military hero when they entertained General A. Sebouh on September 19, 1921. A caption under a photo with an article appearing in a Philadelphia newspaper states the purpose of his visit to the United States: "Armenian army officer here hopes to obtain United States loan to rehabilitate army."[204]

The Syracuse community feted Sebouh at a banquet held at the Chamber of Commerce building, 433 South Warren Street. An invitation probably intended to be extended to city leaders is signed by the chairman of the reception committee, A. H. Sachaklian, C.P.A. and members S. Nigsarian and K. Shah-lamian. Mayor Harry H. Farmer sent a belated response (September 28, 1921), regretting that a previous engagement prevented him from attending and apologizing for not having acknowledged the invitation earlier.[205]

The mission for Sebouh's tour of the United States, if it was indeed as stated in the Philadelphia newspaper article, appears to have been somewhat quixotic. By early summer Armenia had been taken firmly under Soviet control, its Republican leaders killed, imprisoned, or dispersed, the remnants of its army melting away like the snows in springtime, moving toward Persia from their retreats in the mountains of Zangezur. Sebouh continued his tour of the United States as a field worker for the ARF which was trying to keep the dream of independence alive, but it was all over.

The "general" had not actually received that rank, but had been elevated in popular terminology in recognition of his many years of service to the Armenian people. Sebouh was a sturdy man of medium height with piercing blue eyes, a commanding mustache, and a shock of thick hair which had been blond in his youth. Born in 1872, Arshag Nersesian, later given the pseudonym Sebouh, became involved in the revolutionary movement while still very young. He became a Hunchag and assassinated a traitor on the party's orders. Later, as a member of the ARF, he became a commander under General Antranig. At the time of his visit to Syracuse he was head of the secret "special mission" in the United States, having taken over its direction at the request of Armen Garo (Pasdermadjian).[206] Sebouh eventually settled permanently in Detroit where he maintained a grocery business. He died in 1940, a venerated member of the community.[207]

The Sovietization of Armenia introduced a new issue of contention for the Armenian people. The ARF remained unreconciled to the loss of its Republic and continued to oppose the Soviet regime through most of the long years that

---

204.*Public Ledger*, August 22, 1921. Clipping in Sachaklian collection.
205.Letter in Sachaklian collection.
206.Derogy, p. 110.
207.Biography in Kevorkian, p. 393–94.

General A. Sebouh. Photo taken in Syracuse in 1921 by Jasper Abajian.

followed. Opponents of the ARF, however, accepted Soviet rule claiming that only a strong Moscow could protect little Armenia. Arguments often broke out even during social visits and the political parties found it increasingly difficult to find common ground. The disputes of yesterday were only dress rehearsals for a major division of the Armenian communities which was to occur about a decade later.

America Is Home

Armenia's glory days in the world scene were rapidly coming to an end. Very few Armenians were left in Turkey, and with the Sovietization of what was left of Armenia, the Armenian Question was "resolved," at least in the minds of those negotiating the peace treaty. The Treaty of Lausanne, concluded in 1923, ignores Armenia entirely. Not one mention of its name appears in the document.[208]

The Armenians who had expressed their eagerness to be considered Armenian citizens now turned their faces decisively from east to west. America was their destiny and that of their children. Here is where they would build their homes, churches, schools, and community centers. Their prime concern now became the perpetuation of the Armenian nation through their youth. They spoke of the new generation as though it were in physical danger and needed rescue. Indeed, assimilation was referred to as the "white massacre." Efforts had to be made to teach their children Armenian language and history. Trained teachers were few and the community drew on volunteers to conduct Saturday schools for the reluctant children.

208.Gidney, pp. 247, 251.

II

World War I to 1933: Community Rebuilt, Community Destroyed

Resettlement

The decade of the 1920s was a period of movement and consolidation for the Armenian people everywhere. Evicted from their ancestral homelands, robbed of homes and possessions, even deprived of their bank accounts (the Turks confiscated them, charging the Armenians with abandonment), the survivors clung to any life raft within reach.

Hundreds of thousands of exhausted refugees gathered in areas of Turkey and the Middle East that were now under French and British administration. After the war came to an end, the British moved out of Cilicia to be replaced by French troops, as provided by the Sykes-Picot Agreement of 1916. Both the British and the French had encouraged—even commanded—the Armenians remaining from the enforced marches toward the Syrian desert to return to Cilicia. Perhaps they wished to relieve themselves of responsibility for housing and maintaining the refugees. The French forces in Cilicia were weaker than the British troops whose places they took. Seeing this, the Turks began harassment. As the conflict swelled to warfare, the French began to withdraw in secret, leaving a terrified Armenian populace that scattered pell-mell in flight from reinstated Turkish rule.[209] The outbreak of war between Greece and Turkey led to the burning of Smyrna in 1922, when many more Armenian lives were lost.[210]

---

209. Akaby Nassibian, *Britain and the Armenian Question, 1915–1923* (London & Sydney: Croom Helm; New York: St. Martin's Press, 1984), pp. 241–43.

210. Marjorie Housepian, *The Smyrna Affair* (New York: Harcourt Brace Jovanovich, Inc., 1966).

Appealing to every agency available to them, the Armenians in America sought news of relatives and compatriots, hoping to find survivors in the various camps and gathering places known to harbor Armenian refugees. The search continued for many years. Advertisements seeking news of lost family members appeared frequently in the Armenian press of that period.

Homeless Armenians were scattered from the Caucasus to Europe. Some had even drifted eastward, as far as China, coming together in clusters in Harbin and Shanghai. Large numbers of survivors gathered uneasily in self-governing camps in Greece, under constant pressure by the overburdened Greek government to move out of the country. Colonies that formed in Syria, Lebanon, Iraq, and Iran became permanent communities, while new communities sprang up in South America. A few hundred Armenians made their way to Havana, Cuba, clinging in hopeful proximity to the United States, waiting there for the miracle that would get them past American immigration barriers.[211]

The following letter to Aaron Sachaklian from a travel agent in Syracuse provides interesting information concerning immigration restrictions at that time:

Mr. A. H. Sachaklian
423 ½ S. Salina St.
City Oct. 6, 1923

Dear Mr. Sachaklian:

I have taken up with my Head Office the matter of your bringing in Armenians to Canada, and they state as I have already told you, it will be necessary to have the affidavits signed by someone who can guarantee them a farm job in Canada, either a resident or property owner in Canada.

However, what would be much quicker and more simple, would be to bring your friends to Cuba, a United States possession. No affidavits are required. The Cuban vise [*sic*] is easily obtained in Constantinople, and the Holland-America service to Cuba is regular and excellent. The Holland-America have an agent in Bucharest who has a sub-office in Constantinople.

---

211. Ramela Martin was one of the Armenian refugees who waited in Cuba in hopes of going on from there to the United States. See her autobiography *Out of Darkness* (Cambridge, Massachusetts: The Zoryan Institute, 1989).

The third class rate, Constantinople to Cuba is $95.00, and it is necessary to deposit $30 Cuban Landing Money, making a total of $125 per passenger. The $30 is handed to passenger on arrival at Havana. The second class fare is approximately $125, plus landing money. If you will get in touch with Armenians here and explain the situation to them, I am sure it would be the quickest way to send them to Cuba. They can be naturalized U.S. Citizens in Cuba in five years, or after one years residence, are eligible to enter U.S. in the quota, but this seems to me to be the quickest way to get them out of Constantinople, inasmuch as there would be delays in securing Canadian affidavits, copy of which I enclose herewith for your information.

Trusting I may handle this business

Yours very truly,
Helen E. Rutledge[212]

The married men who had left families behind when they immigrated to the United States prior to the war now sought to bring over those who survived, while the early bachelor immigrants searched for brides among the newcomers or among pools of unseen orphan maidens awaiting rescue from their temporary havens abroad. It was common for marriages to be negotiated on the basis of photographs and the recommendations of go-betweens. Many women submitted to an unknown future with a man whom they had not met, or about whom they knew little more than name, age, or home town or village. Under such circumstances misrepresentations sometimes took place, with the surprise of discovery confronting the bride on her wedding day.[213] In some cases, marriages were negotiated solely for the purpose of entry to the United States, with the understanding that the union would be dissolved later.[214]

About one hundred thousand Armenians are estimated to have come to the United States between the years 1880 and 1924.[215] During the 1920s there was another rapid increase in the American communities as families were reunited and marriages took place, followed soon by many births.[216] Most of the new arrivals during the decade of the 1920s joined established

---

212. Sachaklian collection.
213. Khachadoor Pilibosian, coauthored and edited with additional information by Helene Philibosian, *They Called Me Mustafa* (Watertown, Massachusetts: Ohan Press, 1992), p. 3.
214. Martin, 98.
215. David Waldstreicher, *The Armenian Americans,* The Peoples of North America (New York, New Haven, Philadelphia: Chelsea House Publishers, 1989), p. 13.

communities in the Northeast, Midwest, and southern California. Settlements formed in some of these locales have lasted to this day. Others, especially those in smaller towns without a strong economic base, remained fragile and soon dissolved, as the resident Armenians discovered more attractive areas in which to settle. For example, the Bridgewater community in Massachusetts was near death by 1931. Its Armenian library, founded only four or five years earlier, was reported as not serving its purpose and constituting a burden on the community.[217]

Of the cities in upstate New York, Troy-Watervliet, with the appeal of jobs in the shirt factories of the region, and Niagara Falls attracted the largest number of the early Armenian immigrants. Syracuse, then with a bustling economy and a diverse manufacturing base, may have ranked third. Communities in Binghamton and Massena, where jobs were available in the shoe factories of Endicott and in the aluminum plants, respectively, were never large, but were lively at their peak. Smaller groups gathered in Utica and Rochester.[218] From the times of their formation, the central and upper New York State communities formed ties with each other that have survived a changing generation and are maintained to this day.

Those who left the central New York area sought larger Armenian communities as in Detroit, Chicago and California. As the Armenian communities there grew larger and more vibrant, the prospect of joining a more active Armenian environment grew too attractive to resist. Most of those who remained made Syracuse their permanent home. Eliza Sachaklian came to Syracuse with her three children in 1920 to join her husband who had arrived in 1919. She recalled that there were about one hundred to one hundred fifty Armenians at that time. Agishe Minasian estimated that of the seventy-five or so families during 1914–15, only about forty remained after the war. This estimate may be more accurate for 1920–21 than for 1924–25. Several new families formed during the interval. By the end of the war, the Armenian community in Syracuse appears to have gone through a period of transition, with some families moving out and others moving in or becoming established.

A 1922 photograph of a picnic at the Babikian farm, shows a small group, most of whom remained in Syracuse and formed part of a permanent community.

---

216. S. Vratzian, *Hairenik Darekirk Donatsuytz, 1945* [Hairenik Yearbook Almanac] (Boston: Hairenik Press, December 1944), p. 252.

217. *Hairenik Amsakir,* April 1931, p. 174.

218. These are my judgments based on my knowledge of the institutions established and maintained in those communities.

Picnic at Babikian farm, about 1922. At the center in the back is Abraham Nigolian wearing a mock policeman's uniform.

Another photograph taken the next year at the Babikian farm shows a youthful gathering of thirty-seven Armenian men, thirty-three women, and twenty-nine children. Of the men, only Mihran Babikian and two others appear to be elderly. Several of the men were unmarried. Seven of the women were elderly or at least mothers of adult children and only two of the younger women were unmarried. Most of the children ranged in age from infants in arms to about five or six years.[219] Absent from the photo were at least seven Armenian families known to have been living in Syracuse at that time.

Also present in the photo and not included in the above count were several members of a Turkish-speaking Greek family, émigrés from western Turkey, who felt closer to the Armenians from the same region in Turkey than they did to many of the Greek community. Charlie Theodosiou, a lifelong bachelor, was the head of the family, and a tender, loving son to his widowed mother. With his brother, Steve, he operated a shoeshine and hat blocking shop on East Fayette Street. A cheerful, jolly person, he became a familiar figure to the many Armenian shopkeepers in the downtown area. When Steve

---

219. Benjamin collection.

Picnic at Babikian farm, about 1923.

married a young Greek woman from Detroit, some Armenians paid calls on the young couple. There were several Armenian families among the invited guests when their daughter was married.

Forming Families

The new decade was ushered in quite auspiciously for the Syracuse community with a long-remembered triple wedding in 1920. The couples were George and Mary Hamamjian, Karnig and Barkevouhi Shahlamian, and Karekin and Louise Choghanjian.[220]

The first two couples were compatriots, all from Papert (Baiburt), but the Choghanjians were from Sepastia and Smyrna, respectively. After losing his parents in the 1915 massacres, Choghanjian escaped and came to Syracuse in 1918 or 1919. Upon the death of the woman he had planned to marry, he turned to an intermediary to find some young orphan whom he could save. He stipulated that the marriage would take place only if the intended, after arrival, should agree. Their daughter recalled hearing from her parents that the

220.Elizabeth Markarian Avakian; Alice Choghanjian Hagopian.

intermediary had requested extra payment to assure comfortable passage on the long voyage, but substituted much poorer quarters and pocketed the difference.[221] Unfortunately, the exploitation by Armenian agents and brokers of their own countrymen was a tradition reaching back to the earliest waves of emigration out of Turkey. Abuses persisted despite the efforts of authorities to eradicate them.[222]

Khosrov Kyoomjian sought a wife from an orphanage and sent funds for the unseen young woman to travel to Syracuse, also offering to release her should she decide to refuse the marriage. All went well, however, and their wedding in 1923 was the beginning of a happy union.[223] Many of the couples marrying at this time remained in Syracuse, where their children became part of the rising generation.

Marriages such as these may seem strange to today's generation, but the brides and grooms themselves were very likely the products of arranged unions. Dating was unheard of in conventional old-country Armenian society and young couples had little opportunity to make their own choices. An American-born second generation Armenian wag observed, "An American marries the one he loves; an Armenian loves the one he marries."[224]

A few men never found mates and, like Dick Chelian, Jasper Abajian, Missak Der Ohannesian, and a few others, remained bachelors all of their lives. They were nevertheless firmly bound into the community, and made to feel welcome wherever they went. Der Ohannesian, a tailor, was a self-taught artist, featured in several newspaper articles. He produced large charcoal drawings on American patriotic themes, one of which he gave to the Americanization League. His gift to the President of a pencil sketch of Franklin D. Roosevelt, whom he greatly admired, was acknowledged by Louis McHenry Howe, the President's secretary. At Der Ohannesian's death, several large framed pieces were placed in a closet in the Armenian Community Center where they still remain, awaiting disposition.

Gradually, the Armenian community in Syracuse gained new strength, as surviving families left behind in the homeland before the war were now reunited with husbands and fathers, and as the bachelors found brides and formed families. Of the fifty men from Divrig profiled in the Aramtagh book, forty-eight had come to the United States before World War I. Of that forty-eight, seventeen settled permanently in Syracuse. Six of the Syracuse men had been married before the war, but only one had brought his wife and family

---

221. Hagopian.
222. Mirak, *Torn Between Two Lands,* p. 63.
223. Zephyr Kyoomjian Minasian.
224. Harry A. Sachaklian.

before war broke out. Three of the married men were not reunited with their families until 1927. One lost his family and later remarried and one early arrival married a non-Armenian woman of Irish descent. It was rare for the bachelor immigrants to take non-Armenian wives. At first, they were too poor to consider marriage, often living in clusters of four or five to save expenses.[225] When their financial situations improved, they preferred to seek Armenian wives. Three of the eleven bachelors from Divrig were married in 1920, and four and a widower were married later in the decade. No marriages were recorded for four men.[226]

The few Armenian women of marriageable age living in Syracuse during the World War I period and through the early 1920s had abundant suitors. Mianzara Zahrajian and her older sister, Aghavni, had become familiar figures in the community through their performances at Armenian functions. As stated previously, the oldest sister, Mannig, died soon after her marriage. Aghavni was married at eighteen, but Mianzara had other ideas. After attending Lincoln School and North High School, Mianzara took flute, voice, and piano lessons from Professor Lyman and others at Crouse College, Syracuse University. As a flute-player, she joined the Music Settlement Orchestra. There she caught the eye of Walter Eckhoff, who played violin. Walter's discerning sister, who played viola in the same orchestra, gave a party for the orchestra, giving Walter a suitable opportunity to approach Mianzara. For Mianzara, there was no comparison between the polite and gentle-mannered Walter and the earnest, but unpolished, Armenian émigrés. Although her parents at first opposed their daughter's marriage to a non-Armenian, they were soon won over and mutual love and respect prevailed between them and their son-in-law. Mianzara not only continued her Armenian activities, but brought her non-Armenian husband to Armenian affairs, as well.[227]

Everyone arriving in those days had experienced anxiety, fear, deprivation, and severe emotional trauma. Yet, perhaps because everyone had a harrowing tale of survival to recount, their stories were seldom voiced at that time. They may have wished to put the unhappy past behind them, in order to devote full energies to building a better future. It was only in later years, as they aged and as their children and grandchildren grew to adulthood and began to ask questions about "the old days," that they gradually revealed what had happened to them so long ago. The few first-person experiences outlined below cannot

---

225. Told by Khachperoony Gozigian to his son Karl, who recounted the story to me.
226. Aramtagh Book.
227. Information drawn from Mianzara Eckhoff's letters, notes, and phone calls. I remember Walter very well. Many times he sat waiting patiently and without complaint for the long speeches in Armenian to come to an end.

possibly convey the full depth of the feelings behind the simple words, yet in every case the account was told in an unadorned and direct manner.

Elise Hagopian Taft has relayed some of her stories to me but, better still, they are recorded in her colorful autobiography, *Rebirth*.[228] Still a small child when she and her family were driven from their home in Banderma in western Turkey, Elise was the family's only survivor. Her baby sister and beloved older brother died during a harrowing journey of hundreds of miles by cattle car and on foot. Elise describes numerous forms of brutality inflicted on the helpless Armenian deportees by their Turkish guards. Starved, exhausted, and ill with typhus, the remaining members of the family reached the Syrian desert where Elise's father buried two more children and his wife, then lay down and died himself. Elise calls her own recovery from typhus and eventual survival a miracle. She eventually made her way to Smyrna where she was placed in an American orphanage. Here she was sponsored by Mary and Robert Dey, co-founder of the Dey Brothers department store in Syracuse.

When the Turks set fire to the Christian quarter of Smyrna in 1922, Elise escaped with others to Athens. After several years in an American mission school in Greece where she learned English, Elise came to Syracuse in 1927, at the invitation of Mary Dey, in order to enter Syracuse University. The Deys welcomed Elise into their mansion at 950 James Street and provided the support she needed to continue to graduation in 1931. A few months later she married Zarmair Tohafjian. He later changed his name to Taft.

The wedding of Elise Hagopian and Zarmair Taft took place on October 10, 1931, in St. Paul's Episcopal Church in downtown Syracuse in an Episcopal ceremony. Robert Dey gave away the bride, who had three attendants and two flower girls. Guests included a busload of little girls and their house mothers from the orphans' home, Elise's college dean, many professors with their families, and the entire Armenian community. The church was filled to capacity. The reception was held in the ballroom of the Yates Hotel just across the street from the church.

Originally from Van in eastern Turkey, part of ancient Armenia, the bridegroom, Taft, had survived adventures of his own. He had completed two years of medical schooling in Constantinople when, in 1915, after desperate efforts to escape, he was thrown into a Turkish prison and tortured. He was then a member of the ARF. Taft suffered a permanent hearing impairment as a result of the beatings inflicted upon him while held by the Turks. By this time, Turkey had entered the war as Germany's ally. Taft's knowledge of French,

---

228.Elise Hagopian Taft, *Rebirth: The Story of an Armenian Girl who Survived the Genocide and Found Rebirth in America* (Plandome, New York: New Age Publishers, 1981).

Turkish, and Morse Code came to the attention of a German officer who arranged his conditional release so he could be put to work as a telegraph operator. After he recovered from his injuries with the aid of an Armenian woman who befriended him, Taft was escorted daily back and forth from prison to work at the telegraph office.

For four years Taft and his family had no communication with each other. After the Armistice, Taft learned that his family had fled to Erevan, Armenia, where his mother and brother had died and his father had remarried. By this time, Taft was engaged in business in Constantinople. Eventually, the family was reunited in Constantinople, but it was decided that all would emigrate to the United States. The group consisted of Taft's father, stepmother, her daughter from a previous marriage, Taft's sister, Shooshanig, her two small children, and her father-in-law. Shooshanig's husband, Vagharshag Shahinian, who had left his job at the Oberdorfer Foundry in Syracuse in 1914 to fight in the Armenian army, had returned six months earlier to go back to work and to prepare a home for the reunited family. After concluding his business affairs in Constantinople, Taft joined his family in Syracuse in 1921. He opened a tailor shop, which later expanded into a dry cleaning business with as many as a dozen branch stores.[229] Soon after their arrival, Taft's stepsister married Khachperoony Gozigian, from Palou, eastern Turkey. Gozigian had come to Syracuse in 1912 and had his own tailor shop on Fayette Street and then in the Hotel Syracuse when it opened in 1926 or 1927.[230]

Other Syracusans who survived the Smyrna fire were Takouhi Dabanian and Anitsa Chakerian. It was courage and enterprise that saved Takouhi from the chaos that prevailed in Smyrna in 1922. Her experience is recounted in *The Smyrna Affair*.[231] An attractive, petite, quick-witted, blue-eyed blonde, she managed to save her family from the flames by demanding French protection, claiming to be French. She spoke French fluently. After coming to Syracuse in 1923 as the bride of Setrak Kalebdjian, with unflagging determination she brought her sister and brother from Tunis in 1928, then her mother, her sisters, and their families, also from Tunis, in 1942.[232]

Anitsa Chakerian was a teacher in the American College in Smyrna at the time of the fire. With Elise Taft, they were taken in an American boat to Greece.[233] Anitsa was a few years older than Elise and took a protective

---

229. Taft provided much autobiographical information in an interview on July 24, 1983.
    He died in February 1993 at the age of 98. See also Elise Taft, *Rebirth*, pp. 122–34.
230. Karl Gozigian.
231. Housepian, p. 158, pp. 162–63.
232. The Eckhoff collection contains newspaper clippings lacking source and date reporting the family's reunion.

interest in her. Under the auspices of an American mission school, Anitsa was sent to Oberlin College to study music, one of twenty-five girls from her school sent to college in the United States. While at Oberlin, she renewed her acquaintance with Rev. H. K. Khachadourian, whom she had met while in Smyrna.

Khachadourian was a widower, aged forty-two, still in anguish over the deaths of his wife and three sons in a massacre in Hadjin in 1920. His own life had been spared because he and a few other leaders of the town had been sent to appeal for French help at Adana. A week later, at Adana, a government communique announced the massacre of Hadjin. The minister's family was among the dead. Khachadourian completed work for the Doctor of Divinity degree at Auburn Theological Seminary. Immediately afterwards, despite twenty years difference in age, he and Anitsa were married on May 28, 1924.[234] At the invitation of the Gertmenians in Syracuse, old friends from Hadjin, the newlyweds visited Syracuse while on their honeymoon. They liked the area and Khachadourian agreed to become the pastor for the small Armenian congregations in Syracuse and Binghamton.

After some time had passed, Anitsa paid a call on Mrs. Dey to give her news of the student she had sponsored, Elise Hagopian, who was still in Greece. It is likely that Anitsa hoped for Mrs. Dey's assistance. If so, she was not disappointed. Complaining that "We send money but the Turks kill them," Mrs. Dey wrote a check for $500 to pay for Elise's passage to Syracuse, on condition that Elise should stay with Anitsa. She also expressed concern that Anitsa, then six months pregnant, had not yet seen a doctor and urged her to seek care. Mary S. Dey had been for many years closely involved with the Harmony Circle, founded in 1888 as an auxiliary to assist the Women's Hospital, which became the Memorial Hospital in 1918. When Elise finally arrived in 1927, she stayed in the university dormitory while school was in session and with Anitsa during vacations.

The Khachadourians remained in Syracuse for thirteen years, leaving in 1937. At the time of their departure there was a colony of twenty-five Armenian Presbyterians.[235] Robert Koolakian recalls that among the congregation were the following families: Azadian, Koolakian, Khanzadian, Aiqouni, Hovnanian, Adjemian, Jamadanian, Gertmenian, Hagop Yessaian, Ayanian.

Araxi Khanzadian (maiden name not known), from Marsovan, recalled that her family had lived in a large, beautiful home. Deported to Samsun, on

---

233. Anitsa Chakerian; *Syracuse Herald,* February 28, 1937, clipping from Eckhoff collection; Taft, p. 96.
234. Record of Service, Presbyterian Church.
235. *Syracuse Herald,* February 28, 1937.

the southern coast of the Black Sea, the family there suffered the loss of two daughters. Araxi, a small child at the time, was stolen by a Turkish family. An older daughter's beauty had caught the eyes of the local Turks and her parents were forced to allow her to become a Turkish bride. Fearful that rejecting the Turks would bring harm to his family, the father had her many suitors place their names on slips of paper, out of which he chose her future husband, like a lottery. As Araxi told the story, the lucky winner was a wealthy and educated man who spoke French. The sister also knew French and English.

Meanwhile, the Turks learned that the father was a master tailor. Because his skills were needed to prepare uniforms for the army, the Turks allowed the family to return to Marsovan. From there, the mother made repeated efforts to find her missing child and finally succeeded. The family did not remain together very long. The father was killed by the Turks and in 1922 bandits attacked Marsovan, after which Araxi was separated forever from her mother. She was eventually sent to an American school in Greece and went from there to Egypt, where she worked as a baby sitter with an Armenian family.

While in Egypt, Araxi became acquainted with a woman and her daughter. The woman's son, Mr. Khanzadian, had come to the United States before the war to study dentistry. His schooling was interrupted when the war broke out, so he went to Binghamton to start a business. He invented a rug cleaning machine and moved to Syracuse. Araxi became interested in Khanzadian and offered to write a letter to him in place of one by his sister. Khanzadian was so taken by Araxi's letter that he decided to marry the writer, who was only fifteen at the time. He returned to Egypt to see his mother and sister, married Araxi, and in 1930 brought them all to Syracuse.

Mrs. Khachadourian added the information that when Araxi was about to give birth, the kindly Mrs. Dey again responded to Mrs. Khachadourian's appeal for help. Araxi had not seen a doctor during her pregnancy and there was no one to assist her. Through Mrs. Dey's efforts, Harmony Circle of Memorial Hospital sent an ambulance to take Araxi to the hospital and arranged for her care.

Also from Marsovan were Sumpat Kaishian and his wife Sirouhi. In 1914 Sumpat was enrolled in the School of Architecture at Syracuse University. He graduated from the Syracuse University College of Forestry in 1918 and went into the United States army. After a brief course of study at Edinburgh University in Scotland while still in uniform, he returned to Syracuse and opened an oriental rug business. Sumpat went to Cuba for his bride, whom he brought to Syracuse after their marriage in Havana in 1928.[236] According to

---

236. Biographical information is from their son, Edward Kaish.

Antaram Desteian, the rest of the Kaishian family came "in relays starting 1923."

Haigouhi Hanessian (married name) was another survivor of that terrible period. Born in 1906 in Tarsus, she lost her entire family in the 1915 deportations. After wandering in the desert between Damascus and Jerusalem, she and others returned to their homes in Cilicia at the urging of the French, only to experience another massacre in 1920–21. She recalled that one hundred fifty girls perished in an orphanage fire which they themselves had set in despair after their director, an American woman, was captured by the Turks and led away on a horse with her hands tied behind her back.

After such cruel experiences, Mrs. Hanessian came to Syracuse in 1923 with the assistance of her cousin, Mr. Mangurian, and found a temporary home with Mary Gertmanian, a distant relative. Haigouhi had had only two and one half years of schooling and longed for an education, but her entry to the United States was with the objective of marriage to John H. Hanessian, so she became a reluctant bride at seventeen.

The family of Dickran Dumanian was another one of those reunited after a long separation. Their story was told to me by their daughter, Eugenie Dumanian. Dickran was a native of Kughi in Kharpert province and a member of a wealthy family engaged in the export business. His father and uncle bought hides, nuts, and walnut burl veneer from India for export to Europe. Their central office was in Marseilles, but they traveled frequently to Asia. After many years abroad on business, Dickran returned to his home village and was married in 1910 to a girl in her mid teens. Born in 1872, Dickran was now almost forty years of age. After the birth of two children, he returned to the Orient—family documents place him in Peshawar, now Pakistan—and the couple remained separated for long years. They even lost contact with each other for a period of time, according to a document held by the family which reveals the wife's search for her husband. Interned by the British because he was a subject of the Ottoman Empire with which the British were at war, Dickran was finally released when war ended. He returned to Marseilles, settled his affairs there, and came to Syracuse where his cousin Levon Dumanian had an oriental rug business.

In Kughi, Mrs. Dumanian faced deportation along with other Armenians when the massacres broke out. Her sister-in-law, overwhelmed with despair, took poison rather than face the prospect of forced marriage to a Turk. Fortunately, Mrs. Dumanian was spared the agony of the long walk to nowhere. Having made her way to Kharpert, she received unexpected help. She and her two children, with five other children aged three to seven (probably placed in her care by their desperate parents hoping for their survival), left Kharpert in the relative comfort of a horse-drawn wagon provided by the Turkish husband of her aunt. Thus they made their way to safety, eventually reaching Constantinople. By some unknown miracle (perhaps through intermediaries at the Marseilles business office), husband and wife managed to establish contact, and Dumanian sent funds to Constantinople to pay for his family's travel to Syracuse. Mrs. Dumanian arrived about 1920. Her husband had arrived a little earlier. Two more children were born after they were reunited.

Often other members of the family accompanied wives and children being brought to the United States. Khachig Parghamian, who had come in 1912, sent for his wife, Baidzar, in 1927. She was accompanied by Parghamian's niece, Yepime, renamed Sarah, whom Parghamian claimed as his daughter Sarah, who had died earlier. Sarah recalled that in 1915 she and her mother left Divrig and traveled to Arabgir. When the French moved in to occupy the Cilician region, her family returned to Divrig. They found Turks occupying Armenians' homes. The Turks were moved out so Armenians could reoccupy their homes, but the Turkish officials informed the Armenians they could not own their own homes. Sarah recalled that their orchards and fields were devastated. The Turks had cut down the plum orchards for firewood.

After living uneasily for a short time, the Armenians felt that they were not safe and moved out. They went to the city of Samsun and after waiting several days boarded a ship for the seven-day trip to Constantinople. Sarah was accompanied by Lucia and Antranig Nigolian (children of Abraham Nigolian who had come to Syracuse in 1913), Krikor Bedigian (son of Arakel Bedigian, who came to Syracuse after going to Iowa as a laborer in 1911), and others from Divrig. All came to Syracuse in 1927. While in Constantinople they went to an Armenian school. Sarah remembered that for a time the Armenian flag flew above the school, but later it was taken down. Not long afterwards, Setrak Minasian, whose family had been lost during the war, brought Surpouhi, Sarah's mother, to the United States and married her. The union produced a son and a daughter.

These are only a few examples of the trials experienced by a generation of Armenians. There was not an Armenian who came to Syracuse during this period who could not tell a similar story of his or her own.

Employment

The Erie Canal had promoted Syracuse's early economic development and the city's industrial growth continued into the twentieth century. The Armenian newcomers were quickly absorbed into the labor market, but many of them preferred self-employment.

By the 1920s, the Armenian men who had arrived in the United States before World War I had become familiar with Syracuse and with American ways. Industrious and enterprising, many had opened their own businesses before the war and even more did so during the decade that followed. A major section of the *Armenian Encyclopedic Almanac* of 1925 is devoted to listing results of a census, carried out in 1924, of Armenian enterprises in the United States and Canada. The volume acknowledges the assistance of S. Minasian in securing information about Syracuse.[237]

Headings in Armenian and English identify professions, after which individuals are listed by first initial and last name in Armenian, often so badly misspelled as to be incomprehensible. Addresses of the places of business or home are given in English, also badly misspelled. Fortunately, I had the use of the volume from my parents' library, in which my mother, Eliza Sachaklian, had noted corrections for some of the Syracuse listings. Professions and names are as follows:

Tinsmith: Gh. Zahrajian, K. and M. Shahlamian.

Rug dealers: S. Jigarjian, A. Gertmenian, L. Dumanian, (Sumpat) Kaishian.

Meat markets: H. Azoyan, S. Minasian, S. Nigsarian, M. and S. Kalebdjian.

Tailors: Y. Ayanian, B. Abajian, Apikian brothers (Minas, Krikor, Harry), K. Koolakian, O. Enfiejian, H. Telian, G. and Z. Tohafjian, K. Gozigian, H. Haigazian, H. Ohannesian, B. Roomian, H. Jemerdjian, A. Mangurian, D. Chelian, A. Barmaksuszian.

Barbers: C. [Jasper] Abajian, H. Parunagian, M. Casparian, M. Ajemian, N. Tufenkjian, A. Garabedian, Kh. Minasian, A. Sarkisian, A. Kupelian.

Restaurant: G. Muserlian, N. Dickranian.

Bakers: H. Aintablian, J. and G. Aintablian.

Grocers: A. Parghamian, G. Medigian, Kh. (Khachadour) Aghaian, Hoosig Minasian, A., V., and H. Sheperdigian.

Misc.: H. Azadian, gauge manufacturer; A. Sachaklian, accountant; R. Keledjian, forester (My mother's notation reads "photographer." Most likely this was Robinson Keledjian, who was indeed a

---

237. *Amerigahai Hanrakidag Darekirk, 1925* [*Armenian Encyclopedic Almanac*] (Boston, MA: Hairenik Press, 1924), pp. 694–95; 503.

Setrak (Sam) Jigarjian in his oriental rug store, mid-twenties.

photographer, not a forester.); K. Keledjian, house painter; K. Keledjian, electrician (same person as the house painter); H. Yessayan and A. and Gh. Tufenkjian, merchant; A. Gulgulian, shoe repair; R. Pirenian, machinist.

There was a strong Armenian presence in the downtown area. Most of the establishments were located in the center of the city with some clustered together on the same block or even side by side on South Warren Street, East Fayette Street, West Water Street, East Washington Street, East Jefferson Street, Butternut Street. Some businesses shared the same quarters, such as Levon Dumanian, rug dealer, and G. and Z. Tohafjian (Taft), tailors, both at 504 Midland Avenue. Several tailors were listed at the Apikian shop at 202 West Water Street. In addition to the three Apikian brothers, B. Abajian and H. Haigazian were also at that address. Abajian later opened his own shop. The Apikians moved to South Clinton Street and finally to 214 West Genesee Street. They specialized in men's clothing and also made the uniforms for the Manlius School, a military academy.

As mentioned earlier, Koolakian was generous toward Armenian newcomers, taking in and training those with aptitude for tailoring. Many of his trainees eventually opened their own shops. Some, like the Apikian brothers, emulated Koolakian in accepting and training apprentices who then opened shops themselves. There were many tailors within the Syracuse community for several decades. Only the Koolakian business, now in the hands of the third generation, maintains its name today. The B. Abajian tailoring business, transformed to a dry cleaning establishment and owned by a granddaughter and her husband, continues in operation under a different name.

In many communities Armenians tend to be associated with oriental rugs and this was true in Syracuse. Philibosian, the earliest Armenian oriental rug merchant in Syracuse, is missing from the listing in the Armenian Almanac because he was no longer in Syracuse. Each of those named in the list of rug dealers had his own store. The shops may have been run by the owner alone, the repairs and service sometimes being done by wives or employees behind the scenes.

In addition to the two restaurants listed, Leon Vetzikian recalled that Paul Chaijian (Chahijian?) had a restaurant on the State Street side of the Flatiron Building. That may have been at a later time. Robert Koolakian remembers Paklavouni Gebelian who had a restaurant on Washington Street where he lived. It is my impression that the Dickranian restaurant did not last very long, but for many years the Muserlian restaurant remained on Warren Street.[238]

Each of the many barbers had his own business. Ajemian's son, Stephen (Archie), became a skilled barber and women's hair stylist. The beauty salon he opened with a partner, Archie and Ella's, on the second floor of a building at the southwest corner of East Fayette and Warren Streets, built up a loyal clientele. Archie then opened his own shop on the ground floor of a building on Warren Street one block south of the former location. He later developed the Liverpool Golf and Public Country Club, now operated by his two sons.

The list in the almanac falls far short of serving as a full census of Armenian workers in Syracuse in 1924. At that time, many were working in area factories or as laborers. Among them were the following natives of Divrig, according to the Aramtagh Book: Arakel Bedigian, Yeghia Der Boghosian, Massis Arayan, Panos Bedigian, Khachig Parghamian, Krikor Nigolian, Abraham Nigolian, Setrak Minasian. Many of these men eventually opened their own grocery stores, probably aided by compatriots who were operating stores themselves. Among others known to have been in Syracuse in 1924 were the Babikian brothers and Mr. Markarian, a cabinet maker from Kharpert, who had been

---

238.It was a favorite resting place for my parents and their small children, after a tiring shopping day downtown. I was always glad to see Dick Chelian who would buy me a piece of blueberry pie and ice cream. A bachelor, Chelian was probably rewarded by my happy, blue-stained face.

living in Syracuse since 1911. Rev. H. Khachadourian, the first resident Armenian Protestant minister, began his service in Syracuse on July 5, 1924[239] which was perhaps too late for inclusion in this survey.

Also not mentioned was K. Aiqouni, musician and violin teacher. He had been a Syracuse resident since before the war. Popularly called "Professor," he was a talented violinist, teacher, orchestra conductor, and arranger of Armenian music. According to Mianzara Eckhoff, "He had a studio in one of the buildings across from Edwards store on Salina Street. He was teaching during the first World War or right after it."[240] He became associated with the Syracuse Music School Settlement, founded about 1915 with Professor Harry Vibbard as director. Aiqouni formed an orchestra which met for rehearsals and concerts in the YWCA hall. His concerts were presented three or four times a year. Mrs. Eckhoff played flute in the orchestra from 1923 through 1927. A program of musical performances sponsored by Morning Musicals on February 23, 1927, at the Temple Theatre includes selections performed by the Music Settlement Orchestra, conducted by Krikor H. Aiqouni.[241] Haig Koolakian, Aiqouni's pupil, is listed as first violinist and Mrs. Eckhoff appears as one of two flute players. Haig Koolakian also played later in the Syracuse Symphony Orchestra.[242]

Aiqouni was dedicated to his music. Eckhoff tells us, "He never gave a concert for the Armenians. But whenever he was asked to play a solo for Armenian meetings for both side [sic], he always did and right after his solo, he put his violin in the case and left. He hardly mingled with the Armenians."[243] Aiqouni died in the early 1930s while still young, of a brain tumor. The circumstances were tragic. He died in the same hospital at the same time that his wife was giving birth to their second child. The community was profoundly saddened by his death and talk about it remained fresh for many years.

The 1924 listing includes three Armenians in outlying areas: Hagop Topouzian, a farmer in South Otselic; Mugurdich Bedrosian (who lost his young bride, Mannig Zahrajian, in 1919), tailor, in Oswego; K. Tartanian, tailor, in Sherburne.

Farming had an appeal for the Armenians who had immigrated from rural areas. Some, such as Khachig Minasian and Hagop Dumanian, made the attempt but were unable to farm successfully. Harry Menasian purchased land

---

239. Record of Service, Presbyterian Church.
240. Letter, Eckhoff to Mesrobian, May 3, 1983.
241. Program in Eckhoff collection.
242. *Syracuse Herald American,* April 24, 1977.
243. Letter, Eckhoff to Mesrobian, May 3, 1983; the "sides" referred to opposing political factions.

for that purpose, but went no further. Harry Apikian planted some mulberry trees with the intent of developing sericulture, but that too ended in failure. According to Robert Koolakian, his grandfather had a mulberry orchard at his Beattie Street farm in 1916. Koolakian was assisted by Krikor Yessaian, a friend from Banderma, who had raised mulberry trees and had had a silk industry in Banderma. Koolakian informed me that Yessaian later achieved fame, receiving an honorary doctorate from the University of California. In the second half of the 1920s and during the 1930s a few more Armenians came to the area to operate farms. Tufenkjian (Cannon) family members were engaged in dairy farming in Jamesville and Cazenovia, and the Narsasian and Bozoian families maintained farms in DeRuyter and Georgetown respectively.

Most of those who established their own businesses became modestly successful and continued to retirement. Those who did not meet with success tried other ventures and some moved away. Nishan (Mark) Dickranian was one who made several attempts in business. He opened the Arax Photo Studio in 1915. In the course of five years his studio had at least five addresses, according to the listings in the city directories for 1915–20. The Eckhoff collection contains many photographs printed as postcards, with the photography studio's name and address on the back. This information facilitated dating many of the photographs. In 1920 he opened the Star Photo Studio at 214 Montgomery Street, at which he installed Jasper M. Abajian as manager. The directory for 1921 lists Mark Dickranian at the New York Market at 211 East Fayette Street. In 1920 this was the address for the Arax Photo Studio.

Abajian remained in the photography business for only a short time. He had been a barber previously and soon returned to his former occupation. The 1923 directory lists him as a barber at 104 South Warren Street, room 4. In the same directory, Dickranian's non-Armenian wife, Katherine, listing herself elegantly as "DiCranian," is identified as proprietor of a restaurant at 417 East Washington Street, the same address given in the *Armenian Encyclopedic Almanac* for 1925.

Mianzara Zahrajian Eckhoff recalled working in the Star Photo Studio on Fayette Street for a while "in the 1920s," but after 1921 no listing for Arax Photo or Star Photo appears in the city directories. She remembered that "Mr. Dickranian had a partner who had the other Star Photo Studio on South Salina Street just below Dey Brothers department store. I don't remember partner's name or the Armenian girl's name who worked with him. After a while the building was torn down so the partner and the girl went to Albany, N.Y. and opened a Star Photo Studio there."[244] The directory for 1918 identifies Harry Dickranian and Syria Dickranian as artists, living at 940 Cortland

---

244. Letter, Eckhoff to Mesrobian, May 3, 1983.

Avenue, as did Mark Dickranian. The 1919 directory reports that they moved to New York.

During the early decades of the Armenian community in Syracuse, few wives were employed outside the home. Occasionally married women with certain skills, such as dressmaking or alterations, worked at home or assisted their husbands. For example, Araxi Khanzadian was probably introduced to oriental rug repair through her husband's business. Widowed in 1943, she found employment at Charles V. Jacobsen Oriental Rug Company where she was trained by a highly skilled elderly Armenian man. She became so proficient in rug weaving and repair that she used to give demonstrations.

Leah Bayerian Armen, who became a widow only a few years after her marriage, was employed for many years at Niagara Mohawk Power Corporation, eventually rising to "a man's job." She remarked that male co-workers resented the fact that a woman was carrying out a task requiring rather complex computations.

Unmarried women often became office workers and clerks. Antaram Desteian was a teacher. Before her marriage, Mianzara Zahrajian Eckhoff worked as a clerk in Dey Brothers department store and in the Boston Store. Also, as noted previously, she assisted at the Star Photo Studio. She did not work after her marriage in 1924 in deference to her husband's wishes.[245] With her children in school, she went back to work during the Second World War.[246] Like Mianzara, Margaret Menasian worked for a while in a photography studio. Her main task was portrait coloring. After her marriage to Maurice Topalian she assisted her husband when he opened a grocery store.

Reinventing the Armenian Home

For the family-oriented Armenians, the home had very special significance. Just as it had been when Armenians lived in a Moslem country, the home was the bulwark against the foreign world and the sanctuary within which Armenian values were to be nurtured. Chief designer and defender of this fortress was the Armenian housewife and mother, the keeper of the hearth and the pillar of the Armenian family. The Armenian mother was expected to help preserve the Armenian Christian faith, teach her children the Armenian language and traditions, and even to support the menfolk in times of strife. The theme stressing the women's maintenance of feminine values even while bearing arms at the side of their fighting men was symbolically expressed during the revolutionary period by the portrait of a reclining Mother Armenia, cradling

---

245. Letter, Eckhoff to Mesrobian, February 19, 1983.
246. Letter, Eckhoff to Mesrobian, April 19, 1983.

a rifle with one arm and (to my infinite embarrassment) a nursing infant with the other. This image was popularly depicted in paintings and sometimes rendered in fine embroidery or tapestry and displayed on the walls of living rooms or the Armenian club.

The young brides who started to form families in an environment that was at first entirely strange to them usually sought to maintain the traditional values, putting particular stress on teaching their children the Armenian language. It was not uncommon for children of the early immigrants to enter kindergarten speaking only Armenian. Alice Choghanjian Hagopian, born in 1921, recalled that she was sent home from kindergarten because she could not speak English. Her mother, who had learned to read and write English in the old country, a relatively unusual skill, refused to teach her daughter English, probably maintaining, as many other parents did, that she would learn soon enough once she went to school. Alice finally started school at the age of seven, still not speaking English. Of course, not every family was as steadfast and in some cases once the children started school the parents seized the opportunity to learn English from them.

The Armenian home bore the same outward appearance as most American homes of the period, but a keen eye soon discerned some distinctive touches. There were, of course, the inevitable oriental rugs. At the very least, even in less affluent homes, one could expect to see the 8 × 10 Herez, usually in vibrant reds and blues, on the living room floor. The overstuffed sofa and matching chair proudly bore antimacassars, hand crocheted by the housewife, on their arms and backs. Also made by the housewife were Armenian needle lace doilies, incredibly fine webs of knotted white or ecru thread, which decorated the tops of lamp and coffee tables. A few homes displayed a tall, hooded Victrola cabinet in the corner, with a carefully preserved store of thick Columbia records. Among them were sure to be the resonant songs of Armenag Shah Mouradian, the famous Armenian tenor, and the rather reedy sounds of the sopranos (Armenian taste tended to favor the high ranges). Favorites were Armenian folk songs of love and longing, or instrumental music with *sirink* (flute) and *dumpeg* (drum) for Armenian circle dancing. When a record was played, often the first sound heard was the announcement, in a strongly accented voice, "Co-lom-bia re-cord!" Turkish music was banished in some homes, but in a few others it was still enjoyed as a reminder of happier days in the past.

In homes where a highly nationalistic atmosphere prevailed, one would sometimes see a display of photographs of national heroes, such as General Antranig or the founders of the Armenian Revolutionary Federation, or even a framed print or hand-embroidered rendering of the ARF insignia, the pen, sword, and spade, against the background of the Tricolor, all hung high up on the wall, well above eye level.

Few Armenian homes contained libraries in those days—not surprising in view of the circumstances. Over the years some individuals accumulated fairly extensive book and journal collections which clearly reflect differences in religious and political outlook. The large collections of Aaron Sachaklian and Maurice Topalian contain many volumes on the Armenian revolutionary movement, memoirs and biographies of revolutionary leaders, and numerous volumes of Armenian literature, including books by nationalistic Armenian authors, such as Raffi and Avedis Aharonian. Publication dates indicate that they continued to acquire books through the later years of their lives, often responding to drives for book sales carried out by the Hairenik Press. Smaller collections owned by Hoosig Minasian and Khachig Minasian were generally of the same character, but with fewer volumes of fiction or recent publications. Khachig Minasian, who was an archdeacon, also had several books pertaining to the Armenian Apostolic Church. All four men were members of the Armenian Apostolic Church and devoted supporters of the Armenian Revolutionary Federation.

The fifteen books owned by Mr. and Mrs. George Koolakian that came to my attention do not represent their entire Armenian library. They do, however, display totally different reading interests. Eight of them are religious volumes, of which three are in Turkish language but using Armenian letters. These belonged to Mrs. Koolakian. Most of the remainder are very old textbooks. Koolakian did not belong to a political party. Born in the Apostolic faith, he became Protestant at his marriage in accordance with the wishes of his father-in-law.

Armenian newspapers were avidly sought in the earlier days for news of national and world events as well as Armenian affairs. Some sought free papers in the reading room of the Armenian club, but others considered it a duty to support the Armenian press with individual subscriptions. There were Armenian publications ranging over a variety of political and religious interests. The newspapers or periodicals that entered an Armenian home clearly signalled the political leanings of the subscriber. Stirred by the strident tones of the editorials, especially when some issue was being hotly debated (which was often), the men (and sometimes the women as well) argued with vigor and passion, without swaying each other's views. Few women had much interest in world events. With rare exceptions, wives loyally took their husbands' positions on debated issues, but were generally less inclined to dwell on politics.

Homemaking involved considerable effort in those days, and the Armenian housewife bore the additional burden of trying to recreate an environment for which there were inadequate supplies or Armenian ingredients in the American world. The women showed considerable resourcefulness in the search for and adaptation of products and materials with which they could achieve the amenities of the remembered past. For example, how was one to secure a heavy woolen comforter to keep warm in this cold climate? Eliza Sachaklian went to the New York State Fair, straight to the building where the sheep were sheltered, and negotiated the purchase of freshly sheared wool. She brought the wool home, placed it in firmly sewn sacks for washing in her shiny copper-sided Easy Washing Machine, after which the cleaned wool was put in the spin drier. The wool was fully dried on a clean sheet outside in the sun and then thoroughly beaten into a fluffy mass with a strong stick, probably a broom handle. All the children were pressed into service for this chore. Meanwhile, she had sewn a quilt liner, the size of the comforter, which she placed flat on the floor, turned inside out. She distributed the fluffed-up wool evenly over the face of the liner and taking one lip herself, with her daughter at the other end, she carefully rolled the top sheet outward along with the wool, meanwhile turning the lower sheet under. After considerable fumbling, this resulted in a liner that was now right side out, the wool evenly distributed inside. With the piece still on the floor, she tacked down the wool carefully with needle and thread. The comforter was now ready to be enclosed in a pretty fabric cover. In some homes, the sheet was carefully folded over the four edges of the comforter and sewn into place. The comforter was laid on top of the bed, not tucked in at the foot. In our home, it became the custom to lay the comforter on the sheet, tucked in at the foot of the bed, with the top of the sheet folded over the comforter and held in place with large safety pins. This practice had its hazards. The sheets could tear and the pins sometimes opened, with predictable results.

Much to the despair of their American-born children, the women also reached back into their memories for favorite home-style remedies. Colds, fevers, and vaguely defined illnesses brought forth a variety of treatments. Perhaps the least objectionable was that for chest congestion, a mixture of olive oil and black pepper to be rubbed vigorously on the chest. Of course, one then had to be swathed in several undershirts or towels to protect the bed covers. Perhaps it was this extra warmth that helped the sick to recover.

If more rigorous treatment was in order, one would face *shishe kashel*, literally "pulling the bottle." With a small bottle at the ready next to the patient's chest, the practitioner would set fire to a small wadded up piece of paper, usually toilet paper, thrust up into the bottle. This would create a vacuum in the bottle which was then placed quickly against the chest. The suction would presumably break up the congestion, after which the bottle would be removed with a tug, leaving a red circle to dissipate in time.

Most disgusting of all were the leeches, swimming lazily in their bottles of water, that were brought into the house only when other methods failed. It was usually impossible to persuade children to remain still for this treatment. For the most part leeches were applied, by request, to adult bodies.

The kitchen was, of course, the heart of the Armenian home and practically every Armenian housewife took pride in offering the traditional foods and pastries to her family and guests. I feel sorry for young people today who do not remember, as I do, arriving home from school to be greeted by the welcoming fragrance of freshly baked *pideh* (round bread) or flat cracker bread or *katah* (rolls) or *lahmajoon* (meat pastry). Sometimes there were exquisite syrupy trays of paklava, cut into diamond shapes, or rolls of *bourma,* sweet flaky pastry and nuts. I recall hearing my mother's melodic soprano voice, trilling loudly in the freedom of her solitude while she worked, a signal even before I entered the house that treasures awaited me.

As orphans or young brides, many of the housewives learned cooking and homemaking not at the sides of their mothers, except for a few precious fragments remembered from childhood, but rather from experimentation in search of remembered tastes and textures or from each other. A tattered old Armenian cookbook owned by my mother lacks adequate measurements or cooking instructions and would be useless to someone unacquainted with the desired end product. She carefully preserved a packet of cooking tips, information probably gleaned from others or occasional items in the Armenian press.

There were then no local stores from which to purchase the special ingredients needed for Middle Eastern cookery, so the women often imported the necessary supplies from Armenian stores in New York City or Boston. Some substitutes were discovered—for example, shredded wheat could be made to pass for *khadeif,* a much finer and softer product, ready to be prepared with nuts and sugar syrup. For the most part, however, the cooks preferred authentic materials. Certain ingredients tended to be used most often. Lamb, rice, bulgur—ground in three different sizes—onions, eggplant, tomatoes, formed the basis for many of the dishes, but there were regional differences in flavorings and methods of preparation and serving.

For preparation of breads and pastries certain tools were also needed and were often made with the help of the husbands. A carefully sanded and buffed broomstick, cut to the proper length, provided the long thin pole required for rolling out the cracker bread dough or for preparing *bourma.* The carpentry was more complex for the wide flat wooden spatula, in evidence today for pizza-making. The flat part and the wooden handle had to be shaped separately and then bolted together.

Invitations to dinner offered opportunities to sample regional dishes and Armenian women quickly picked up appetizing additions to their repertoire of menus. Everyone prepared certain foods like rice pilaf and yogurt. The preparation of yogurt, called *madzoon* in Armenian, also provided an opportunity for social contact, because the housewife inevitably stopped to chat while seeking a starter culture from her neighbor. *Madzoon* was used in many ways: eaten straight at breakfast, lunch, or dinner, as topping for *dolma* (vegetables, especially tomatoes, peppers and eggplant, stuffed with ground lamb and rice) and *sarma* (meat and rice filling wrapped in leaves from wild grape vines), pressed to a soft paste by straining out the liquid and eaten as a dressing on moistened flat cracker bread, diluted in water and chilled with ice cubes for a cooling hot-weather drink called *tahn*, and *jajukh*, with chopped cucumbers and a sprinkling of crushed mint leaves. Who prepared the first yogurt culture? According to Karl Butler, a scientist and writer on agricultural topics, yogurt was brought to the United States by an Armenian named Setrak Boyajian when he came to this country in 1906.[247] Since then, the beneficial attributes of yogurt have gained recognition and it has become very popular, although in a sweetened form that was unknown to the immigrants of yesterday.

The expeditions in June and early July to pick the wild grape leaves, while still tender on the vines of springtime, should be mentioned as well. Even though it meant that the young ones were expected to contribute to the harvest as well, it was an opportunity to run and jump in the countryside. For the housewife, there was further work on returning home. The leaves had to be arranged neatly in packs, soaked in hot water, then packed in brine in canning jars or wide-mouthed bottles with caps. This would preserve the leaves through the long winter for use as needed.

Anyone who has never tasted Armenian hors d'oeuvres has not lived life to its fullest. Here we find some of those grape leaves, transformed into delicious delicately flavored rolls stuffed with rice and onions, tender white brick cheese soft and fresh from tubs of brine, Greek olives, various versions of Armenian meat sausages spicy and tasty, crisp cucumbers and sweet tomatoes from the kitchen garden, and that wonderful Armenian flat bread, crunchy when dry and rendered tender with moisture.

The Armenian cuisine, complete with pilaf, dolma, and many other delicacies, has made a successful transition to the present day. Even non-Armenians have adopted some of these dishes. However, it seems that the foods—however tasty—that are prepared today with the aid of carefully detailed cookbooks cannot compare in full flavor and fragrance with the dishes produced with casual abandon—the measure of *achkee chap* ("the measure of the eye"), a sprinkle of this and a dash of that—by the wonderful ladies of the immigrant generation. Or is it because they were prepared by our beloved

---

247. *Syracuse Post-Standard,* September 21, 1991.

The smiles of the group gathered in August 1927 are in sharp contrast to the somber faces of the earlier years.

mothers that the lush meals of yesterday can never be replicated by our own forever inexpert hands?

A Close Community

Based on the information provided earlier, it does not seem unreasonable to estimate that there were as many as eighty adult Armenian males in Syracuse in 1924, many of whom had wives and families by this time. Even greater growth appears to have taken place through to the early 1930s. Group photographs taken in the early to mid-1930s show about two dozen children aged four or five to the early teens, all born in Syracuse. With the great increase in marriages and births through the decade and the arrival of families relocating to Syracuse from abroad, many of whom soon produced additional children, the community grew quickly. By the early 1930s, there could have been close to three hundred Armenians in Syracuse.

Referred to as "the South Siders," there were a dozen or more Armenian families living on or in the vicinity of South Avenue, up to Valley Drive and Glenwood Avenue, including Rev. and Mrs. Khachadourian and the Tohafjian-Taft family.[248] Armenians also lived in clusters in the East Washington Street and East Genesee Street areas, in Eastwood, and along

Butternut Street and other sections of the city, but no ghetto ever developed. The warmth that had characterized the Syracuse community during the previous decade continued through the 1920s. Many years later, Haigouhi Hanessian, who had come to Syracuse in 1923, remembered the closeness of the community she had joined. Rose Zahrajian Benjamin recalled, "We had no phones. We walked everywhere. Wherever we visited, we were always welcome." Close associations developed within the youthful, growing community, already linked by ties of blood, marriage, compatriotic relationships, and friendship. Assistance was freely extended whenever needed, without concern for return. The old-timers helped newcomers to find jobs and homes and to learn the ways of their new environment. Not only newcomers sought help. Years later, stories were told of numerous unpaid loans having been made to certain longtime members of the community. The men who had advanced these sums were themselves far from affluent, but no consideration ever appears to have been given to litigation to force repayment.

Women had their own ways of assisting each other. On Sunday mornings Rev. Khachadourian would officiate at services in Syracuse. In the afternoon, with his wife, he would go to serve the Binghamton congregation, returning to Syracuse the following morning. Every Sunday, Mrs. Khanzadian would care for their three children, Mrs. Khachadourian told me.

In 1924, Mianzara Zahrajian Eckhoff, then a newlywed of six months, and her mother paid a visit to Mrs. M. Ajemian. They found her ill in bed, unable to care for her little baby. At her mother's suggestion, Mianzara took the infant home with her and gave him loving care for nine months until the mother was well enough to take him back.[249] The question of remuneration was never raised.

A friendly temporary home was always found for the prospective brides who arrived, undoubtedly confused and apprehensive, to meet the men to whom they were to commit their lives. It is likely that the hostess provided comforting words of advice and encouragement, as well as food and shelter. As noted, Mrs. Gertmenian received Mrs. Hanessian and also befriended the Khachadourians. The hospitality of the Divrig people extended beyond their own abundant clan. When Kyoomjian's intended, Dickranouhi, arrived, she was received and befriended by Nazeni Minasian—"as usual," said her daughter, Zephyr Kyoomjian Minasian. The generous-hearted Mrs. Minasian had also tried to nurse Mannig Zahrajian Bedrosian back to health at the Minasian farm.

---

248. Taft, p. 122.
249. Letter, Eckhoff to Mesrobian, May 3, 1983.

Families living in close proximity visited each other frequently and warm friendships developed between some of them. The home of Khachig and Nazeni Minasian on East Washington Street was within comfortable walking distance of the downtown area. Warmed by Mrs. Minasian's easy hospitality, the home invited constant visitors, whether single or married, who would gather there in groups, Zephyr Minasian recalled. Even if families differed in tastes and outlook, the presence of an Armenian neighbor, however incompatible, warranted formal acknowledgment. Generally, however, as is usual in social affairs, certain groups tended to form within the community. In particular, relationships by blood, marriage, and compatriotic origin continued to link families.

A visit was always the occasion for serving oriental coffee. The Armenians hated to call it Turkish coffee. Preparations started with roasting the beans in one's own oven. After the beans cooled, the housewife placed them in a beautifully decorated brass hand grinder which ground the whole beans into a fine powder. Next, the powder and water were mixed in a long-handled fluted pot. True coffee drinkers eschewed sugar. The mixture was brought to a rolling boil several times and poured into the tiny cups while there was still considerable foam on top. For some, the foam was mandatory decoration. The coffee had to be poured carefully, in small amounts among the cups, so the sediment would be evenly distributed. After drinking the coffee slowly in small sips, the drinker allowed the cup to cool slightly, and then turned it upside down on the saucer to dry out, in preparation for fortune telling. A few ladies, among them Pergrouhi Jigarjian and Eliza Sachaklian, became noted readers of coffee cups, gaining fame with their accurate predictions.

Alcoholic beverages such as beer and hard liquors did not usually take a prominent place in the hospitality that was offered, at least in my memory. *Raki* (the Greek "Ouzo") was a more familiar drink. Often cherry cordial prepared by the housewife would be served. Consuming such drinks tended to be of a ceremonial nature and customarily toasts would be offered before sipping.

On very formal visits, sweets were occasionally served in the old country way. The housewife or her daughter—sometimes even a small son—would pass a tray containing a dish of rose or apricot jam or quince preserves, all homemade, with a cluster of brightly polished silver spoons. The guest would eat a spoonful of the sweet and then place the empty spoon in a glass of water provided for that purpose. Very likely the rose jam had been prepared by the housewife from petals taken from an old-fashioned rose bush in her own back yard. The sequence of service had its protocol, with the first offering to be made to the eldest or most distinguished guest. One reason for using children as servers may have been to teach them deference to their elders. Usually the child doing the serving would have been instructed by his or her mother, but

Karnig Shahlamian with hookah pipe, about 1915.

often the guests, attempting to outdo each other in politeness, would wave off the tray designating someone else, and causing the child to return to the kitchen in exasperation.

Certain customs from the old days persisted for a long time, finally disappearing with the aging of the immigrant generation. A photograph of Karnig Shahlamian, taken at the Arax Studio in about 1915, shows him with a hookah pipe (called *narghilé* in Armenian) of elaborate design.[250] Such pipes were in evidence in some Armenian homes through the 1920s and would sometimes be brought out for the use of special guests, but they had mostly disappeared by the middle or late 1930s.

Amusements

This was a youthful community with little opportunity for amusement and social interchange except for what they themselves could provide. At this time few of the adults were sufficiently fluent in English to feel comfortable in a non-Armenian setting, so they were largely absorbed with Armenian affairs.

---

250. Eckhoff collection.

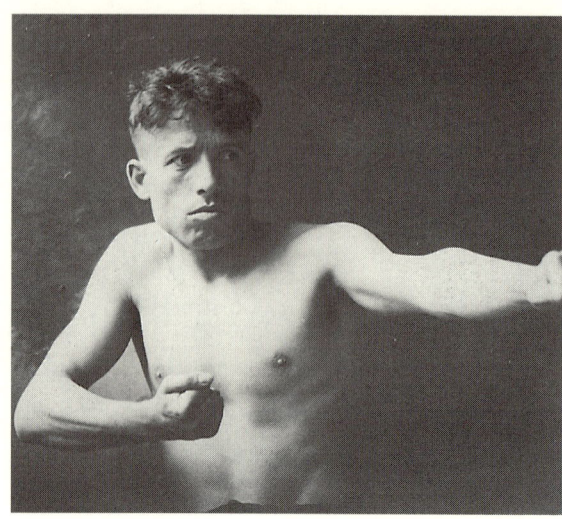

Hagop (Jack)
Bezirjian, 1921.

The Yeprad Athletic Club that had offered in 1915 an instructional program under the direction of H. Terzian seems to have disappeared by the
1920s, perhaps because of the departure of Mr. Terzian. Nevertheless, several
young men found ways to engage in regular physical activity. Missak
Kalebdjian was a skilled wrestler, while a photograph of Hagop Bezirjian in a
militant pose, bare-chested, fists clenched, commemorates his boxing career.
Mianzara Zahrajian's notation on the back of the photograph records an
important event: "Syracuse Fighter, Heavyweight Champion, Hagop
Bezirjian, First Fight, Monday Night, 11 July/1921, at Onondaga Park."[251]
Perhaps it was Mianzara's enthusiasm that conferred a championship after
only the first fight.

Social gatherings in homes were frequent and card-playing was very much
in evidence. When Aaron Sachaklian came to Syracuse in 1919 he soon
became part of a men's group calling itself unexplainably the *Tiv Dasni Meg*
club ("Number Eleven"). In 1921, while he was away on a business trip, his
friends sent him a commemorative photograph of themselves along with a
mock petition signed by the eight men in the photograph beseeching God's
favor on the club's absent *scambile* champion.[252] Later a men's pinochle group
developed.

Scambile, a card game that was always the occasion for jokes and loud
laughter, was also a favorite with the women. It was played with four, six, or
sometimes even eight players, divided into two teams. The hands were shown

---

251. Eckhoff collection.
252. Sachaklian collection.

Tiv Dasni Meg (Number Eleven) club, 1921.

freely between partners, but passed in great secrecy and plays were called by facial signals or voiced instructions. The game has not survived the transition to a new generation. It has not been played in the Syracuse community for many years.

Well known throughout the Middle East, backgammon has always been a favorite, especially with the men, and it is rare for an Armenian home not to own a *tavloo* board, often one elegantly inlaid with mother of pearl and colored woods. To this day, backgammon is a familiar amusement in Armenian clubs or at Armenian picnics and informal gatherings.

Music was very much present in those days. Mary Apikian, a tall, beautiful, fun-loving, and vivacious young woman, always drew a close circle around her when she played the *oud* (a stringed wooden instrument with a big belly and long neck, like a lute) and sang the Turkish folk songs that most of her audience knew from their childhood. Although there was some antipathy toward anything Turkish, sentiment sometimes overcame principle. As the younger generations grew older, the music changed to Armenian and American folk songs, with singers clustered around the piano.

Aaron H. Sachaklian, Syracuse city checker champion, 1928.

Gradually, Armenian songs inspired by the American setting began to emerge, such as "Catskillin Jampan" ("The Way to the Catskills"), referring to a resort area popular with the Armenians during the 1930s and 1940s, "Marsilliayen Minchev New York" ("From Marseilles to New York"), and the gay "Dari Lo Lo," generally sung when guests were preparing to leave a home after an evening's partying. Its rhyming refrain acknowledged the hospitality that had been enjoyed: "This was an enjoyable evening, the housewife's work for tomorrow has increased."

The emerging younger generation introduced novelties such as parlor games and amateur performances. On one such occasion, when it was Karnig Shahlamian's turn to perform, he remarked, "I can't sing, I don't have a story to tell, but I can swear wonderfully." He could, too, but as it was mostly in Turkish the young people could not appreciate his skill.

Picnics were undoubtedly the most popular social and organizational event. Photographs of large and small groups from the 1920s and 1930s may be found in almost every Armenian home from that period. The Babikian farm continued to be used, although not as frequently as it had been in earlier years, and groups also met in Onondaga Park or in some green spot chosen as a meeting place with the small Armenian communities in Auburn, Rochester, or Utica. A photo of twenty-one adults and six children with the ARF field worker, A. Vanarian, was taken at the Babikian farm in 1920.[253] A photo marked June 14, 1925, was taken of fifteen young adults at the Babikian farm.[254] In another, at least twenty-five people in family groups are shown seated on the grass before a well-laden picnic offering. The photo, taken August 1927, Geneva, New York, includes Armenians from the communities in Syracuse, Auburn, and Rochester.[255]

A Widening Gap

As war came to an end and the world entered the 1920s, the Syracuse Armenian organizational scene began to reflect the changes that had taken place in Armenian affairs. Most notably felt was the impact of the fall of the Armenian Republic. The red banner bearing the Soviet hammer and sickle had replaced the Tricolor of the Armenian Republic. Armenians who had supported the short-lived Republic observed developments in Soviet Armenia with suspicion and apprehension, while those who had welcomed Russia's

---

253. Eckhoff collection.
254. Ibid.
255. Gift of Ara Saxenian to Mesrobian.

"protection" minimized destructive aspects of Soviet rule and emphasized efforts to develop and stabilize the country.

Although community members continued to maintain close ties of friendship with each other, disputes over Armenian political affairs constantly simmered beneath the surface. The Armenians sought to keep the peace and to build a tight network that would help to preserve their identity and, in particular, the identities of their children in what was still seen as a foreign environment. Despite their efforts, however, this undercurrent of disunity, a continuation and exacerbation of the attitudes that had been expressed a decade or more earlier, continued to bubble with occasional outbursts from time to time.

Even during its brief existence, "not all Armenians supported the Armenian Republic."[256] Philosophical differences turned into political conflicts over the question of Armenian independence. While the vigorously anti-Soviet ARF sought to keep the Armenian Question alive, those taking an opposing position argued that with the imposition of Soviet rule the Armenian problem had been resolved. Opponents of the ARF even held it against the party that the ARF-dominated government of the Armenian Republic had strenuously resisted the Soviet invasion. Opposition to the ARF, a revolutionary party, was especially strong among those espousing the position of the Ramgavar party, whose orientation was that "revolution or resistance as a means for solving the Armenian problem were impractical or delusional."[257] The Marxist Social Democratic Hunchagian party easily made the transition to a pro-Soviet and anti-ARF position. Thus it was that the conservative Ramgavars and the revolutionary Hunchags made common cause in their opposition to the ARF in an unsteady union of convenience that lasted many decades.

The few individuals in Syracuse with Ramgavar sentiments gradually abandoned the party, while the Social Democratic Hunchagian committee in Syracuse, which had previously joined with the ARF on occasion to protest the Turkish deportations and massacres, became less visible through the 1920s. Members of both groups now turned to "Hayasdani Oknoutyan Gomide" (Committee to Aid Armenia) or HOG. This group was founded in Armenia in 1921 with the purpose of gaining sympathy and material support for Soviet Armenia from the communities in the diaspora.[258] It claimed to be a nonpolitical organization, dedicated to the reconstruction of Armenia, but its pro-Soviet views were transparent. Its chapters did "celebrate the anniversary of

---

256. Letter, Eckhoff to Mesrobian, February 19, 1983.
257. Atamian, p. 273.
258. Kevorkian, p. 159.

Soviet Armenia and similar observances which are recognized by all organizations having sympathy for Soviet Armenia, whether political or not."[259] HOG was dissolved in 1937.

The Syracuse committee of the ARF had been formed in 1913 and for seventy years it remained the strongest Armenian political organization in the community. The committee lost a few members in the fallout over the Sovietization of Armenia, but new members quickly refilled the ranks. Continuing the pattern of activities described earlier, it regularly sponsored programs and events throughout the year. The ARF club rooms were even made available to a visiting speaker, Mr. Kasparian, for two hour-long speeches on December 5 and 12, 1929, in praise of Bolshevism. In a rebuttal delivered on December 19, 1929, A. H. Sachaklian corrected errors in Kasparian's account describing how Armenia became subject to Bolshevik rule.[260]

Depending on the type of program, events intended to attract a large audience were held at the Boys' Club on East Fayette street, later in the Syracuse Museum of Fine Arts on James Street, and in the Ukrainian Hall. Mianzara Zahrajian Eckhoff also recalled "lots of meetings in the YWCA" on East Onondaga Street before she was married.[261]

As in Armenian communities elsewhere, Syracusans annually commemorated April 24, Armenian Memorial Day, May 28, the anniversary of the founding of the Armenian Republic in 1918, and ARF Day in October. Syracuse was among the communities that observed the fortieth anniversary, in 1930, of the founding of the ARF.[262] Now, however, part of the Armenian community remained conspicuously absent from observances considered to be purely celebratory of the ARF, such as ARF Day or even Armenian Independence Day on May 28. With the expectation of a diminished audience, such observances were held at the ARF club rooms.[263] The ARF press observed, "What should be universally celebrated [May 28] is unfortunately seen as a political event."[264] Internal party rebellions sometimes occurred. "In a few communities the local Ramgavars, going against instructions of their central leadership, also participated" in observances commemorating Armenian Memorial Day and Armenian Independence.[265]

Picnics were sometimes dedicated to heroic deeds of the past. In 1923 a picnic sponsored by the ARF in remembrance of the Khanasor Expedition

---

259. *Hairenik Amsakir,* July 1927, p. 159.
260. Text of Aaron H. Sachaklian's speech in Sachaklian collection.
261. Letter, Eckhoff to Mesrobian, February 6, 1983.
262. *Hairenik Amsakir,* June 1927, p. 159; March 1931, p. 175.
263. Postcard announcement dated May 29, 1932 in Eckhoff collection.
264. *Hairenik Amsakir,* June 1927, p. 159.
265. Ibid., June 1929, p. 176.

raised $150 to send to the ARF Central Committee in Boston.[266] The commemoration honored ARF fighters who, in 1897, retaliated against Kurdish forces who had ambushed and slain Armenians attempting to defend the city of Van against Turkish attacks. Except for the April 24 observance, fundraising seemed to be continuous throughout the year. Sympathizers gave generously to underwrite activities on behalf of the Armenian cause.

Aaron H. Sachaklian, who had been a member of the secret group seeking revenge against the Turkish leaders responsible for the Armenian massacres, apparently continued his efforts behind the scenes. His inquiry received the following response dated August 9, 1926, from F. C. Nichols, Vice-President, Colt's Patent Fire Arms Manufacturing Company, Hartford, Connecticut as follows: "At the present time we know of no restrictions affecting shipments to the Levantine. . . ." The letter writer adds that he is sending catalogues for automatic machine guns and automatic machine rifles.[267] Although Sachaklian's intent is not known, he does not appear to have envisioned active resistance to Soviet might. He wrote in 1930 that the ARF does not propose to take up arms against Communism. Looking with confidence into the future, he asserted that Communism will crumble. When it collapses in Russia, then Armenia will be free.[268]

The ARF club rooms in the downtown section of the city provided a regular meeting place for members and friends. A. H. Sachaklian's papers contain a receipt from the Syracuse Lighting Company dated July 13, 1925, addressed to the "A R F Pub Library, 307 E. Genesee St., 3FL." This appears to have been in the Myers Block, still in use by the Armenians for more than a decade. The rooms were used for visiting, card-playing, backgammon games, and meetings of the ARF and its women's affiliate, the Armenian Red Cross. A lending library of Armenian and English-language books was also available, although there were few users.

Many Syracusans today, children then, still recall the third floor walk-up in a triangular structure across the street from City Hall. Invariably, the recollection also brings back the memory of the smells of the Chinese restaurant on the second floor which had to be endured before reaching the final elevation. According to Mianzara Zahrajian Eckhoff,[269] the club was opened sometime between 1918 and 1920, but meeting notices in the Azadian collection give evidence that the Myers Block was used as early as 1913. When the building

---

266. Copy of letter in Sachaklian collection written by Aaron H. Sachaklian to ARF Central Committee.
267. Sachaklian collection.
268. Ibid.
269. Letter, Eckhoff to Mesrobian, February 6, 1983.

was torn down in the early 1930s, the club rooms moved to a clean and cheer-ful suite of rooms on the second floor of a building on the southeast corner of Warren and Fayette Streets.

The Armenian Red Cross, the benevolent organization formed in the United States in 1910 under the auspices of the ARF, was at first supported by "everybody" when a Syracuse chapter was organized in 1915, Mianzara Zahrajian Eckhoff remembered. Even strongly anti-ARF Mrs. Azadian lent her presence to the organizational meeting. "Then things began to change. We got separated. The Tashnags formed separately."[270] The effort collapsed.

The chapter was reestablished in 1920 under strong new leadership. The new president, Eliza Sachaklian, had become a charter member of the Hartford chapter of the Armenian Red Cross in 1914. She then moved to Boston and joined the chapter there. Coming to Syracuse from the large Armenian community in Boston, she brought fresh ideas and enthusiasm. However, the membership of fifteen to twenty women[271] was no longer representative of the community at large. Members were primarily the wives of ARF members or women associated with families who did not oppose the Armenian Republic or the ARF. Many of these early members, with dates of joining, are pictured in a commemorative album published in 1930.[272] Other early members, whose names Eliza Sachaklian recalled in a talk given on May 8, 1960, were Nazeni Minasian, Nazeni Kupelian, Siranoush Kupelian (later Parnagian), Mannig Enfiejian, Haigouhi Nigsarian.[273]

The Armenian Red Cross later changed its name to the Armenian Relief Corps and then in 1946 to the Armenian Relief Society (ARS). The organization proved to be an important influence in the lives of its members, as well as a welcome source of support for needy Armenians, especially those in the Middle East. Official publications—*Arpi: A Magazine for the Armenian Family*, first issued in January 1932, *Hai Garmir Khach* (Armenian Red Cross), and *A.R.C. Quarterly* initiated in January 1939—contained articles on health,

---

270. Ibid.
271. Eliza Sachaklian, 1983.
272. Mary Apikian (1920), Satenig Apikian (1920), Siranoush Apikian (1920), Dickranouhi Kyoomjian (1923), Zarouhi Zahrajian (1922), Varteni Zahrajian (1915), Mianzara Zahrajian Eckhoff (1922), Hripsime Tufenkjian (1923), Philomena Garabedian (1924), Mary Hamamjian (1924), Jouhar Mangouni (1911), Barkevouhi Semerjian Shahlamian (1920), Araxi Shakarian (1928), Aghavni Boyajian (1915), Eliza Sachaklian (1914), Anna Kupelian (1916). *Albom Hai G. Khachi Ir Ksanamyagin Artiv* [*Album of the Armenian Red Cross on Its Twentieth Anniversary*], (Boston: Hairenik Press, 1930), pp. 125–26. Jouhar Mangouni must have become a member before coming to Syracuse.
273. Text of talk in Sachaklian collection.

child care, selected topics from Armenian history, information on ARS chapters in other parts of the world, poems and skits that could be taught to children, even a few songs and music scores. Within a few years, articles in English by American-born youth began to appear, dealing with topics of special concern to the younger generation. One of the names occasionally appearing in the ARS publications was that of former Syracusan, American-born Stella Sachaklian Rustigian, now a young matron in Hartford busy with her own family.

The ARS was a school for its members, Mrs. Sachaklian used to say in later years. For many women it was their first opportunity for public activity. They learned how to plan organizational affairs, to budget, to work in cooperation with other members, to speak and perform in public. At a time when the Armenian women had few other outlets, the ARS provided opportunity to grow and develop.

In the 1920s, another organization emerged which stood in competition with the Armenian Red Cross. The "Hayasdanyaits Garmir Khach" (Red Cross of Armenia), sister organization to HOG, was espoused by those sympathetic with Soviet Armenia. Before long, the name was changed to "Bedagan Garmir Khach" (State or Federal Red Cross). A Syracuse chapter of the Bedagan Garmir Khach maintained a shaky existence for a few years, according to Haigouhi Hanessian. Only three members are named in the *Hunchagian Yearbook* of 1931: Mother Kalebdjian (Elise), her daughter-in-law, Takouhi, and Mrs. Desteian. Neither the Bedagan Garmir Khach nor the HOG, seems to have made much headway in Syracuse. Few of those I interviewed remembered them.

In contrast, the Armenian Red Cross had already become an international organization by 1929. In 1931, its convention drew sixty delegates from the United States, Canada, Cuba, and several countries in Europe and the Middle East. In 1932, it claimed an American membership of fifteen hundred plus five hundred in a youth group. Foreign membership totalled thirty-eight hundred.[274]

The Armenian General Benevolent Union (AGBU) had a strong structure and a steady following and seemed to emerge without harm from a tentative association with the Bedagan Garmir Khach and the HOG. The Syracuse branch, founded in 1914, sponsored plays and programs, sometimes bringing speakers from out of town.[275] Events were held in locations familiar to the Syracuse Armenians, such as the Boys' Club (the favored choice for plays), the YWCA hall, later the YMCA on Montgomery Street,[276] and the Museum of

274. *Hairenik Amsakir,* August 1932, p. 171.
275. Gozigian, Avakian, Desteian.

Fine Arts on James Street for smaller gatherings. Although ostensibly non-political, the AGBU had been founded by the Ramgavar leader Boghos Nubar and tended to obtain its support from people with Ramgavar sympathies.

Despite the existence of many organizations and groups seeking to raise money to help Armenia and the Armenians, the needs were never-ending. Even while efforts were continuing to find lost Armenian orphans and refugees and to aid and resettle them, word came from Armenia of a catastrophic earthquake in the region of Shirag in October 1926. Alexandropol (Leninakan, now Gumri—the same city that was devastated in the earthquake of 1988) was 80 percent destroyed and twelve villages had disappeared. One thousand people were dead and eighty thousand had lost their homes. Damage was estimated at sixty-five to seventy million dollars. The Armenian communities in America sought to organize a unified campaign to secure help, but squabbles erupted practically from the beginning. Despite such problems, half a million dollars was raised, a remarkable sum in a short time.[277] The Syracuse Armenians came together in a cooperative campaign and in a strongly worded letter to the Armenian-American press expressed their objection to the disarray in the central leadership of the fund-raising drive.[278]

The lack of a central governing body to control and manage the many campaigns for funds was deplored in the press. Even the many compatriotic societies, down to the level of ancestral village, carried on independent fund-raising campaigns. Without the structure that centralized planning could have provided, the communities were bombarded with appeals for funds for various causes. The AGBU and ARS raised money to pay for Armenians to return to their "homeland," Armenia, from various communities in the diaspora (*nerkakht*). The ARF sought to find and rescue Armenian women in Turkish harems and to help convert the Armenian refugee camps in the Middle Eastern countries into stable communities with their own institutions. Fundraisers came from abroad seeking support for schools in Armenian communities in Europe. A HOG representative came from France to travel around soliciting funds from the communities in the United States, leaving controversy in his wake. Even as late as 1929 came news of the discovery of small groups of starving Armenians in Turkey who needed help.[279]

276.According to Desteian, the Armenians used the YMCA "in the Khachadourian era," September 7, 1992.

277.*Hairenik Amsakir,* December 1926, p. 141.

278.Ibid., January 1927, p. 159–60.

279.Ibid., January 1927, p. 159; April 1927, p. 144; September 1929, p. 175; February 1926, p. 144; July 1928, p. 176; April 1927, p. 144; January 1929, p. 176; April 1929, p. 175.

The Young Ararat Club, directed by Zarmair Taft, seated in center front, about 1924.

Meanwhile, the Armenian-American communities, concerned about losing a younger generation of thirty thousand, made strenuous efforts to fund the construction of Armenian schools and churches and to establish a diocesan center.[280] By 1930, however, the effects of the depression were being felt, hampering such campaigns.[281]

In Syracuse, efforts to organize the young people started early. Young adults were first brought together in the nonpolitical Armenian Students Association, established in Syracuse in 1915. In the early 1920s, the group was transformed into "The Young Ararats," consisting of late high school and college students and young adults.[282] One of the organizers was Zarmair Taft.[283] A photograph uncertainly dated 1924 pictures twelve young men and six

280.Ibid., May 1926, p. 143; February 1929, p. 176.
281.Ibid., December 1930, p. 176.
282.Koolakian.
283.Desteian.

young women, many of whom appear to be in their early twenties.[284] The Ararat group did not last long, being supplanted in the mid-1920s by the Junior League of the AGBU. According to Antaram Desteian, at that time Armenian organizations had deteriorated and the Junior League was dominant. Miss Desteian had no affiliation with the ARF and ARS, both of which were active in Syracuse at the time.

The Junior League was a social organization supposedly for people up to the age of eighteen, but the age limit does not seem to have been enforced. This technicality was disposed of by calling the older ones seniors. Mianzara Zahrajian Eckhoff recalled that she did not belong to the Junior League because she was married then and was too old.[285]

The lighthearted Mary Apikian, a married woman, apparently had no such compunctions, because she appears in a 1929 photograph of "The Syracuse N.Y. Juniors" in *Hoosharar*.[286]

According to the text that accompanied the photo, the Syracuse chapter came into existence in June 1928 at the initiative of Mrs. Z. Kalemkerian of New York City, growing from five young people to twenty-eight. The group maintained an active program of dances, picnics, and even the presentation of a play. They met at members' homes twice a month, once for business and once for social purposes, conducting the meetings in Armenian. After Nevart Dabanian joined the community in 1928, the group often met at her home for Halloween parties, programs, and dinners.[287]

A photograph dated December 17, 1933, records another Junior League event. It shows nine young women and a young girl in Armenian peasant costumes and a young man in his twenties, the popular Onnig Keshishian, in Arab costume. Onnig was a dashing fellow with a Rudolph Valentino kind of flair and many of the young women considered him romantic. On the back of the photograph is the notation: "Play held at Boys' Club. Rehearsals held at Victoria Roomian's and the Z. Taft's apartment."[288] Elise Taft tells us, "Zarmair directed local Armenian plays for many years. The rehearsals now

---

284. Benjamin collection.

285. Letter, Eckhoff to Mesrobian, February 19, 1983.

286. Pictured are: Karnig Keledjian, Haig Menasian, Rose Muserlian, Sarkis Kaishian, Ardemis Desteian, Mary Khoubeserian, treasurer; Zarouhi Zahrajian, Mary Apikian, Hilda Sachaklian, recording secretary; Vartan Bahoukian, Missak Kalebdjian, Arshag Sarkissian, Onnig Keshishian, vice president; Malcolm Abajian, Harry Menasian, president; Antaram Desteian, corresponding secretary; Mary Muserlian. Desteian collection.

287. Desteian.

288. Benjamin collection.

AGBU Junior League, 1929.

took place in our new home and it soon became a center for much of what went on in the Armenian community in Syracuse."[289]

Well, not entirely. Organized under the auspices of the AGBU, which had Ramgavar orientation, the Junior League may have been intended to serve as the training ground for membership in the senior agency. In any case, it was avoided by youth from staunch ARF families. Stella Sachaklian Rustigian recalled that her father prohibited her from joining.

Americanization League

Although divided over political issues, the community was united in the desire to maintain its cultural and religious identity. Differences were set aside in the efforts to maintain their church, history, and language, and to transfer national values to their children. At every opportunity, the Armenians came together to display their heritage to the American community, to teach their

289.Taft, p. 134.

AGBU Junior League Halloween party, about 1930.

children the Armenian language and the nation's history, and to organize their parish to participate fully in the activities of the national church.

The Americanization League proved to be an ideal forum for the Armenians to present themselves to the American public. The plan for Americanization of new immigrants was suggested by the Bureau of Naturalization, United States Department of Labor, and was carried out in numerous cities. [290] The purpose was to develop sympathy and understanding between the various ethnic groups and also to assist immigrants to learn the English language and to become naturalized American citizens.

In Syracuse, the Americanization Committee of the Chamber of Commerce sponsored a meeting of foreign-speaking residents of the city "for the purpose of forwarding the Americanization movement."[291] Mr. and Mrs. Azadian were members of the inner circle from the beginning. The organizational meeting which brought together "a group of civic minded people" took place at their home.[292] Mr. and Mrs. Azadian became members of the board

290. *Syracuse Journal,* November 13, 1916.
291. Ibid.
292. Article by Ramona B. Bowden, *Syracuse Herald-American,* October 23, 1966.

Play at the Boys Club, December 17, 1933, presented by the AGBU Junior League. Rose Zahrajian Benjamin's notation on the back of the photo reads: Rehearsals were held at Victoria Roomian's and Z. Taft's apartments.

and served as representatives of the Armenians.[293] Mrs. Azadian was recording secretary of the board at one time.[294] This local league was the first of its kind in the country, attracting nationwide interest.

One of the earliest and most ambitious ventures of the Americanization League in Syracuse was a week-long series of tableaux presented at the New York State Fair in September 1919 by a number of ethnic groups picturing important events in their history. The program culminated on September 13, which had been designated as Americanization Day. With the support of the Armenian Students Association, the Armenians presented a lavishly costumed pageant depicting the historic Battle of Avarair.[295] Also on display throughout the week of the Fair was an Armenian booth organized under the

293.Koolakian, "Mr. Azadian Came to America," p. 165.
294.Letter dated May 28, 1930 in Eckhoff collection.
295.*Syracuse Post-Standard,* September 13, 1919.

chairmanship of Mrs. Azadian. The exhibit presented an unusual collection of handiwork brought from Europe, such as several rugs and a hand woven and embroidered altar panel, several hundred years old.[296] Attending the pageant was Dr. John H. Finley, state superintendent of education. Dr. Finley was also associated with the American Committee for Armenian and Syrian Relief and was scheduled to be in Constantinople during late summer to assist the committee's relief program, according to a letter sent to George Koolakian from Charles V. Vickrey, executive secretary in New York. [297]

A pageant of nations was also presented through the week at the 1920 New York State Fair and September 17, 1920, was especially observed as Americanization Day. It is likely that Armenians participated in the event, although memories are somewhat unsteady. Eliza Sachaklian recalled Mrs. Kalebdjian's joyful exclamation, "My boy horse!" at seeing her son Missak on horseback during the parade. Antaram Desteian remembered her own role as Mother Armenia, while Paklavouni Gebelian, popularly known as "Mendz Agha," pretended to be a Turk, holding Mrs. Daniel Markarian and Ardemis Desteian by the hair, threatening to cut off their heads.[298]

While the pageants and programs were enjoyable, learning English required serious effort. Eliza Sachaklian recalled that when she first came to Syracuse in 1920 Armenians were going to a church (Fourth Presbyterian Church) to study English. There were also English tutors, supplied by the government, who came to the homes. The Americanization League offered regular teaching programs. Elise Taft remembered that Belle Dickenson, for many years a missionary in Turkey, was a volunteer teacher for the Americanization League. She had a class of nine Armenian boys, all newcomers.[299]

The fourth annual edition of "The Home Class Review," published in June 1927 by the Home Classes of the Americanization League of Syracuse and Onondaga County, notes "the progress being made by the members of the Home Classes at Syracuse, N.Y. in connection with the Americanization League of Syracuse and Onondaga County, N.Y."[300] Among the short articles written to demonstrate the authors' accomplishments were three by Armenian women: Shooshanig Gozigian, Pergrouhi Jigarjian, and Pearl Toofangjian.

---

296. *Syracuse Post-Standard,* September 9, 1919.

297. Letter dated January 22, 1919 in the Koolakian collection.

298. There was also considerable excitement when child movie star Jackie Coogan visited Syracuse in 1925. The Armenians participated in the welcoming ceremonies at Clinton Square, where nine-year-old Arpena Abajian presented him a bouquet of flowers. It is not known whether the event was under Americanization League auspices.

299. Taft, p. 123.

300. Booklet in Jigarjian collection.

Reenactment of the Battle of Avarair at the New York State Fair Grounds, September 1919. From left to right: Paklavouni Gebelian, Abraham Kurdian, Setrak Kalebdjian, Sam Minasian, Krikor Aghaian, Dickran Desteian, George Koolakian, Krikor Apikian, Ghazaros Choghanjian, Missak Kalebdjian, Haig Koolakian, Mary Philibosian, Vahram Rejebian, Zarouhi Zahrajian, John Enfiejian, John Finley, Yervant (Robinson) Keledjian.

The Home Classes were evidently dominated by women, because only one article bears a man's name. A news item on the formation of "The Home Class Club of Syracuse" names only women as officers and members. Shooshanig Gozigian was appointed temporary chairman and Sirouhi Kaish was elected president.

Members of the Home Classes who received their citizenship during the 1926–27 school year included Siranoush Minasian, Shooshanig Shahinian, Alice (Elise) Kalebdjian, Shooshanig Gozigian. Among those scheduled to appear in the June naturalization court were Pergrouhi Jigarjian, Takouhi Kalebdjian, Arousiag Telian. Pearl Toofangjian was among those filing their Declaration of Intention or First Papers. Those commended for perfect or almost perfect attendance included Virginia Kalebdjian, Mary Dumanian, Nesly (Nazeni) Kupelian.

Representatives of each participating country also put on dinners according to Antaram Desteian and Mianzara Eckhoff. Mrs. Eckhoff added that at the Armenian dinners she sometimes played the flute and the Azadian daughter Arshalouis played piano. In addition, the younger generation was soon organized into singing and dancing groups for participation in mixed ethnic programs. In 1934 an Armenian folk dance group consisting of eleven young women and one young man took part in an Americanization League program involving two hundred persons representing sixteen nations.[301]

The Americanization movement has not been universally praised. According to one scholar, it sprang, in part, out of the fear felt by nativist groups that an intrusion of foreigners would change the country. It was also prompted by humane considerations for easing the social integration of the new immigrants. These two sides to the Americanization movement are called "the impulse of fear and the impulse of love." One current demanded conformity, while another was moved by considerations of the immigrant's welfare.[302]

In Syracuse, the Americanization League program appears to have avoided both the unreasoning fear of something foreign as well as the stifling, pompous benevolence prompted by pity felt for people who are "different." Rather, the program provided opportunity for the immigrants to display their own valued traditions, while learning about those of others with growing understanding and respect. Also, a most important component of teaching independence: they received an education in the language and governmental structure of their new country.

Another positive result, appreciated in hindsight, was the impact on the American-born young people (myself included) who participated in the various performances as representatives of a culture which they themselves did not fully understand. By making their own contribution to the medley that is America and viewing the enjoyment and respect with which their songs, dances, costumes, and foods were received, the youth felt pride in themselves and appreciation for their parents' efforts to teach them their own heritage. The results of efforts to resist assimilation have been examined in a dissertation whose author concludes, in part, that "the empirical data tends to support the contention that cultural pluralism for the Armenian-Americans is beneficial to the ethnic individual and culture as well as the majority culture. Conversely, assimilation, when defined as the *rejection* of one's own ethnic group, tends to be neither beneficial to the individual nor the majority culture."[303]

---

301. *Syracuse Herald,* April 22, 1934; program from Sachaklian collection; newspaper clippings from Sachaklian and Eckhoff collections.

302. John Higham, *Strangers in the Land: Patterns of American Nativism 1860–1925* (New York: Atheneum, 1981), p. 237.

School

One of the prime concerns of the immigrant Armenian communities was the retention of their children within the traditions of their nation. Being able to speak, read, and write the language was accorded prime importance. In effect, language was equated with nationhood. Next in importance came knowledge of Armenian history. In the words of Elise Taft:

> To those of us born in Turkey (or under any regime that persecuted minorities) one's religious faith, language and cultural identity were the factors which made for his survival as a human being. If these had been destroyed the Armenians as such . . . would have been destroyed long ago.[304]

In 1932 a census of sorts revealed that there were sixty Armenian schools with five thousand pupils and one hundred teachers for a population of 151,140 Armenians in America, excluding California.[305]

There were few trained teachers anywhere and none were available in Syracuse, so the community relied on volunteers to take over the fewer than two dozen children of varied ages and levels of attainment who met once a week, on Saturday mornings, in a changing series of locations, starting in the basement of the Fourth Presbyterian Church. There appeared to be no planned program of study or syllabus, except that prepared by the teacher. As the teachers changed often, so did the program. The history course became a joke with the older students, who complained of starting every fall with the story of Haig and Bel (the legendary beginning of the Armenian nation) and ending in the spring with the encounter between Ara the Handsome and Queen Semiramis.

Much of the emphasis during the school year was usually placed on teaching the children Armenian songs and recitations to be performed at the annual or semiannual school *hantes* (program). Sometimes there were elaborate skits or plays, with children in costume. The totally uncritical public took huge delight from these performances, enjoying a mistake as much as polished delivery.

The early community schools lacked textbooks appropriate to the ages, intellectual levels, and cultural backgrounds of the students. The only printed materials available to the teachers were old texts brought from Armenian old country schools. Aghavni Zahrajian Boyadjian's library contained *Tbrotsi*

303.Paul Kernaklian, "The Armenian-American Personality Structure and Its Relationship to Various States of Ethnicity," Ph.D. dissertation, Syracuse University, 1966.
304.Taft, p. 139.
305.*Hairenik Amsakir,* September 1932, p. 168.

Kirke (The School Book), a book of readings published in Constantinople in 1902, and *Maireni Lezoo Tavtian* (The Tavtian Mother Tongue), title page missing, on a lower level of difficulty. *Tankaran* (Treasury), a book of poems and short selections, belonged to Mannig Zahrajian Bedrosian. It was published in Constantinople in 1908.

Teachers had to work diligently to improvise methods and materials that would bridge the gap between early twentieth-century Turkey and urban America of the post World War I era. What may have been the earliest attempt to produce a textbook for Armenian-American students was *Meghraked* (River of Honey), published by the Hairenik Press in Boston in 1917. A brief foreword stated that the volume on two levels had been produced in response to numerous appeals for texts suitable for the new student generation. The books contained poems and short, sometimes amusing, often didactic reading selections. They were widely used in many American communities for more than a decade.[306] Aghavni Zahrajian Boyadjian owned the 1917 edition and her sister Rose used the 1927 edition. The text was somewhat too advanced for many of the students, however, and books on a much more elementary level began to appear, such as *Oshagan Nor Keragan* (Oshagan New Grammar), published in Constantinople in 1930. Aghavni Boyadjian's son, Sarkis, owned a copy. It used large print, contained illustrations, and provided demonstrations of handwriting, which differs from the printed letters.

Despite many handicaps, the young people did learn to speak the language, generally using the dialects of their parents and often, like their parents, unknowingly mingling Turkish words. They managed to learn to read a little too, but only those who continued to study independently ever made much progress. Nevertheless, during World War II, many a young American-born soldier of Armenian descent wrote letters in a broken, error-filled Armenian script to his parents that to their dewy eyes rivaled the most beautiful pages of Armenian literature.

Attempts appear to have been made to oversee the management of the Syracuse school and run it in an orderly fashion. Report cards in my possession dated December 1931 and January 1932 bear the label "Sirakusi Hai Azkayin Tbrots" (The Armenian National School of Syracuse). Others bear the stamp on the back: "Sirakusi Hai Dignantz Yegeghetsasirats Miutiun" (The Armenian Women's Church Union of Syracuse).[307] The neatly prepared cards, adorned with colored ribbon bows, recognize punctuality, deportment, and

---

306. These books were used in Armenian schools in Canada during the 1920s. See
    Polyphony: The Bulletin of the Multicultural History Society of Ontario, vol. 4, no. 2,
    Fall/Winter 1982, special issue "Armenians in Ontario," p. 71.
307. Sachaklian collection.

achievement in the study of history. Slips dated November 1931–32, December 1931–32, January 1932, and February 1933 give precise grades within a tenth of a percentage point for my accomplishments in reading, writing, spelling, and grammar, translation from English to Armenian, punctuality, and deportment. It is my impression that the report cards were prepared by Mrs. Robinson Keledjian, whom I remember as an uncompromisingly stiff marker. I recall her remark that she gave us low grades "to encourage us" to work harder.

There is no evidence that parents were ever charged tuition for the various school programs that were offered, but Nevart Apikian recalls that teachers who taught in the Armenian school in the basement of Fourth Presbyterian Church received pay for their efforts. She said that on payday Mr. Chookasouzian would sit at a desk, like a paymaster, and require the teachers to line up for their money. The practice stopped after Nevart's father, who was a church official (he was the community's delegate to the National Representative Assembly), heard the teachers' complaints.

Many Syracuse Armenians now in their seventies and eighties have recollections of the various locations where Armenian school took place during the 1920s and early 1930s, and of the teachers, but it has not been possible to determine precisely when each person taught and where. Several people remember that the earliest Armenian classes in Syracuse were held in the basement of Fourth Presbyterian Church, which provided the Armenian newcomers with a place for worship and social gatherings.[308] Agishe Minasian recalled that at the age of twelve in 1921 he was himself a pupil at the Armenian school in the basement of Fourth Presbyterian Church. Later in the 1920s there were about fifteen students, he said. In 1922 a building permit was issued for the Syracuse Hotel, and the Fourth Presbyterian Church was subsequently demolished to make way for it. After that, the Armenians held classes in several schools in the downtown area.

Agishe Minasian said Plymouth Church was used by the Armenians, but he must have been in error. Antaram Desteian said they did not, and there is no evidence that they did. Azad Minasian thought that Putnam School was used before Fourth Presbyterian Church, but this too is not supported by the general testimony. Several people mentioned Prescott School, at the corner of Willow and North State streets, and particularly of Montgomery School between Adams and Jackson streets. Montgomery School, now demolished, was a small two-story building, dating from the 1850s. Armenian classes were held in a classroom on the second floor. Some remember Clinton School on

---

308. Eliza Sachaklian, Stella Sachaklian Rustigian, Agishe Minasian, Arpena Abajian Mechigian.

Lodi Street. James Abajian is the only one I interviewed who remembers going to Armenian school in a school building on the corner of Salina and Colvin Streets, where a post office now stands. He said his teacher was Takouhi Kalebdjian. He remembered that an Armenian inventor lived across the street. The Azadian family lived on Colvin Street next to the South Presbyterian Church on the corner. Abajian was born in 1921 and came to Syracuse in 1923. He would have been going to Armenian school in the later 1920s and early 1930s.

Stella Sachaklian Rustigian remembered that one of the earliest teachers was Arshag Sarkissian, who taught Armenian history. Orphaned by the 1915 massacres, he worked at the tailor shop of the Apikian brothers during his college years until his graduation from Syracuse University in 1929. He later attained a doctor's degree and joined the staff of the Library of Congress. Sarkissian entered into Armenian community life in Syracuse and was a member of the Junior League. He appears in the photo in *Hoosharar* July 1929. According to Mrs. Rustigian, during his lectures, Sarkissian would fix his eyes on anyone who seemed to be paying attention and continue in that manner to the end of the talk. On one occasion, speaking before an Armenian audience at the Boys' Club, he praised the Soviet Union. The audience rose up in indignation and drove him from the stage.

Many remembered Takouhi Kalebdjian.[309] Mrs. Kalebdjian, who was devoted to the Armenian Apostolic Church, made a point of teaching about the Armenian Church and its history. In one of my composition books on Armenian history and geography, several pages are devoted to the story of Armenia's conversion to Christianity. Her students learned to recite the Lord's Prayer in Armenian and to sing the main hymns. I recall her instructions for making the sign of the cross, with the thumb, index, and middle fingers brought together, moving from forehead to the lower part of the chest, and stressing that the hand should then move from left shoulder to right, not from right to left like the Greeks. For several years a group of us children would tour Armenian homes at Christmas time to sing the hymn *Khorhoort Medz* ("Great and Glorious Mystery") and receive holiday offerings for the church.

Many also remember Zvart Markarian, who started to teach soon after coming to Syracuse in 1926 to be married. Mrs. Rustigian associated Mrs. Markarian with the classes in the Fourth Presbyterian Church basement, but Mrs. Markarian's daughter said she taught at Putnam School. Mrs. Rustigian remembered that Mrs. Markarian taught the Armenian letters by sound, not by name, and wondered whether she had received German pedagogical

---

309.Azad Minasian, Elizabeth Markarian Avakian, James Abajian, Karl Gozigian. Gozigian also named Hmayag Kassabian as a teacher, the only one to do so.

training. Her daughter confirmed that Mrs. Markarian had graduated from a German seminary in Kharpert. Among other early teachers, all volunteers from the community, were Anitsa Khachadourian,[310] Mrs. Robinson Keledjian, [311] and Sirarpi Mardigian.[312]

As the years rolled through the 1920s and into the 1930s, the Armenian Church became increasingly politicized, becoming the vehicle for penetrating and disrupting Armenian community interrelationships and institutions. The school, which was under the management of the women's church auxiliary, did not remain immune. What happened then to the schools and the church is a melancholy story.

A Hostage Church

The importance of the national Armenian Apostolic Church in Armenian affairs cannot be overemphasized. Their Christian faith sustained the Armenian people during their sufferings at the hands of hostile neighbors. Moreover, it was the national church that gave the stateless Armenians political as well as religious identity. The Sovietization of Armenia had a profound impact on the Armenian Church and, through the church, on the Armenian communities abroad, especially in the United States. Although it is not possible here to detail the complex history of the Armenian Church during its period of captivity under Soviet domination, the trials of the Armenians in America cannot be understood without some appreciation for the destructive effects of Communist policy during this sad period in Armenian history.

In Turkey, the church's position of leadership was validated by the Ottoman *millet* system, which placed jurisdiction of certain civil, educational, social, and administrative matters in the hands of the various ethnic religious leaders.[313] Because membership in the Armenian Apostolic Church defined nationality as well as religion, in Turkey Armenians of Protestant or Catholic faith became officially excluded from nationhood.

In Syracuse for a time "everybody went" to the Protestant services conducted by the early Armenian ministers and later by Rev. Khachadourian,[314] but Apostolic Armenians did not feel comfortable there. Only the national church with its familiar rites and traditions could satisfy their spiritual needs. It was the national church, as well, that the immigrants looked to for leadership in forming schools and for guidance in issues of national concern.

---

310. Stella Sachaklian Rustigian.
311. Eliza Sachaklian, Zephyr Kyoomjian Minasian.
312. Eliza Sachaklian, Alice Choghanjian Hagopian, Arpena Abajian Mechigian.
313. Atamian, p. 26.
314. Haigouhi Hanessian.

Church affairs in the United States had had a troubled history up to the 1920s and matters were to get worse, rather than better. Local parish councils composed of laymen included partisans of the various factions and the political differences that disrupted the communities invaded church affairs as well. Soon events in Armenia were to provoke further divisions among the Armenians in America.

With the arrival of the Red army in Armenia in autumn of 1920, Soviet power prevailed over the Transcaucasus. Little Armenia and its meager resources fell subject to Communist rule. The same types of coercive and propaganda methods that were carried out elsewhere in the Soviet Union to destroy religion were introduced into Soviet Armenia. First to feel the harsh consequences was the one national institution remaining to the Armenians, their Apostolic Church. In December 1920, one month after taking command in Erevan, the Communists separated the schools from the church and confiscated the buildings, fields, and properties of the Etchmiadzin monastery, as well as the church treasures which were to be directed to the state museums.[315]

The removal of the monastery's possessions not only clearly signalled the anti-religious policy of the new order, it also had the practical result of depriving the church of a major means of support, thereby hastening the desired decline. By February 1921, other ominous signs appeared with the imprisonment of two vartabeds (priests).[316]

As news of such developments filtered into the diasporan press, ARF supporters pointed to them as confirmation of their worst fears. Opponents of the ARF brushed off such news, taking solace in the gradual rebuilding of Armenia, the establishment of collective farms, the opening of factories, the enlargement of schools. True, these were all Communist institutions, but they were, at least, for Armenia. How could Armenia have aspired to such development had it not been for the resources of the big Russian brother?

In 1922 the government encouraged and gave recognition to a "Free Church" formed by a group of priests whom the Catholicos excommunicated for their "uncanonical" teachings.[317] In the meantime, seeing that their crude attacks on the Armenian Church were ineffective in undermining traditional loyalties, the Soviet leaders reassessed their policy toward religion in Armenia. They soon realized that "it was more profitable from their point of view to

---

315. Stepan Stepaniantz, *Hai Arakelagan Yegeghetzin Stalinian Prnabedoutian Orok* [*The Armenian Apostolic Church Under Stalinist Tyranny*] (Erevan: Abolon, 1994), p. 8.
316. Ibid., p. 10.
317. Mary Kilbourne Matossian, *The Impact of Soviet Policies in Armenia* (Leiden: E. J. Brill, 1962), p. 93.

penetrate the official, traditional Church rather than to build up a rival body which, being a Soviet instrument, was suspect from the outset."[318]

As they began to look beyond the boundaries of the Soviet Union, they took into consideration the significance of the Catholicos, Supreme Patriarch of All Armenians, and of Holy Etchmiadzin (the seat of the church), among the seven hundred thousand or so Armenians throughout the diaspora.[319] The Catholicos of Etchmiadzin is a national symbol, respected by Armenians universally, but he has a coequal, the Catholicos of Cilicia or Sis. Deported from Turkey, like his people, the Catholicos was now residing in the village of Antelias, just north of Beirut, Lebanon. Until the fifteenth century, the Armenian patriarchal seat changed frequently, moving to at least seven places to keep pace with the movements of the Armenian kings and princes.[320] The Catholicosate of Cilicia had been established many centuries earlier to serve Armenians at a time when distance or disruptions of war prevented communication with the Catholicosate of Etchmiadzin. It was the only See for a time when the Catholicosate of Etchmiadzin remained unoccupied. Its administrative territory encompassed the immediate region, not the far-flung diaspora, as did the authority of Etchmiadzin.

The Soviet leaders recognized that they had a powerful tool within their grasp. By retaining the Catholicosate within Soviet territory, there was the opportunity of influencing Armenian public opinion throughout the diaspora. At the same time, the exploitation of this opportunity did not weaken Communist resolve to destroy religion and church authority within the Soviet Union.

> So it became Soviet policy to reduce to a minimum the influence of Etchmiadzin inside the Soviet borders, whilst giving the Catholicos the maximum of support in his endeavours to maintain his influence over the Armenian diaspora. [321]

Taking church affairs firmly into their own hands, the Soviet leaders established a Commission for the Affairs of Religious Cults to supervise the churches and to act as the intermediary in all official affairs. These bodies were "but a facade for the Cheka-GPU-NKVD-MVD and its ecclesiastical section."[322]

---

318. Walter Kolarz, *Religion in the Soviet Union* (London, Melbourne, Toronto: Macmillan; New York: St. Martin's Press, 1966), p. 150.

319. Simon Vratzian, *"Haieri Tivn oo Vijage"* [The Numbers and Condition of the Armenians], *Hairenik Amsakir*, December 1925, p. 95.

320. Kolarz, p. 151.

321. Ibid., p. 152.

The Communist campaign of intimidation and destruction of the Armenian Church and clergy within Armenia and the Soviet Union was not enough. As news reports of Soviet attacks on the church began to appear in the diasporan press, the Communists made use of the Soviet press to hurl accusations against the church and its leaders, both within Armenia as well as in diasporan communities. They put pressure on the Catholicos, demanding the cooperation of their hostage church leader to make public denials of what everyone knew to be true.

Even America was not far enough away to avoid Communist scrutiny and censure. In a letter bristling with indignation, Archbishop Tirayr Hovhannesian, primate of the diocese in eastern United States, wrote to Catholicos Kevork V on April 1, 1926, to deny charges that had appeared against him in a Tiflis newspaper.[323] In vain, the Catholicos sought to defend himself and the church against Soviet accusations. His long letter dated October 7, 1927, addressed to the president of the central commissariat of Soviet Armenia, Ardashes Garinian, listed actions taken with regard to bishops in charge of several foreign dioceses and pointed out that he has instructed Bishop Balakian (Paris) and Bishop Tirayr in America that they are not to participate in any political activities and that they are always to support the great task of reconstruction of Soviet Armenia.[324]

He also stated that he learned only from Garinian's speech (appearing in the official newspaper *Khorhourtayin Hayasdan*) that Bishop Tirayr had taken the "Tashnagtsagan Garmir Khach" (Tashnag Red Cross) under his sponsorship. In that connection, he has already demanded an explanation from the Prelate. The Catholicos pointed out that in 1922 and in 1925 he had issued encyclicals instructing Etchmiadzin's representatives to support Armenia's Red Cross.[325] (This is the so-called Bedagan Garmir Khach.)

These protestations evidently did not satisfy the Soviet officials. Would they be content with the Catholicos's declaration of total surrender? A directive dated June 26, 1929, issued under the authority of the Catholicos informed all the diocesan primates of the Armenian Church that the Church

> is far from adhering to any party nor will it protect the interests of any faction, but . . . states her loyalty and friendship towards the Soviet regime and advises all the Diocesan Primates as well as the

---

322. Ibid., p. 54.

323. Sandro Behboudian, *Vaverakrer Hai Yegheghetsu Badmoutian (1921–1938)* [*Documents from Armenian Church History*], (Erevan: Government of the Armenian Republic, Archival Office, 1994), p. 78.

324. Ibid., p.119.

325. Ibid.

religious jurisdictions and the clergy subject to them to be likewise and friendly towards the Soviet regime. Having as a guide the principle of division of church and state, they are asked not to allow speeches against the state or to permit the exploitation of Church functions and institutions for anti-Soviet propaganda. The Armenian faithful must be advised to follow the same course. It should be made known that the opposition course is and will hereafter be disapproved and subject to censure.[326]

This is a strange application of the principle of separation of church and state. Speeches are not to be made against the state (i.e., the Soviet Union), nor would the church allow anti-Soviet propaganda. Instead, only expressions of friendship toward the Soviet regime are to be allowed. Even for slow learners, it must have become evident that the church was not remaining outside politics, but was in fact totally enmeshed in it. Under pressure from Communist authorities, the church was forcing the diasporan communities to choose between pro-Soviet and anti-Soviet positions.

The strain was apparently too much for the American primate. Archbishop Tirayr resigned from his position in 1928.[327] It was reported that he withdrew because he was not able to continue under current conditions.[328] Archbishop Tirayr, a frequent guest of Mr. and Mrs. Minas Apikian, became a familiar and respected, if not warmly loved, figure in Syracuse. Austere, scholarly, and uncompromising in manner, he was somewhat intimidating. His integrity, however, was never doubted. The charismatic Arsen Mikaelian, ARF field worker who had made visits to Syracuse, was his nephew.

With the church fully under their control, Soviet leaders pressed to implement the plan for collectivization. Resistance was punished by the deportation of as many as twenty-five thousand peasants from their homes. This provoked further resistance. "Tashnags appeared in some areas, and only with the intervention of the army were the main uprisings crushed in early 1932."[329] As the main support for the ARF tended to come from the simple countrymen, collectivization helped to destroy the ARF base remaining from the period of the

---

326. *Documents,* pp. 20–21; for Armenian version see Behboudian, pp. 187–88.
327. *Documents,* p. 18.
328. *Hairenik Amsakir,* November 1928, p. 176.
329. Ronald Grigor Suny, *Armenia in the Twentieth Century* (Chico, California: Scholars Press, 1983), p. 56.

Republic. Communist leaders maintained an enduring hatred for the ARF.[330] The church was also finally to be broken.

> All basic institutions of traditional Armenian culture were assaulted in the period 1929–36, and the Armenian Church was no exception. The anti-religious campaign was at a height between 1929 and 1931, when the collectivization campaign was in its most critical stage.[331]

By 1932 the church had been so severely decimated that Soviet leaders could afford to become more lenient.

> A petty Armenian government official told a visitor to Armenia that this change was ordered by Moscow and was partly motivated by the desire to mollify Armenians of the Diaspora who sent financial aid to Soviet Armenia.[332]

A new Catholicos was elected on November 14, 1932, filling a seat that had remained vacant since 1930. Only seven of the seventy-three electors were from abroad. There were no delegates from the Catholicosate of Cilicia, the patriarchates of Istanbul and Jerusalem, or the large dioceses of the Middle East, Europe, and California. A proposal to move the seat from Etchmiadzin to Jerusalem was defeated.[333]

The office of primate in eastern United States[334] remained vacant until 1931 while the communities tried to decide what course to take. After considerable dispute, the National Representative Assembly, composed of laymen representing the parishes, meeting on January 31–February 1, 1931, elected Bishop Levon Tourian, pastor of the small Armenian parish in Manchester, England, and, for approximately eight years, bishop of the Armenian Church in England with headquarters at Manchester.[335]

Those with ARF sympathies were troubled by Tourian's election. The minority group that had opposed him pointed to disruption and controversy that had erupted during some of his previous assignments. They also

---

330. While I was in Beirut, Lebanon, in 1937–38, it was possible to tune in short wave broadcasts from Erevan and listen to the ARF being castigated in the harshest terms. Stepanian mentions Communist hatred of ARF; see p. 11 and elsewhere.

331. Matossian, p. 147.

332. Ibid., p. 150.

333. Ibid.

334. The California diocese was separately administered. At that time the eastern United States diocese encompassed parishes in the rest of the United States, all of Canada, and Cuba.

335. *Syracuse Post-Standard*, February 8, 1932.

disapproved of his attitude toward Communism. In an article appearing in the religious yearbook, *Datev*, and dated June 10, 1928, while Soviet authorities were carrying on their campaigns against the church, Tourian brushed away confiscation of Armenian Church properties by the Soviet Armenian government. He argued that church is not buildings and material possessions, but unity, love, and the spirit of Christianity. These qualities are strengthened when freed of material ties, he argued. He also asserted that Soviet Armenia does not oppose the church in principle and that freedom of faith and religion is not hampered.[336]

This was the background of the Prelate who was expected to bring peace and order to the American communities. At the welcoming banquet on June 5, 1931, the blunt words of Khosrov Babayan, speaking on behalf of the Central Executive, proved to be prophetic. Warning that he would be frank, Babayan stated that he had not voted for Tourian, but that he supported the decision of the majority. This was a fortunate land where criticism was open and the bishop should expect to hear it, he warned. But he advised that the new primate should also be open and direct, and keep his resignation ready, as a way of stilling passions. Babayan concluded with an appeal to maintain harmony and peace. In his response, Tourian pledged always to be guided by his responsibilities and to respect church law.[337]

The new Prelate proceeded to tour the communities, visiting the larger parishes first. Syracuse finally had its turn. He arrived on February 6, 1932, and was greeted by a large delegation, including Mihran Babikian whom he had met "more than fifteen years ago" in Constantinople, according to the news account.[338] If the two men had indeed met in Constantinople, it must have been as very young men, because by this time the Babikian brothers had been Syracuse residents for twenty-nine years or more. Another Syracuse acquaintance was Harutun Azadian, who recalled that he and the bishop as young boys had attended the school of the Armenian Patriarchate in Constantinople.

Tourian was imposing in appearance, six feet tall and weighing 215 pounds. A photograph of him taken during this Syracuse visit shows a handsome person in full ecclesiastical garb, wearing a tall miter. He had a pleasant face, with dark eyes and eyebrows, a graying mustache and small beard.[339]

336.A. Bardizian, *Hai Yegeghetzvo Daknabe yev Anor Badaskhanadounere* [*The Crisis in the Armenian Church and Those Responsible for It*] (Boston: Hairenik Press, 1936), pp.180 and 325.

337.Ibid., 186.

338.*Syracuse Post-Standard*, February 7, 1932.

339.Ibid.

An informal reception on the evening of the bishop's arrival took place at the home of Mr. and Mrs. Minas Apikian. Mr. Apikian, Syracuse's delegate to the National Representative Assembly, had met the bishop at the church convention in New York City on October 11, 1931. The following day, Sunday, the bishop conducted services at the Church Of The Saviour. At that time, he conducted the ordination of two women, Eliza Sachaklian and Arousiag Telian, as acolytes. It was rare for women to receive this rank. A tea in his honor was held on Monday evening at the Yates Hotel. Members of the board of trustees of the Syracuse parish were Setrak Kalebdjian, president, Vartan Sheperdigian, Karnig Shahlamian, S. S. Kaish, and Krikor Apikian. [340]

Mr. Apikian's status as delegate gave him the honor of having the bishop as his house guest during the Syracuse visit. The Prelate received a warm welcome from the Apikians' dog Teddy, who invited him to play. Miss Apikian remembered that Teddy stole the bishop's slipper and their guest was hopping around in the parlor on one foot until her mother rescued the slipper. During his visit the bishop was also entertained at the home of Mr. and Mrs. A. H. Sachaklian, according to a warmly expressed note of appreciation in the bishop's handwriting, addressed to Mr. Sachaklian. [341]

With renewed enthusiasm, on February 5, 1933, the Syracuse Armenians put on an elaborate performance at the Boys' Club depicting the Christianization of Armenia. The program, its first (and only) such production, was sponsored by the Women's Auxiliary of the Armenian Apostolic Church which had been organized three years earlier. Mrs. S. S. Kaish was president. According to the news report, the play "was presented in the native language, and several hundred Armenian men, women, and children packed the small hall and enjoyed the production." [342] The cast included all political and religious elements of the community. [343] The lavish costumes using Armenian designs were created and executed by Stella Sachaklian, then a senior in the College of Fine Arts, Syracuse University. [344]

While the communities proceeded with their activities, the new Prelate began to introduce changes. A few months after his arrival, Tourian's new book of the liturgy, in both English and Armenian, was published by *Baikar*, the Ramgavar press. The customary prayer for the Republic of Armenia

340. Ibid.

341. Letter, February 11, 1932, in Sachaklian collection.

342. *Hairenik*, February 11, 1933, clipping in Sachaklian collection.

343. Khachig Minasian, Samuel Minasian, Minas Minasian, Azad Minasian, Antranig Nigolian, Eliza Sachaklian, Aghavni Boyadjian, and misses Arpena Abajian, Mary Khoubeserian, Arpena Sachaklian, Nevart Apikian, Beatrice Enfiejian, Rose Zahrajian, Rose Gebelian, Mary Tashjian, May Edison, Alice Koolakian.

344. Ibid.; *Syracuse Post-Standard,* February 1, 1933.

appeared in the English version, but in the Armenian version the word "Soviet" had been inserted.[345] The ARF press objected, but the Ramgavar press came to the Prelate's defense. The ARF press also objected to other innovations not in accordance with church law such as the invention of church awards.[346]

More serious issues soon developed, as Tourian prohibited the participation of the church in public events in observation of April 24, the day set aside to honor Armenia's martyrs. Bishop Tourian not only refused to chair the 1932 Armenian Memorial Day observances in New York City, but he also prevented the former primate, Archbishop Tirayr, from accepting. He explained that

> a special solemn requiem service commemorating the Martyrs will be conducted on April 24 in all the Armenian churches. . . . Since the Armenian clergy will have completely fulfilled their duties in the Holy Church, their presence at such [i.e., public] commemorative functions is unnecessary for various reasons.[347]

He also said that he feared "disturbances." This was to become a familiar excuse as further incidents broke out during the coming months.[348] Promoting unity had been one of the important objectives for Bishop Tourian's mission in the United States. Instead, the bishop's actions were widening the divisions within the communities. At the National Representative Assembly meeting in New York City on January 21–23, 1933, there were intense arguments over the bishop's actions.[349]

Controversies among Armenians in the Middle East and in Europe were beginning to erupt over the matter of the flag of the Armenian Republic which had been generally accepted as the national banner since 1918. Similar incidents began to appear in the United States Armenian communities. The escalating controversy finally exploded on July 1, 1933, during Armenian Day festivities at the Chicago World's Fair. The bishop who had prohibited the clergy's participation in public commemorations of Armenia's honored dead had hastened to appear at Armenian Day festivities at the Chicago World's Fair. As he entered the stage, he demanded that the police remove the Armenian Tricolor so he could give his greeting.[350]

---

345. Bardizian, p. 187; *Documents,* p. 22.
346. Bardizian, p. 191.
347. *Documents*, pp, 22–23.
348. Bardizian, pp. 194–95.
349. *Hairenik Amsakir,* February 1933, p. 157.
350. Bardizian, p. 200; see also *Documents,* pp. 24–31 concerning the flag issue.

As news of these events spread, the people responded with rage. The communities "are in turmoil," it was reported. Petitions of protest demanding the Prelate's resignation were put into circulation and Armenian communities had split from California to Canada, Cuba, and Mexico. According to the press, the Prelate defended himself, claiming that he was following instructions from the Catholicos.[351] Thereafter, events quickly accelerated toward the tragic climax.

When the National Representative Assembly convened on September 2, 1933, the issue that dominated the agenda was the status of the primate.[352] Pleading illness, Tourian designated another bishop to chair the meeting in his place. When the third session convened, not all delegates had returned to the meeting site. It was revealed that the minority group which wanted to retain Tourian had gathered at another site to meet separately. There they voted to retain him, while the original meeting voted to censure and remove him. Both meetings sent their reports to Etchmiadzin. A response that surprised even the sympathetic Ramgavar newspapers with its speed recognized the minority group's decision. A message from the Supreme Spiritual Council followed, advising Tourian to invite all delegates to a new meeting.[353]

Thereafter, the entire affair moved decisively to the political arena. Meeting in the Armenian Church hall in New York City on September 24, 1933, only three weeks after the abortive church convention, the Armenian Bureau of the Communist party and the Committee to Aid Armenia (HOG), declared war against the Tricolor and the ARF and invited others to join them in a United Front. The major participants were Communists, Ramgavars, and members of the Hunchagian party. Similar United Front groups were formed in Armenian communities throughout the United States and abroad. They called for direct and indirect actions, including a whispering campaign, with the purpose of undermining and ultimately destroying the strength of the ARF.[354]

In Syracuse, too, the community had divided on this issue. All were invited to a meeting at the ARF club on November 2 to hear the parish's delegate, Minas Apikian, give his report on the church convention.[355] In view of the fact that Mr. Apikian had remained with the original meeting and that he was

---

351. *Hairenik Amsakir,* September 1933, p. 171; October 1933, p. 172.
352. A detailed examination of this crucial period in Armenian life lies beyond the scope of this study.
353. Archbishop Mesrob Ashjian, *The Armenian Church in America* (New York: Armenian Prelacy, 1995), p. 28. See also Document 12, Official Statement of the Diocesan Council, September 20, 1933 in *Documents,* pp. 34–38.
354. Bardizian, pp. 374ff.
355. Postcard invitation, Eckhoff collection.

known to be a member of the ARF, it is not likely that those opposing the ARF would have come to what they perceived to be a den of iniquity to hear a report which they no doubt considered to be irrelevant, at the least, or even seditious, at the worst.

In this hubbub, little notice was given to an encyclical dated November 12, 1933 from Catholicos Khoren, urging peace and harmony for the sake of national unity.[356]

Midst all this unfortunate turmoil for the Armenian people, the United States decided to extend formal recognition to the Soviet Union.[357] It was expected that trade opportunities would help the United States economy, which at that time was suffering from a severe depression.[358]

The Prelate's days of glory, however, were soon to end. On Sunday, December 24, 1933, in the Armenian Church in New York City, Archbishop Levon Tourian was assassinated as he walked down the aisle during church services.[359] One of the parishioners battered in the melee that followed was Garabed Giragosian, mentioned earlier as a native of Divrig and formerly a Troy resident. A New York City resident, he returned home from church that day with his clothing torn.[360]

The terrible news burst upon the Syracuse community, as in other communities, causing sorrow, dismay, and confusion. In a long article in the local press, it was announced that plans for Armenian Christmas services on January 6, to be conducted by a priest whom the archbishop was to send from New York, were suspended. A member of the local board, S. S. Kaish, attempted to explain what had happened. He stated that there were approximately three hundred Armenians in Syracuse, and, according to him, most of them were members of the Armenian Church and none of them were of the faction which opposed the archbishop for his support of Soviet Russia. The article quoted him as follows: "I suppose this affair is the climax to dissension over the Soviet." He continued,

---

356. *Documents*, p. 44.

357. The United States never withdrew its recognition of the Armenian Republic, nor did the State Department issue an explanation reconciling that fact with recognition of the Soviet Union. See [James H. Tashjian], *Crisis in the Armenian Church: Text of a Memorandum to the National Council of the Churches of Christ in the United States of America on the Dissident Armenian Church in America* (Boston: Prepared by The Central Diocesan Board Armenian National Apostolic Church of America, 1958), pp. 52–53.

358. When the first Soviet envoy, Maxim Litvinoff, arrived in America, the Armenian primate sent a telegram greeting him, and was the lone religious figure attending the welcoming banquet—despite the controversy swirling around his head.

359. *The New York Times*, December 25, 1933.

360. Sarah Minasian.

> Ninety percent of the Armenians in this country are satisfied with
> conditions such as they are today.
>
> Armenia is a small country, surrounded by enemies. It is natural
> and for Armenia's good that she should be one of the Socialist
> Soviet Republics. Armenia sends her representatives to Moscow
> who have a voice in the government.
>
> But 10 percent of the Armenians belong to a faction which for-
> merly was in power in Armenia. That was just after the war. A
> republic was set up. When the Bolshevists came, they were ousted.
>
> It is only natural and diplomatic for Archbishop Tourian not to try
> to antagonize the Soviet, since Armenia is part of the Soviet.[361]

The above statement is representative of the anti-ARF position commonly
expressed at the time. It reflects no dismay over the destruction of the church
and nation under Soviet rule, expresses the belief that Soviet rule has been
"good" for Armenia and that Armenians "have a voice in government," justi-
fies Tourian's activities, and unrealistically minimizes the influence and extent
of the pro-ARF sentiment in the United States.

Certainly, at that time far more than ten percent of the estimated three
hundred Armenians in Syracuse were members of the ARF or sympathized
with the ARF position. The ARF was the only Armenian organization in Syracuse that up to that time, and for many years thereafter, was large enough and
strong enough to maintain its own club rooms. The ARF committee and the
ARS continued regular activities long after the Bedagan Garmir Khach and the
HOG had disappeared. Furthermore, Kaish's statement that none of the
church members "are of the faction which opposed the archbishop for his support of Soviet Russia," implies that even before the assassination the opponents of the ARF in Syracuse had already responded to the United Front calls
to make war against the ARF.

The article also reports that frequent attempts to form a permanent Armenian Church in Syracuse had failed, principally for financial reasons. The
Armenians were assisted by Rev. Carl Schwartz, a former rector of the Church
Of The Saviour, and the current rector, Rev. Arthur B. Merriman, but failed
in an attempt to form a church about eighteen years earlier.[362]

Just in case passions had not yet risen to the boiling point, the Armenian
Communists hastened to add fuel to the fire. A protest meeting held on

---

361.*Syracuse Post-Standard,* December 26, 1933.
362.Ibid.

December 31, 1933, in New York City under the sponsorship of the Friends of the Soviet Union reiterated a declaration of war against the ARF. The participants resolved to expel the ARF from Armenian community life, to boycott the ARF organ, *Hairenik*, to appeal to ARF members to abandon their leaders and join them, to form a United Front against the ARF and in defense of Soviet Armenia and the Soviet Union.[363]

Similar meetings and widespread boycotts, law suits over ownership of churches, disruptions among families and friends, and destruction of Armenian communities everywhere followed in city after city. The following report of a meeting in Troy is typical of events in other communities. Under the heading "Troy Leaders Move to Boycott Tashag [*sic*] In Armenian Church" appeared this story:

> Leaders of the Armenian Church of St. Peter and Paul were compiling a list today of members of the congregation believed to belong to the secret political organization Tashag, the group the church aeges [*sic*] is responsible for the assassination of Bishop Leon [Levon] Tourian in New York while he was holding Christmas services.
>
> Church leaders said that persons on the list would be boycotted.
>
> Decision to compile the list came after a surprise move last night, when 400 members of the congregation gathered under police protection and ousted four trustees alleged to belong to the Tashag group. They were replaced by four others chosen by the congregation.
>
> Church leaders said there were about 80 members of Tashag in the church.[364]

It apparently did not seem unreasonable to the enemies of the ARF to believe that complicity for the attack on an Armenian Prelate in church during the Christmas season could have been shared in remarkable secrecy by every rank and file ARF member in all the far-flung communities. Nor did it matter that expulsion from the church of those considered to be members of the ARF also meant the banishment of their spouses and children.

In Syracuse, the schism caused painful breaks in friendships of many years. Family and compatriotic relationships were disrupted and the institutions that had been built up over the years with such self-sacrifice and effort were torn

---

363. Bardizian, p. 375.
364. *Syracuse Herald,* January 15, 1934.

apart practically overnight. In the community that had been so loving, "like one family," now bitterness and hatred prevailed. Passions cooled as the years went on, but memories of those bitter days still linger among the few remaining older folks, while the younger people carry on the divisive traditions without fully understanding their origin.

Some ARF members were arrested and several were imprisoned, although it was never clear what had happened or who was responsible. A scholar concludes:

> But whoever was the immediate culprit, there can be no doubt that a great deal of the moral guilt for the crime lies with the Soviet Government for it was they who had forced the Armenian Church into a position where it ceased to be the traditional guide of the church and had become a fighting ground for political factions.[365]

---

365. Kolarz, p. 155.

III

1933 to 1956:
Living Apart

A Divided Community

With the dawn of 1934, the divided Armenian communities assessed the wreckage around them and began to make plans to live separately. It was imperative to retain what remained of the ruined foundations of community life, especially the church and school, and to build on them to ensure survival.

In Syracuse, the immediate effect of the break in the church was felt deeply. The ARF and its related institutions had been pointedly ostracized since the previous September, but now all social relationships were affected as well. Saddest of all was the loss of communal love and friendly intimacy. Disrupted friendships poisoned the atmosphere and those holding differing political views, including the women, avoided each other or exchanged harsh words if they chanced to meet. Even worse, previously suppressed personal animosities, having nothing to do with the church or politics, now sprang into view. Unlike some other communities, however, no legal wrangles or public disturbances took place in Syracuse.

Disputes over ownership of churches raged for months in some communities, but in Syracuse the only property held for church use was the small bank account of the women's auxiliary and some vestments, which Mrs. Jacob Telian refused to relinquish.[366] The money remained in the bank for many years, out of anyone's reach. Its release required the joint signatures of representatives of the opposing factions, and at the time they were not speaking to each other.

Ejected from their church, those holding ARF sympathies strove to organize themselves. Convinced of the legitimacy of their position, they formed

---

366. Reported by Stella and Arpena Sachaklian in *The Blat,* summer 1934, family newspaper in Sachaklian collection.

new parish councils and continued communications with the Central Executive remaining from the September 1933 meeting. The National Central Executive managed church affairs in America (except for California) from 1933 to 1957, cut off from the administrative and spiritual leadership of the Catholicos in Etchmiadzin. Several priests had objected to the illegalities that had been sanctioned by Etchmiadzin's recognition of the rump meeting which voted to retain Archbishop Tourian as Prelate, and refused to banish the ARF community. They were punished by being ejected from the church as well. They rallied to the side of the Central Executive Council, and for many years served as pastors of the churches remaining in the hands of the anti-Tourian segment and as visiting priests for the parishes without resident pastors.

Through the spring of 1934, while their opponents attempted to continue the attacks of the United Front, ARF sympathizers held huge mass meetings in the larger communities. A meeting in New York attracted three thousand people, one in Worcester drew two thousand, Union City had five hundred. People demonstrated their support by coming forward to join the ARF or the ARS.[367]

This was a time of severe economic depression throughout the country. Despite that, the pro-ARF segment gave generously in a nationwide drive to help defray the expenses of an appeal in the case of two men convicted of killing Archbishop Tourian. The Syracuse community contributed $800. The extent of their sacrifice may be shown by comparison with the sums collected in Los Angeles and Newark, cities with large Armenian populations, $840 and $832 respectively.[368] Ten men had been arrested and two were convicted for taking part in the killing. According to the news report about the Syracuse rally, "Speakers charged that the murder was committed by Bolshevists who were seeking to discredit the Armenian Nationalists and they allege none arrested had anything to do with the crime."[369]

The appeal failed and the two men faced execution on April 11, 1935. As the fatal day approached, dozens of petitions signed by Armenians in cities throughout the United States flooded the office of Governor Herbert H. Lehman. Among the many petitioners asking for clemency were "several hundred members of the Armenian-American Citizens Club in Syracuse."[370] The Governor commuted the sentence seventy hours before the final moment.[371]

367.*Hairenik Weekly,* March 1, 1934.

368.*Hairenik Amsakir,* November 1934, p. 148.

369.*Syracuse Herald,* October 8, 1934.

370.Undated newspaper clipping and copies of variously worded petitions are in the Sachaklian collection.

371.*Hairenik Weekly,* April 12, 1935, p. 1.

In 1934, Rt. Rev. Mampre Calfayan was designated by the Supreme Religious Council in Etchmiadzin as locum tenens to fill the vacant seat of primate.[372] He continued in that capacity until 1939. In ARF circles he was considered a troublemaker.[373] As acting Prelate, he visited Syracuse in August 1934 to celebrate the first *badarak* (full service) of the church in Syracuse since the assassination.[374] Symptomatic of the paranoia of the time, a police escort had been "requested as a precaution against disturbances by any of the Tashnag group, who were blamed for the assassination of Rev. Calfayan's predecessor, and who subsequently seceeded [*sic*] from the church."[375] Among those greeting Rev. Calfayan on his arrival at the train station were Y. S. Saxenian, a trustee of the Syracuse church, D. Desteian, and M. Keshishian.[376]

A rebuttal appeared in the Syracuse press on the following day. A group of Syracuse church officers asserted that Calfayan is a member of "the insurgent" group and is not "acting Prelate" of the church. The officers were identified as A. M. Kupelian, chairman of the local church, V. Sheperdigian, secretary, and K. Apikian, treasurer. They charged that Rev. Mampre Calfayan "has appropriated the title of bishop, whereas he has never been ordained as such." The group also claimed that those who brought the cleric to Syracuse are "a few Armenians who met in the YMCA after the regular annual meeting last spring, and elected themselves as the governing body of the church." The news report added that the convention to elect a successor to the late Bishop Tourian will take place in September in New York City. Delegates from Syracuse will include M. Apikian. Others identified as trustees were Jacob Telian, Karnig Shahlamian, and Robinson Keledgian.[377]

In October, the National Representative Assembly met in New York City, with Apikian in attendance. The temporary primate, Rev. Nishan Papazian, called the meeting to order. In attendance were eighty-seven delegates representing forty-seven parishes. Before the assassination there were sixty-five parishes, of which eleven were now practically dissolved. The convention devoted particular attention to an examination of church bylaws which, having been prepared in Soviet Armenia, were considered by the delegates to be in conflict with conditions in the United States. The convention passed changes restricting the authority of the Catholicos to matters of faith, worship, and creed,

---

372. *Hairenik Amsakir,* April 1934, p. 173.
373. Ibid., November 1934, p. 147.
374. *Syracuse American,* August 26, 1934; *Syracuse Herald,* August 26, 1934.
375. *Syracuse American,* August 26, 1934.
376. Ibid.
377. *Syracuse Journal,* August 27, 1934.

reserving administrative matters to the National Central Executive in the United States.[378]

Following the abortive church meeting in September 1933, the Supreme Religious Council in Etchmiadzin had directed Tourian as primate to call the delegates to another meeting. This directive was never obeyed, neither by Tourian nor by his successors. The church remained administratively divided, with each group meeting and conducting its affairs separately.

Political matters had for many years become entwined with church affairs and now it became impossible to separate them. The issues were so closely interwoven that an individual's position with regard to Armenian matters could be determined simply by knowing which church he or she attended or which Armenian newspapers entered the home.

Meanwhile, Communist oppression continued in Armenia. From 1933 to 1940, purges were carried out against Armenian "nationalists," becoming most intense from 1936 to 1938, and culminating in 1938 with the strangulation and secret burial of the Catholicos by the Cheka.[379]

By the end of the 1930s, the HOG had disappeared from the Armenian-American communities. In its place arose the Harachtimagan or Progressive League, the name taken in 1939 by the Panvoraganner (The Workers) which had emerged in the early Twenties. At the same time, the party organ *Panvor* adopted the name *Lraper* (Herald).[380]

The Progressive League found active support among Syracuse Armenians with anti-ARF sympathies. Adherents referred to the Progressive League as being "pro-Armenia,"[381] while opponents called it "pro-Soviet" or Communist.[382] The Progressives sought to increase sympathy for Soviet Armenia and for the Soviet Union. Antaram Desteian identified the following families as belonging to the Harachtimagans: Gozigian, Markarian, Hanessian, Kassabian, Chengerian, Boghosian. In many cases the wives were members as well. The Syracuse group sponsored programs and occasionally brought speakers from out of town.[383] Activities continued into the 1940s and early 1950s. The same people also supported the AGBU, arranging meetings and programs, and bringing in speakers.

While supporters of the ARF continued annual observances of May 28, the anniversary of the Armenian Republic, their opponents celebrated the

---

378. *Hairenik Amsakir,* November 1934, p. 146–47.
379. Matossian, p. 161.
380. *Hairenik Weekly,* December 11, 1947, p. 1.
381. Gozigian.
382. *Hairenik Weekly,* December 11, 1947, p. 1.
383. Gozigian and Avakian.

Republic's Sovietization. The Syracuse chapter of a short-lived organization called the Armenian National Council of America sponsored a celebration of the "thirty-second anniversary of Armenia" on December 7, 1952. A circular announcing the event urged that "it is the . . . duty of every Armenian to be present at this celebration commemorating Armenia's emancipation from tyranny." Only in the Armenian portion in small type do the words "S. Armenia" appear. [384]

The thirty-fifth anniversary of Soviet Armenia was also recognized by the Syracuse Armenian National Council in a "lavish observance" on December 4, 1955. The program at the Odd Fellows Hall offered a speech by *Unger Oksen Sarian* (presumably from out of town), recitations, and three films: *Burial of the Catholicos, A Leading Farm Station,* and *Armenia Today*. The program notice carries no names of Syracuse participants. It does, however, display a claim for the Armenian provinces of eastern Turkey, in addition to Kars and Ardahan. [385] Shortly afterwards, to the disappointment of all Armenians, the Soviet Union discontinued voicing claims against Turkey.

The anti-ARF community never had its own club rooms, but rented space as needed. As the years passed, they used a room on the second floor of a building at McBride and Madison streets and a club off Westcott Street. On occasion, they had picnics at the Narsasian farm in DeRuyter. [386]

The Bedagan Garmir Khach did not develop deep roots in the community and few informants mentioned it. The *Hunchagian Darekirk* of 1931 credited Elise Kalebdjian, her daughter-in-law, Takouhi, and Mrs. Desteian for providing the leadership in maintaining the Bedagan Garmir Khach in Syracuse. [387] It seems likely that the ladies' church auxiliary had much more appeal for the women.

To sum up, the anti-ARF group recognized the legality of the rump National Representative Assembly in September 1933, faithfully upheld the directives emanating from Etchmiadzin, supported the United Front, the AGBU, and, while they existed, the Bedagan Garmir Khach, the HOG, and the Progressive League. ARF sympathizers, having been ejected from the Etchmiadzin church, maintained a National Central Executive, conducted National Representative Assembly meetings, and conducted church services in their communities with the help of sympathetic clergy, while continuing their customary efforts to keep the Armenian cause alive. This situation continued to 1957.

---

384. *Syracuse Post Standard,* December 21, 1952.
385. Program notice in Sachaklian collection.
386. Gozigian.
387. P. 277.

Separate Schools

Despite the fracture in the community, efforts had to be made to ensure the continuation of the Saturday Armenian school program. The two segments carried on separately, using city school facilities at times and volunteer teachers. Stella Sachaklian Rustigian recalled that during a discussion about the possibility of the two factions coming together to operate a school, Zarmair Taft objected. He pointed out that history is taught in school, and that the ARF segment would want to include "politics" in the teaching of history, whereas his side did not want that. Therefore, the school should be kept separate.

By the early 1930s, small advances had been made in the production of teaching materials. One of the most sophisticated efforts was the series of textbooks called *Hrazdan,* prepared in accordance with a carefully thought out pedagogical design by an experienced educator, Armenouhi Aharonian. (Mrs. Aharonian was married to the son of Avedis Aharonian, the noted author and statesman.) First issued in 1934, the set of books on at least four levels remained in use for several decades. I remember using the lower level volume in the Syracuse school. Students who endured to the fourth level were introduced to short selections from noted Armenian authors and poets. Despite efforts to teach students to read and write, however, school instruction continued to emphasize memorization and performance.

The ARF segment presented a school program in the ARF club on Sunday, June 24, 1934, charging twenty-five cents for admission. The card of invitation bears a bilingual stamp. In English, it reads "Trustees of the Armenian School" and in Armenian: "S. Mesrobian Varjarani Khnamagaloutiun" (Trustees of the St. Mesrob School).[388] The name of St. Mesrob is customarily associated with Armenian schools because he is credited with the invention of the Armenian alphabet in the fifth century.

In the mid-1930s, the ARF had to find new club rooms because the building, constructed in 1850, was to be demolished. They found suitable space on the second floor of a building on the southeast corner of South Warren and East Fayette streets. A large corner room with many windows provided a pleasant site for large groups, while a smaller room was used for club meetings. There was also a small kitchen. This facility became the gathering place for training the children and there was no longer any need to use the city schools. It was also used for public meetings and social affairs. John Enfiejian's tailor shop was across the hall. Next to it was the editorial office of the *Bugle* newspaper, a popular tabloid of the time, whose proximity greatly excited the Armenian young people.

---

388. Invitation in Sachaklian collection.

Operetta presented by Armenian school children at the ARF Club under auspices of the ARS, May 24, 1936. Note that none of these children appear in the picture of Anitsa Khachadourian's school, nor are the Khachadourian school children present in the ARF-sponsored group.

The new club rooms offered ample space for the audiences usually to be expected at the Syracuse gatherings. Although there was no stage, there was sufficient space for an ambitious springtime operetta performed by the children on May 24, 1936. The club was transformed into a flower garden with rambler-entwined trellises, fences, and archways. The operetta was written and directed by Stella Sachaklian and sponsored by the Syracuse ARS. Twenty-six children ranging in age from five to twelve years appeared in the operetta.[389] Not long afterwards, Stella Sachaklian's betrothal ceremonies took place there on October 11, 1936, with one hundred fifty guests in attendance. The men's choir of the Armenian Church sang several religious songs,

---

389.*Hairenik Weekly,* June 12, 1936, p. 7; photograph in Vartkas and Zephyr Minasian collection.

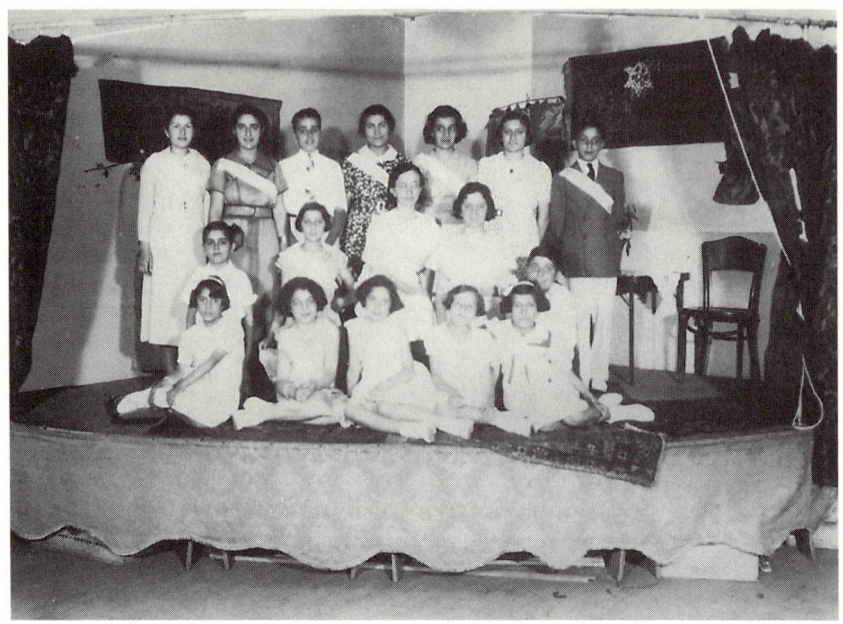

Play presented by children in Anitsa Khachadourian's school, 1936. Mrs. Khachadourian is seated at center.

after which the diamond engagement ring was blessed and placed upon the finger of the bride-to-be by her fiance.[390]

Anitsa Khachadourian opened an Armenian school in the early 1930s which appeared to have been attended by the children of families philosophically opposed to the ARF. Classes met on Saturday mornings at Clinton School, 606 Lodi Street. Teachers were Takouhi Kalebdjian, Antaram Desteian, Sirarpi Mardigian. There were at least twelve students of varying levels, including young adults. The school did not last long, but several people recalled a memorable performance of "Snow White and the Seven Dwarfs" put on by the children in Snell's Hall on Salina Street. Several people pointed out that the girl playing Snow White, Angele Saxenian, and the prince, Karl Gozigian, were later married.[391]

Despite their efforts to work within the entire Armenian community, Rev. Khachadourian and his wife were not received with universal friendship. Many years after the event, Mrs. Khachadourian told me of the hurt she had received from Takouhi Kalebdjian. The two had known each other since

---

390. *Syracuse Post-Standard,* October 18, 1936.
391. Gozigian, Desteian, Virginia Saxenian, Avakian, Khachadourian.

Smyrna (although Takouhi was older, Mrs. Khachadourian carefully pointed out to me). Meeting her former acquaintance again in Syracuse, Takouhi chided Anitsa for marrying a Protestant, telling her that by doing so she had denied her nation. Mrs. Kalebdjian's brother-in-law, Missak, disliked Rev. Khachadourian and, recalled Stella Sachaklian Rustigian, removed him from a gathering at the Yates Hotel by informing him that he was wanted on a non-existent phone call.

When the community became enveloped in controversy, further antipathies were revealed. Mrs. Khachadourian became greatly distressed on the arrival of an anonymous threatening letter advising the *badveli* (minister) to tell his wife to close her school. That night Mrs. Khachadourian dreamed that she was being crucified, but St. Peter leaped up and saved her. The next day they received an invitation to go to California. According to the Record of Service, dated February 22, 1937, in the files of the Presbyterian Church, Rev. Khachadourian terminated his services in Syracuse on October 1, 1936, although he did not leave immediately. He was still in Syracuse several months later, as indicated by a newspaper interview which reported the tragedies that both Rev. and Mrs. Khachadourian had experienced in their past.[392] According to Anna Markarian, the Khachadourians left Syracuse in September 1937.

Rev. Khachadourian's school was immediately followed by the "Tourian School," taught by Aghavni Zahrajian Boyadjian. As a young woman, Mrs. Boyadjian had participated in many ARF events, preparing and enacting skits and delivering speeches, recitations, and poems. According to her sister, she was "excellent in [Armenian] reading and writing." [393] Her formal education was limited to the high school level, completed in night school, but she was a person with considerable drive and self-discipline. Married at eighteen, she embraced the political views held by her husband, who was ardently pro-Soviet.

Aghavni's notebook provides meticulous attendance records for eight boys and eight girls from November through June 1936–37. Among her papers are numerous handwritten Armenian poems, many of them extolling love of mother and nation, and scripts for short plays in Armenian, some bearing notations indicating to whom they had been assigned. According to a handwritten list, the school was divided into three classes. Ages have not been recorded, but, based on my acquaintance with some of the pupils, they ranged widely. The school does not appear to have lasted very long and I was unable to find anyone other than Mianzara Eckhoff who remembered that it existed. According to a handwritten draft notice found among the papers with the

392.*Syracuse Herald,* February 28, 1937.
393.Letter, Eckhoff to Mesrobian, February 19, 1983.

notebook, the unnamed temporary executive body in charge of the Tourian School issued an invitation to the public to elect a new executive for the coming school year, 1937–38, and to express their views concerning plans for the school. The meeting was called for August 24, 1938, at the YMCA hall, but it is not known whether it took place or what resulted, if it did.[394]

The arrival of Rev. and Mrs. John H. Adjemian to Syracuse in 1937–38 brought new resources to the community. Adjemian succeeded Khachadourian as pastor to the small Armenian Protestant community in Syracuse. He was a warmhearted individual, passionately devoted to his people, and an ARF sympathizer. This was not Rev. Adjemian's introduction to Syracuse. Many years earlier he had spent a short time in the city, as indicated by his photograph taken on September 27, 1914 in Syracuse, found in the Azadian collection. He is also probably the H. Adjemian who spoke at a November 1914, event sponsored by the ladies' society.[395]

Adjemian's wife, Zarouhi, had a distinguished educational background, having taught and directed Armenian schools in Constantinople and Greece. Mrs. Adjemian volunteered her help and soon the youth of the community began to gather around her for instruction. As her school was considered neutral ground, all segments sent their children to her.

More than twenty pupils from families with diverse political views participated in an ambitious enactment of the historical play, "Tiridates the Great," performed entirely in the Armenian language in the YWCA auditorium on April 27, 1947. Among the performers were the daughter and son of the late violinist, K. Aiqouni. A large audience, including some from out of town, was in attendance.[396] Two years later, on January 9, 1949, Mrs. Adjemian directed what may have been a repeat performance. The play depicted the conversion of King Tiridates and the Armenians to Christianity in the year 301. Twenty-four young people participated in the program. The audience represented "a cross section of all the Armenians in the community," meaning that adherents of opposing political sentiments were in attendance.[397]

Neither widowhood nor severe arthritis deterred Mrs. Adjemian. She continued to teach in her home, finally terminating her efforts during the late 1950s or early 1960s. For many years afterwards she maintained an active interest in her former pupils, admiring and encouraging them whenever they visited her.

---

394. Notebook and papers from the Boyadjian collection.
395. *Hairenik* newspaper clipping in Eckhoff collection.
396. *Hairenik Weekly*, May 15, 1947, p. 6.
397. Ibid., January 20, 1949, p. 1.

Music and Dance

Under the sponsorship of the city's Adult Education Department and with funding presumably from the Works Progress Administration, the Armenian National Chorus came together in 1935 under the direction of Ernest W. Drake. Stella Sachaklian was secretary of the group and Arthur Fredenburgh, pianist.[398] Although the group was not linked to a political party, singers from the faction opposed to the ARF were noticeably absent. A photograph of the group in Armenian costume shows sixteen women and five men, two of them non-Armenian. The singers are named in an inscription on the back in Eliza Sachaklian's handwriting.[399]

Mr. Drake, a skilled musical director, had conducted for Madame Melba, Anna Held, George M. Cohan, and Lillian Russell. Although he had had no prior acquaintance with Armenian music, he carried out his new duties with skill and flair and, with suggestions from Stella Sachaklian, produced sounds that to Armenian ears were authentic. The pianist was an equally skilled musician.

The group's first performance took place in Lincoln Auditorium in Central High School, then the city's largest auditorium, on April 1, 1936. Wearing national costume, the chorus of thirty-five voices presented well-known Armenian favorites such as "Zeitoontsi Yerk," "Der Getzo," with Mary Apikian as soloist, "Hov'n Anoosh" by Stella Sachaklian and the chorus, and "Im Chinari Yaru" by Eliza Sachaklian and the chorus. A dance was performed by fourteen members of the chorus.[400] In its second appearance, the group presented the same program on April 14 for the music appreciation class at the Syracuse Museum of Fine Arts.[401]

Illness forced Mr. Drake to retire after only a few months. He died on May 31, 1936.[402] Stella Sachaklian replaced Mr. Drake as director and a successful season followed. The group performed several times, providing entertainment on request for private clubs as well as public events. After Miss Sachaklian's marriage and departure from Syracuse in the spring of 1937, the choral group dissolved.

The costumes prepared for the choral group served for many a function thereafter. A newspaper article in 1937 about a series of sessions on war and neutrality sponsored by the Rotary Club with about forty Syracuse

---

398. A newspaper clipping in the Sachaklian collection, lacking source and date, provides details.

399. Photograph in Sachaklian collection.

400. *Hairenik Weekly,* May 1, 1936, p. 1.

401. Ibid.; Syracuse newspaper clipping in Sachaklian collection.

402. Undated obituary notice, newspaper clipping in Sachaklian collection.

The Armenian National Chorus of Syracuse, 1935.

organizations and service clubs participating featured ushers in native costumes representing fourteen different nationalities, including Armenian. Photographs of Arpena Abajian, Louise (Lucia) Nigolian, and Zartar Nigolian in
the costumes of the choral group accompany the articles.[403] The costumes
were also used for programs sponsored by the Americanization League.

Armenians everywhere took pride in the accomplishments of internation-
ally renowned artists such as Rouben Mamoulian, the movie director, who
gained fame with his film *Dr. Jekyll and Mr. Hyde*, Rose Zulalian, who sang
before twenty-five thousand delegates at the 1932 Democratic National Convention in Chicago, and Armand Tokatyan, singer with the Metropolitan
Opera.[404] The achievements of stars such as these encouraged the Armenians
to believe that their small nation was second to none in artistic talent and ability.

Syracuse Armenians envied residents of New York, Boston, and other large
cities who had an opportunity to hear and perhaps meet artists such as these

---

403. *Syracuse Herald,* January 17, 1937; *Syracuse Journal,* January 20, 1937.
404. *Hairenik Amsakir,* February 1932, p. 173; August 1932, p. 171; December 1932, p.
    171.

and others. Not quite at the same level, but exciting nevertheless, was the opportunity to hear a young Armenian baritone from Belgium, who had made his European debut in Antwerp in 1932, in his first American recital. K. Carlo Sourene (Souren Keshishian) appeared in Prescott School in November 1935 under the auspices of the Alliance Francaise, Italian War Veterans, and the Armenian-American Citizens Club. He sang selections in English, French, Italian, and Armenian. A violinist and a pianist, both non-Armenian, appeared with him.[405] Sourene remained in Syracuse for several weeks as the guest of his aunt, Mrs. A. Azoyan, traveling about the area with Mary Apikian as his willing chauffeur and guide.

Another visiting artist was Garo M. Garapetian, who in 1944 directed the Houghton College Choir of forty women in a program of choral music of many lands. Mr. and Mrs. Garapetian were guests of Mr. and Mrs. Khosrov Kyoomjian during their stay in Syracuse.[406] Even more exciting were the two performances given by the noted New York violinist Anahid Ajemian in concert with the Syracuse University orchestra in 1946 and in 1947.[407]

Armenians in Public

Mrs. Azadian's influence helped to neutralize participation in the Americanization League and the two factions occasionally came together in intra-ethnic programs under her direction. Such an event was announced for the Syracuse Elevation and Progress Jubilee for September 24, 25, and 26, 1936. "The folk dances and weird folk songs of the Near East will be sung and enacted by groups of native born Armenians under the direction of Mrs. H. B. Azadian and A. H. Sachaklian," was the rather uncharitable description.[408] The Jubilee was in celebration of the removal of the New York Central train tracks that periodically blocked traffic on Salina Street, the city's main street.

The actual event was far more grand and, in view of its decidedly nationalistic flavor, was undoubtedly carried out without the participation of either Mrs. Azadian or the anti-ARF segment. The Armenians were the only national group to prepare a float for the parade. The scene depicted King Tiridates' acceptance of Christianity. Beneath the glittering dome of a replica of an Armenian cathedral, St. Gregory the Illuminator (N. Garabedian) was seen blessing the kneeling King Tiridates (V. Sheperdigian), the queen (Mrs. A. Nigolian) and the princess (Mrs. K. Shahlamian). Two soldiers (A. Nigolian and A. Abajian), garbed in military dress of the early fourth century, stood on

405. *Hairenik Weekly,* December 6, 1935.
406. Ibid., June 7, 1944, p. 2.
407. Ibid., April 11, 1946, p. 1; August 7, 1947, p. 1.
408. *Syracuse Herald,* 1936, clipping from Eckhoff collection.

guard. Red, blue, and orange streamers—colors that unmistakably symbolized the Armenian Republic—decorated the entire float.[409]

Led by the Armenian Tricolor and the American Stars and Stripes borne by two Tzeghagrons (members of a youth group to be discussed later) and flanked by a color guard, Tzeghagron, and Armenian National Chorus members in costume marched in precision evoking cheers along the line of march. The event was directed by A. H. Sachaklian, member of the Americanization Division of the Parade Committee, and designed by Stella Sachaklian, whose committee included John and Azad Minasian. Mr. Sachaklian received compliments on the fine appearance of the Armenian unit and float from the chairman of the Jubilee Committee and the former commander of the American Legion.[410]

In the person of Mary Louise Karagosian, Armenians were represented in a newspaper article featuring photographs of sixteen young girls from Syracuse who had been located with the assistance of the Americanization League. Children of foreign-born parents, the American-born girls expressed the new year greeting in their ancestral tongues.[411] Apparently the same spirit motivated radio stations WFBL and WSYR whose 1935 broadcast of Christmas greetings in many tongues was sponsored by the Department of Adult Education. Stella Sachaklian spoke in Armenian.[412]

Greek and Armenian foods were temptingly displayed in a photograph accompanying a newspaper article appearing on October 11, 1936, featuring Mrs. H. B. Azadian who is identified as a member of the women's branch of the Rotary Club, of the Order of the Eastern Star and several other women's organizations, and a member of the board of directors of the Americanization League.[413]

In other instances, Armenians participated in a festival to benefit the war relief fund of the Red Cross held in 1940, where Mrs. Arshalouis Azadian Randall, in Armenian costume, sang.[414] Armenians also displayed oriental clothing, embroidery, jewelry, pottery, Armenian manuscripts, and brassware in an exhibit sponsored by the Americanization League presenting cultures of the peoples of the United States. A dance group and a women's chorus performed before an audience of seven hundred.[415]

---

409. *Hairenik Weekly,* October 9, 1936, p. 1.
410. Ibid.
411. *Syracuse Herald,* December 29, 1935.
412. *Hairenik Weekly,* January 31, 1936, p. 3.
413. Clipping in Sachaklian collection.
414. *Syracuse Herald,* June 30, 1940.
415. *Hairenik Weekly,* May 5, 1939, p. 3.

More than two hundred and fifty people attended the Americanization League dinner at South Presbyterian Church on May 24, 1945. Armenian dishes were served. The dinner was sponsored by the Armenian group of the League under the chairmanship of Mrs. Azadian. Rev. John Adjemian of the Armenian Presbyterian Church was one of the guests of honor. A choir sang under the direction of Miss Ardemis Desteian. Other performers were Alice Telian, singer, accompanied by Zephyr Kyoomjian, Krikor Aiqouni (son of the musician) on the violin, accompanied by Anna Markarian, Mrs. Eckhoff on the flute, Alice Jigarjian on piano. Mrs. Randall sang and played.[416]

Armenian young people (of only the ARF faction) were among the twenty nationalities represented at the Centennial Folk Festival of the Americanization League in Grant Junior High School on October 15 and 16, 1948. The singers and dancers used the costumes prepared for performance with the Armenian National Chorus.[417] Photographs in the Azadian collection also provide a record of two Armenian dinners in 1950 carried out under the auspices of the Americanization League. One was in April 1950, and another on October 18, 1950. The latter took place at South Presbyterian Church and Rev. John Adjemian was present.

Mrs. Azadian's death in 1952 not only ended a lifetime of service, but also terminated Armenian community involvement with the Americanization League. She had personified the League for the Armenians and no one could take her place.[418]

The New Generation

Although most Armenian communities attempted to teach their young people to speak, read, and write the language, it was becoming clear that far more strenuous efforts were needed to keep the youth together and to prevent their disappearance into American life. ARF leaders, in particular, were concerned about the preparation of a new generation with the commitment and knowledge to step into positions of leadership in the ARF and ARS as the older generation faded from view. In some communities youth clubs were formed, such as the Detroit Christopher Youth Organization,[419] and san-sanouhi (boys and girls) children's groups were brought together under auspices of the ARS. An Armenian-language periodical for young people called Arpi began publication.[420]

---

416. Ibid., June 7, 1945, p. 7.
417. Ibid., October 28, 1948, p. 5; Centennial Folk Festival program in Sachaklian collection.
418. Obituary notice April 23, 1952, newspaper not identified, in Eckhoff collection.
419. Hairenik Amsakir, February 1931, p. 190.

The older generation began to look more carefully at the needs and interests of the American-born generation which by now ranged up to college age. They came to realize that the obsession with Armenian language as a sort of prerequisite to feeling and being Armenian was threatening to alienate most of the generation that had grown up in the United States. What were the thoughts and interests of those young people? The ARF daily newspaper, *Hairenik*, inaugurated an English-language column where it published a questionnaire in an attempt to find out. The column continued for eighteen months. The response to the questionnaire was "quick and good."[421] Among those who replied was Stella Sachaklian from Syracuse:

To the Editor of Hairenik:

Although each of your questions in the questionnaire is worthy of lengthy discussion, I will attempt to answer them as briefly and concisely as I am able.

I am conscious in my daily life that I am an Armenian.

This consciousness is expressed in our speech, appearance and interests.

I am a college student and am not handicapped because of my Armenian origin.

I do feel an obligation towards the Armenian people in general.

I am very much interested in Armenian life—past, present and future.

I read Armenian newspapers and books, and many books in English about Armenian history, its church and customs, and its art and architecture.

I believe it necessary to publish an English paper for our younger generation. Speaking as one of this class, I can say that there are many Armenians who unfortunately have not been able to learn to read Armenian but who are nevertheless interested in Armenian affairs. There are others, American born, who can read Armenian but not as easily as they can English. Don't you think that if they become acquainted with Armenian life and affairs through the

---

420.Ibid., February 1932, p. 173.
421.Ibid., July 1932, p. 172.

English language, they will become interested enough to pursue it in the Armenian? Although this may be an expensive venture, I believe it will more than pay in the end.

I am interested in Armenian activities and participate in them.

I believe in several of the organizations of the older generation.

I find them most satisfactory. I hope they continue, and also initiate the younger generation into their groups. Their aims are high and the organizations should not be condemned for the actions of individuals.

If, by "the younger generation" you mean American born or American raised children, I think there is a conflict of interests. The older generation is inclined to think of the past and the future. The younger generation thinks of the present.

If the older generation could prepare the younger to take up where it leaves off, and if the younger generation can be made more receptive, this conflict would be eliminated.

Acquaint the young generation with the history and purposes of the Armenian people. Imbue in them a feeling of pride in their race. Encourage them to enter into discussions of the many political and social problems of our people. Let these discussions be conducted in either English or Armenian. You will have made a new generation Armenian-Conscious.

Yours sincerely,
Stella Sachaklian
Syracuse, N.Y.[422]

Soon the Ramgavar organ *Baikar* inaugurated an English-language paper called *Mirror*, after which the *Hairenik Weekly,* in English, began publication on March 1, 1934. But much more needed to be done. The young generation needed to be engaged directly.

The ARF international convention in Paris in 1932 moved to invite General K. Nejdeh to the United States as a field worker. It was hoped that the general would be able to attract America's Armenian youth to the ARF.

---

422. *Hairenik,* June 21, 1932. At the time Miss Sachaklian was a junior in the College of Fine Arts at Syracuse University. Her knowledge of Armenian enabled her to prepare her senior thesis on the topic "Armenian Art and Its Right to Recognition."

ԳԱՐԵԳԻՆ ՆԺԴԵՀ

Under the leadership of General K. Nejdeh, hundreds of Armenian young people came together to form a youth group called *Tzeghagron*, later changed to Armenian Youth Federation.

Nejdeh had received his military training in the Bulgarian military academy in Sofia. As commander of the Armenian forces in the Zangezur region in Caucasian Armenia, he directed a brilliant and valiant defense that led ultimately to the retention of the region as a part of Armenia when the country was Sovietized, unlike the fate of Nakhichevan and Karabagh regions which were lost to Azerbaijan.[423]

Nejdeh was an intense, charismatic leader whose vitality and conviction were infectious, overcoming even the strangeness of his eastern Armenian dialect. He traveled throughout the United States for two years, visiting communities large and small, speaking, exhorting, and exciting the youth with his vision of a strongly united, ably trained cadre prepared to confront the problems of the future. An organization called ARF "Tzeghagron" emerged, animated by the spirits of Armenia's revolutionary heroes. The chapter in each city was called *ookht* ("pledge"), the term he had used for his guerilla forces. The youngest in the groups, like Cub Scouts, were called *kailoog* (diminutive

---

423.Avo, *Nejdeh: Gyankn ou Kordzouneoutiune, Nishkharner, Vgayoutiunner* [*Nejdeh: His Life and Work, Selections, Testimonials*], (Beirut, Lebanon: Hamazgayin, 1968).

term for "wolf"). He had used the same term for his smaller guerilla units, calling them *kailakhoomper* ("wolf packs").[424] Dressed in their blue shirts and orange kerchiefs, colors taken from the red, blue, and orange Tricolor of the Armenian Republic, the young people felt ready to confront any enemy.

Tzeghagron is a coined term, formed by the combination of *tzegh* meaning "race" and *gron* (actually, the word is *gronk*) meaning "religion" or "worship." The term has been interpreted to mean "devotees of the race," "followers of the race," or "believers of the race."[425] Nejdeh's intent was to instill pride and commitment in the minds and hearts of the eager young army that was rising up to follow him. His impassioned creed stressed racial consciousness and pride.[426] The concept was derived from Nejdeh's exhortations as commander, intended to inspire his beleaguered fighters in the mountains of Zangezur. With the emergence of Hitler, Nazism, and the idea of a master race, however, the term Tzeghagron became subject to criticism by friends as well as foes of the ARF. It was difficult to spell and pronounce and even more difficult to explain to non-Armenians. In 1941 the name was changed to the Armenian Youth Federation (AYF).

Before Nejdeh's arrival in the United States, the ARF had begun to report increases in membership. Among the ARF committees reporting membership increases in 1932 were Syracuse with four, Binghamton six, Massena five, Troy seven, Watervliet ten.[427] But, after Nejdeh's arrival, with the controversy over Bishop Tourian's attacks on the Tricolor raging more hotly day by day, those with ARF sentiments came forward with eager enthusiasm to defend their nation's flag. Wherever their leader went the youth rose up in response to his message. In a period of only two months, Tzeghagron chapters had been formed in fifteen cities, among them Syracuse with twenty members, Massena thirty-five, Troy twenty-five, and Binghamton twelve. The ARF press proudly noted these successes in comparison with the decay of HOG.[428]

Finally, it was Syracuse's turn to meet and hear the dynamic general. An eager audience filled the hall of the Boys' Club on September 17, 1933, to be entertained by the usual songs and recitations before the guest speaker was finally introduced.[429] Stirred by the enthusiasm of the moment, at a reception for the general given by the ARS, Hagop Topouzian of Manlius, New York, announced his offer to donate a twenty-five-acre parcel of land in South

---

424. Ibid., p. 81.
425. Atamian, p. 392.
426. *Hairenik Weekly,* January 11, 1935, p. 1.
427. *Hairenik Amsakir,* July 1932, p.172.
428. Ibid., October 1933, p. 174; December 1933, p. 169.
429. Notice in Sachaklian collection.

Otselic, New York, situated about forty miles southeast of Syracuse, to the Tzeghagrons of America for use as a camp and recreational site.[430] Although the site was never used for that purpose, the proposal planted the seed of an idea that led later to the establishment of Camp Hayasdan in Franklin, Massachusetts.

The enthusiasm evoked by Nejdeh's visit bore fruit within a few months. A capacity audience—perhaps one hundred fifty to two hundred people—filled the ARF club rooms on May 27, 1934, when a group of young Armenians pledged themselves to uphold the ideals of the Tzeghagrons. The occasion was the anniversary of the founding of the Armenian Republic celebrated jointly by the ARF, the ARS, the church trustees, and the Tzeghagrons. The newly formed chapter took the name "Nejdeh" in honor of the founder, who had visited Syracuse a few months earlier.[431] The name was later changed to "Navasard."

Stella and Harry Sachaklian, sister and brother from the twenty-three-member Syracuse chapter, were among twenty-seven delegates representing forty chapters at the first annual Tzeghagron convention in Boston on June 1, 2, and 3, 1934. The total membership of the still-growing organization was reported to be over fifteen hundred with forty-eight chapters. With the passage of a constitution and bylaws, the organization was formally founded. By the time of the second convention in 1935, there were sixty-two chapters with a total membership of twenty-three hundred.[432]

The first function undertaken by the Syracuse chapter was a picnic on August 12, 1934, to commemorate Armenian Flag Day. A caravan of eighteen automobiles decorated with American and Armenian flags paraded in the rain through the city to the picnic site, then paraded back to the ARF club rooms on Warren Street where festivities went on far into the evening. Antranig Nigolian, chairman for the day, opened the program and introduced the speakers, Arousiag Telian, A. Kupelian, A. Sarkisian, and Maurice Topalian. An Armenian flag was presented to the chapter by Krikor Bedigian, whose father Arakel Bedigian, presented an American flag. Peter Karagosian became "godfather" to the flag and made a donation to the new chapter. Announcement was made that the expenses for the Tzeghagron uniforms had been provided by Arshag Sheperdigian. Members of the audience participated in songs and dances which followed a gymnastic drill by the Shavasbians (young teens).[433]

---

430. *Hairenik Weekly,* June 7, 1934, p. 1.
431. Ibid.
432. *The AYF Legacy: Portrait of a Movement in Historical Review, 1933–1993* (Boston: Armenian Youth Federation, 1994), p. 5; *Hairenik Amsakir,* August 1935, p. 154.

The vitality of the Syracuse chapter soon radiated to the small Armenian community in Utica, where a chapter of nine members was formed in October under guidance from Stella Sachaklian.[434]

By November, the Syracuse chapter had twenty-four members, eighteen of whom were in attendance at a meeting which opened with games and dancing, after which refreshments were served. Only then did they get down to business. Plans were discussed for the Armenian Youth Day celebration to take place on January 13, 1935. A program committee composed of Nevart Apikian, Arpena Sachaklian, Vahe Aghababian, and Souren Kupelian was appointed to arrange a program of speeches and debates to take place at chapter meetings. It was decided to subscribe to *Arpi* which would be read at each meeting. Azad Minasian was elected "Director of Athletics and Basketball."[435]

At the next meeting it was decided to present a one-act comedy in the Armenian language, "Bashdonus Khrumpal E" ("My Duty Is to Snore") under the joint auspices of the Harachabah (senior) members of the Nejdeh chapter and the Women's Auxiliary of the Armenian Church. Leads were assigned to Rose Zahrajian, Vahe Aghababian, John Minasian, and Harry Sachaklian. Proceeds from the event were to go to the Armenian school.[436]

Another summer approached and again a picnic was planned in observance of Armenian Flag Day. The invitation notice for August 11, 1935 welcomed everyone with or without automobiles to gather in front of Khachig Minasian's home at exactly 10 a.m. in order to participate in the parade to the Cedar Grove picnic grounds, departing at 10:15. The program included an address by the Honorable Willis Sargent, president of Syracuse's Common Council, talks by M. Topalian and A. Sarkisian, and a solo by Mrs. S. Mardigian. All this for an admission charge of twenty-five cents.[437]

Sports were given high priority in the organization, but the Syracuse chapter lacked the numbers needed for team sports. Instead, the members put emphasis on activities involving individual skills, such as track. They purchased fencing equipment and tried to teach each other how to use it. The pool table that was acquired later proved to be very popular.

The public programs presented by the enthusiastic young people typically featured Armenian language skits and plays, short speeches (invariably filled with errors in grammar and pronunciation), musical performances. A chorus performed on a Tzeghagron Day observance on January 24, 1936.[438] From

---

433.*Hairenik Weekly,* August 31, 1934, p. 3.
434.Ibid., November 9, 1934, p. 3.
435.Ibid., December 7, 1934, p. 3.
436.Ibid., January 4, 1935, p. 2.
437.Notice in Sachaklian collection.

time to time the presence of guest speakers brought news and fresh enthusiasm from chapters elsewhere.

Directives emanating from national headquarters in Boston stressed the study of Armenian history, especially the exploits of revolutionary heroes. Study materials were made available for a structured program of study at the chapter level. One of the earliest teaching materials for the study program was the booklet *Highlights of Armenian History*, published in 1938.[439]

On the whole, the young people tried to fulfill their parents' expectations of them, but it was not possible entirely to eliminate cultural and generational differences. On one occasion, the Syracuse youth decided to hold a cake baking contest. For long afterwards they laughed among themselves over the list of entries: two homemade cakes, a store bought cake, a lemon meringue pie, and a plate of *yalanchi sarma* (stuffed grape leaves).

Stella and Harry Sachaklian also attended the second annual convention as delegates and both became people of influence at the national level in the AYF and later in the ARS and ARF. Stella was elected to the AYF Central Executive in July 1937, following her marriage to Jacob Rustigian and move to Hartford, Connecticut. Harry was a Central Executive member for two terms: 1939 and 1940. He was also credited with an educational plan that was instituted by the organization and with the selection of a site and specifications for what became Camp Hayasdan in Franklin, Massachusetts.[440] Harry won a host of followers with his impassioned call to action: "I Am Looking for a Company of Fools." "If only I could find some fools," he yearned. "A company could do what a million wise men would find impossible."[441]

Sachaklian's earnest, if excessively romantic "A Tzeghagron's Prayer" (1937), expresses the intense emotion that characterized the youth movement of that time. Written in Armenian with many misspellings corrected in his father's hand, the prayer is paraphrased as follows: We have inherited responsibilities from our forebears. We ask God to give us the mental powers and strength of character to continue the work they have begun. We ask especially for the means to fight for Armenia. And if it is necessary to sacrifice ourselves, may we meet death with our faces turned toward Ararat, a smile on our faces, joy in our hearts, in the conviction that we are being sacrificed for justice and freedom.[442]

---

438. *Hairenik Weekly,* February 28, 1936, p. 6.

439. James G. Mandalian, *Highlights of Armenian History* (Boston: Hairenik Press, 1938).

440. *The AYF Legacy,* p. 8 and p. 10.

441. Ibid., October 18, 1935, p. 2.

442. Poem in Sachaklian collection.

As it is part of the story, I should mention that Nevart Apikian and I also became known at the national level, largely through the pages of the AYF organ, the *Armenian Weekly*, inaugurated as the *Hairenik Weekly*. Nevart Apikian hosted the Children's Page from 1941 to 1945. I wrote a weekly column on the history of Armenian literature through approximately the same period of time. Also, while in Beirut during 1937–38, I sent news articles to the paper from time to time.

Regional groupings and visits between the AYF chapters led to friendships and (to the delight of the older folks) marriages between young people who may not otherwise have had the opportunity to meet each other. The chapters in Syracuse, Utica, Troy, Massena, and Binghamton formed the Upper New York State Council and planned athletic and social events hosted by the individual chapters. Syracuse was host to a regional track meet at Griffin Field, Liverpool, New York, on August 18, 1940. Participating were chapters from Binghamton, Massena, Niagara Falls, Utica, Troy, and Syracuse.[443]

The annual conventions and the "Olympics" which took place over Labor Day weekends gave the Armenian young people further opportunities to meet each other and to participate in events attended by many hundreds—even thousands—of Armenians. For the youth who lived in small communities, these were exciting experiences that left their impact for many years.

Frequent news reports in the *Armenian Weekly* provide evidence that the Syracuse chapter maintained an active existence for more than three decades. There were many dances and social events, frequent performances of plays and skits (usually in Armenian), participation with speeches, salutations, and singing performances on the occasions that were hosted by the ARF and the ARS, and picnics—always picnics.

But nothing remains the same. The keen excitement of the founding years began to fade and a change of tone is revealed as early as 1937. A report from Syracuse observed, "During last year the chapter had one of the best records in the organization, but recently it has suffered much by losing a number of leading members." Now the next group of youngsters took over, continuing with equal dedication and competence. In 1939, the twenty-one member chapter put on a comedy. The following year the young people presented a historical play, "David Beg," written by Aaron Sachaklian and directed by Arpena Sachaklian. Roles were taken by six young men and six young women in costume.[444]

Demolition of the Warren Street building forced another move of the ARF club. A space was found temporarily on the second floor of a building on East

---

443.Announcement circular in Sachaklian collection.
444.Ibid., October 1, 1937, p. 7; November 24, 1939, p. 7; February 16, 1940, p. 7.

Fayette Street, across the street from the shoeshine shop owned by Charlie Theodosiou. An engagement party in February 1940 given by the AYF in my honor took place at this site. I seem to be the only one who remembers the club at this address. By 1942, better quarters were found: "three large club rooms located on the corner of Townsend and East Genesee Streets."[445]

As war approached, one by one the young men began to depart. The girls carried on, continuing to present skits, songs, and dances. A feature of the tenth AYF anniversary program was reading letters from the servicemen who were once active members of the Syracuse chapter. The girl reporter wrote wistfully, "Somehow, this year, although we are doing our utmost, something in the spirit of all chapters is missing. Many of the older boys have gone into active service and many more are sure to leave in the near future. Syracuse has added two more boys to their list. . . ."[446]

The girls carried on and eventually the boys returned bringing renewed zest to the club. A long-awaited visit from Uncle Bozo (K. Merton Bozoian from Boston) in 1945 was featured at the AYF twelfth anniversary observance. It was held at the YMCA hall, suggesting that the ARF had vacated its club rooms at 332 East Genesee Street.[447]

The activities of the AYF seemed to attract some interest from the children of the opposing Armenian factions. A reporter wrote, "The chapter has given several successful dances in the past year which has brought the Armenian youth of the city, regardless of the faction, to closer relationship. We feel that this is something which we can justly be proud of."[448]

The chapter's most notable accomplishment was serving as host to hundreds of Armenians, both young and old, at the fifteenth annual AYF Olympics, over the weekend of September 5 and 6, 1948. Athletic events were held at Griffin Field near Onondaga Lake and the Olympics Ball was held in the ballroom of the Hotel Syracuse. The members did not rest for long. Their annual picnic at Cedar Grove was held on the following weekend.[449]

The AYF movement continued to grow and develop. A photograph taken about 1948 shows twenty-six young people.[450] AYF graduates—at least some of them—began to take their destined places in the ARF and ARS. It was a great day for older ARF members when a new junior chapter of the ARF was formed in Syracuse on November 16, 1947. A. H. Sachaklian was chairman

445. *Hairenik Weekly*, February 11, 1942, p. 3.
446. Ibid., January 27, 1943, p. 7.
447. Ibid., February 22, 1945, p. 6.
448. Ibid., July 3, 1947, p. 6.
449. Ibid., September 9, 1948, p. 7.
450. Photograph in Vartkas and Zephyr Minasian collection.

The Syracuse AYF in 1948.

of the meeting attended by about one hundred twenty-five persons. Sixteen
young men and women took the membership oath. Another member was
added at the first meeting of the new committee.[451] The young people enthu-
siastically took up their responsibilities, working energetically to plan and
carry out the customary round of programs. The young ARF did much of the
work in preparation for a Flag Day picnic at Cedar Grove in 1953, at which
Gourgen Assaturian, an official at the Armenian section of Voice of America
in Washington, was guest speaker. As the youth took center stage, there were
signs that the community was maturing. About thirty graying heads appear in
a photograph of approximately one hundred fifty men, women, and children;
there are also about fifteen small children being held on adult laps.[452]

The success of the AYF movement was observed carefully by those opposed
to the ARF and through the 1940s and 1950s both ARF and AYF were subjected to constant attacks in the anti-ARF press. For a time, the Communist
Armenian-language newspaper, *Lraper*, sought to promote an opposition
youth group under the name Armenian Youth of America (AYA). The ARF
press, in its turn, headlined the news in 1947 that the Armenian Progressive

451. *Hairenik Weekly,* December 4, 1947, p. 3.
452. Photograph in Sachaklian collection.

ARF-AYF observance of Armenian Flag Day at Cedar Grove (Syracuse), August 16, 1953. Gourgen Assaturian from Voice of America, Washington, D.C. was the main speaker.

League of America, the senior society to the AYA, had been declared a subversive force by the United States Attorney General Tom Clark.[453]

In Syracuse, the AYA had a lukewarm reception among the children of parents with anti-ARF sentiments. According to Karl Gozigian, prior to World War II there were no youth groups within his (anti-ARF) community, other than school. After the war he was in AYA "for a while." He recalled one social event. He mentioned a few other members: Leon Vetzikian, Helen Koolakian, Elizabeth (Keghanoush) Markarian. It was "quite informal," he remembered, and did not last very long. Elizabeth Markarian Avakian recalled that AYA, a Progressive youth organization, was not active.

The ARS, too, gradually gained new members, as several young women moved from the AYF to the ARS. The Syracuse chapter of the ARS observed the thirty-seventh anniversary of the organization's founding in typical fashion on March 30, 1947. A member of the new generation, myself, conducted the meeting as president. Twenty-five-year pins were presented to Siranoush Minasian and Mianzara Eckhoff. Guest speaker was James G. Mandalian, editor of the *Hairenik Weekly*. Young people of the community participated with songs, Armenian dances in the costumes of the Armenian National Chorus, and a comedy skit. The news report of this event further informs us that a cake donated by Mrs. Abraham Nigolian was "auctioned off" by Missak Kalebdjian "who made the audience reach into their pockets to the tune of $317," after which the cake was served to the audience.[454] This was one of the traditional

---

453. *Hairenik Weekly,* December 11, 1947, p. 1.
454. Ibid., April 3, 1947, p. 1.

ways of raising money. Another was to prepare a decorated cake studded with unlit candles which would be lit, one by one, by each person making a donation.

Time was passing and the composition of the membership was changing. At the ARS forty-first anniversary observance in 1951, Eliza Sachaklian read the names of eleven deceased members, asking the audience to stand for a moment in their memory.[455]

Both the ARF and ARS in Syracuse continued to carry out their programs in the usual manner and the younger people continued in the same traditions. The ARF never failed to observe May 28, Armenian Independence Day. The ARS and ARF each celebrated the anniversaries of the founding of their organizations, and the commemoration of April 24, Armenian Memorial Day, was observed by both organizations together, usually with the participation of the church board as well.

The annual report of the Syracuse ARS for the 1951–52 year indicated a membership of thirty, including one new member and none lost during the year. It was reported that the ARS had not sponsored any Armenian school in Syracuse. There was $650.06 in the treasury, including dues, balance from the previous year, donations, income from events.[456]

The years were passing and younger people were beginning to assume more responsibilities in the direction of Syracuse's Armenian institutions. Changes in leadership did not appear to promote changes within or between the communities, however. Rather, old values and traditional modes appear to have been perpetuated. Perhaps wartime and the departure of many young men from the small community drained community energies that might otherwise have produced innovations.

Wartime and Aftermath

The Armenians of Syracuse loyally supported the war effort, as did Armenians everywhere throughout the United States. War and reports about its effects on the Armenian communities dominated the pages of the *Hairenik* and other Armenian newspapers throughout 1942 and 1943.

Midst these dark days, optimism and hope was the message brought by a distinguished visiting speaker, Simon Vratzian, premier of the fallen Armenian Republic, addressing the community at the ARF club rooms. Mr. Vratzian considered the second world war, with its objective of democracy and freedom for all the peoples of the world, as an opportunity for Armenia to

---

455. Text of speech and list of names in Sachaklian collection.
456. Report in Sachaklian collection.

regain its independence. He urged Armenians to unite and work toward that end.[457]

With Aaron H. Sachaklian presiding, Syracuse Armenians bought $10,900 in war bonds at a rally in May 1943 at the YMCA. In addition, the community sent $22 to the Central Executive of the ARS for the war relief effort, a sum contributed by friends on the occasion of Harry Sachaklian's promotion to the rank of major in the United States Air Force.[458]

All Syracusans were saddened with the news that George Garabedian, eighteen, Private First Class, United States Marine Corps Reserve, had been killed on March 7, 1945, on Iwo Jima, in his first action in combat. He had enlisted at the age of seventeen and was believed to be the youngest Armenian-American serviceman to lose his life in World War II. There was a large attendance at the funeral services in Grace Episcopal Church and burial in Morningside Cemetery.[459]

The publication of two books (one for each "side") honoring the Armenian-Americans in the armed forces was pointed evidence that the community schism was alive and well.[460] Nevertheless, everyone recognized that the Soviet Union was an ally in the war effort. Shared concern for the fate of the country, for their servicemen, for Armenians in foreign lands touched again by war and upheaval, and for Armenia itself which could not escape the consequences of Soviet involvement, temporarily softened the mood of the community. Armenians were in need and political lines did not matter. The Armenian communities in America sent packages and financial contributions through existing agencies and supplied private support as well. Two letters written by the Giredlian family of Erevan, Armenia, acknowledge the gifts and assistance provided by Mr. and Mrs. Aaron Sachaklian of Syracuse.[461]

Springing perhaps from a desire to make peace on another front, faint, unstructured attempts emerged in Syracuse to reach out and make contact with individuals from "the other side." A men's discussion group came together a few times to explore possible avenues toward rapprochement. It was discontinued after a few hesitant exchanges. Participants included Zarmair Taft, George Arslanian, Archie S. Ajemian, William J. Mesrobian.

---

457. Newspaper clipping lacking source and date in Sachaklian collection.

458. *Hairenik Weekly*, May 26, 1943, p. 1; *Hairenik*, 1942, clipping in Sachaklian collection.

459. Clipping from Syracuse newspaper lacking source or date in Sachaklian collection; James H. Tashjian, *The Armenian American in World War II* (Boston, Mass.: Hairenik Association, Inc., 1952, p. 285; *Hairenik Weekly*, December 30, 1948, p. 1.

460. Tashjian; "Our Boys" Committee, *Armenian-American Veterans of World War II* (New York: Armenian General Benevolent Union of America, Inc. [1951]).

461. Sachaklian collection.

An effort to bring together all members of the community on neutral ground was made on March 24, 1946, with the reestablishment of the Syracuse chapter of the nonpartisan Armenian Students Association. The national president of the ASA, Negdar Kazazian, was guest speaker. According to the news report, the chapter was founded by Sonia Jigarjian with the assistance of Mrs. Stephen Balakian (Anna Balakian's husband was Stephen Nalbantian) and Mary Arslanian. In actuality, the Syracuse branch had first come into existence before World War I. Miss Kazazian reported on recent activities of the national organization and appointed the following as temporary officers of the Syracuse chapter: Arpena (Sachaklian) Mesrobian, president; Duke G. Ajemian, vice-president; Alice Jigarjian, recording secretary; Alice Choghanjian, corresponding secretary; Sonia Jigarjian, treasurer and public relations director; Ann Boghosian, Elizabeth Markarian, advisors. At the thirty-sixth annual convention in June 1946, announcement was made of the formation of a Syracuse branch with thirty active members.[462]

Within a few months Miss Kazazian returned to Syracuse to attend the first annual banquet (which proved to be the last) of the Syracuse branch. The program included musical performances by singer Alice Telian and pianist Alice Jigarjian. John C. Donahue, principal of Vocational High School, spoke on the Armenian case and the atomic bomb, an interesting combination of topics. Officers for the 1946–47 term were announced: Ann Boghosian, president; Karl Gozigian, vice-president; Alice Choghanjian, corresponding secretary; Elizabeth Markarian, recording secretary; Zephyr Kyoomjian, treasurer; Arpena Mesrobian, advisor; Sonia Jigarjian, program chairman. Soon afterwards another meeting took place with the popular Dean Charles E. Noble of Hendricks Chapel, Syracuse University, as speaker. He urged fighting for peace, as was done for war. His talk was followed on December 12 by Arpena Mesrobian's lecture on "The Role of Students in Armenian History." The next event was a dance at the YWCA on February 8, 1947. Next was a piano recital on June 7 at the Syracuse Museum of Fine Arts. The performer was Marie Kassouny, a student at the Juilliard School of Music in New York. She later enrolled at Syracuse University. A news report on the 1950 annual convention of the ASA includes Syracuse in its listing of branches, but activities in Syracuse had lapsed by this time.[463]

With war's end the Armenian benevolent organizations were flooded with new appeals. Even before the war the ARS had placed a high priority on helping the Armenian communities in Syria and Lebanon. Large numbers of

---

462.*Hairenik Weekly,* May 30, 1946, p. 7; July 4, 1946, p. 5.

463.Ibid., October 24, 1946, p. 3; October 31, 1946, p. 6; January 2, 1947, p. 3; February 13, 1947, p. 3; June 12, 1947, p. 6; June 15, 1950, p. 4.

Levon Shant (center), principal of the Armenian College of Beirut, greeting a former student, Arpena Sachaklian Mesrobian, in Syracuse while on his fund-raising tour of the United States in 1949. At left is Gobernig Tandourjian of Detroit.

refugees from the Turkish deportations had settled there and were still living in deplorable conditions, as I witnessed on my visit to Lebanon in 1937–38. With the slogan "A Plate of Food," the ARS embarked on a fund-raising campaign to provide hot lunches for Armenian school children in Lebanon and Syria. Meals were prepared in school kitchens by volunteers and served to needy children free of charge.

It seemed that only America had the resources to help fulfill Armenian needs. A drive for funds was carried out by Levon Shant in 1949 on behalf of the Armenian College of Beirut, of which he was the principal. The school was then, as now, the foremost Armenian educational institution at the secondary level in the Middle East. It was a delight for me to renew my acquaintance with the dynamic educator during his Syracuse stop. A sum of $535 was collected at a meeting on May 3, 1949 in the YMCA.[464]

A huge new problem for Armenians was revealed when hostilities ended in Europe. Among the large numbers of laborers forcibly brought to Germany for production of the tools of war were numerous Armenians from Greece, Iran, and the Soviet Union, as well as many who were stateless. About thirty-five hundred Armenians remained stranded throughout Germany, Austria,

---

464. *Syracuse Post-Standard,* May 4, 1949.

and Italy. As many as two thousand were gathered in a camp in Stuttgart, Germany.[465]

Through the efforts of a San Francisco restaurateur, George Mardikian, the Armenian National Committee for Homeless Armenians (ANCHA) was created to resettle these displaced persons. Legislation permitting their entry to the United States (with certain restrictions) was put through and the massive enterprise of identifying, processing, moving, and settling the displaced persons was carried out with financial assistance and volunteer help from the ARS. Committees formed in the communities sought volunteers to receive the new arrivals, find homes and jobs for them, and help them get settled in a new country. Because of the involvement of the ARS, the enterprise was seen as being associated with the ARF and was therefore not supported by those with anti-ARF leanings.

It is regrettable that adequate documentation does not exist permitting a full study of the history of this extensive enterprise. At the time, emphasis was placed on the rescue effort which was carried out entirely with the help of volunteers. The information provided in the present work has been gleaned from a packet of materials in the Sachaklian collection. Among them are the following: Armenian Displaced Persons List No. 1, printed January 1, 1949; Armenian Displaced Persons List No. 2, printed August 10, 1949. At the front of each list are names and addresses identifying ANCHA branches in the communities volunteering to help in the effort. Syracuse is the smallest Armenian community to be so identified. There are also a few letters to Syracuse from ANCHA headquarters in San Francisco, copies of letters written from Syracuse, and miscellaneous pieces.

The first contingent arrived in New York City in autumn of 1948.[466] Thereafter work proceeded quickly. A. H. Sachaklian's name appears among the list of ANCHA branches identified in the January 1, 1949, list, indicating that commitment to participate in the enterprise had already been made in Syracuse.

A community-wide meeting on September 19, 1949, at the YMCA set up specific plans. It was decided to form a seven-person committee to handle arrangements and to invite fifteen to twenty people, preferably small families of no more than three persons or single people. Sachaklian, chairman of the committee, informed ANCHA headquarters of the community's decisions and sent a list of thirty-eight names from which the individuals to be sent to Syracuse could be selected. On the list fifteen preferred names were marked. Peter Karagosian, Jacob Telian, Krikor Apikian, and Missak Kalebdjian filled

---

465. *Hairenik Weekly,* December 13, 1945, p. 1.
466. Ibid., November 4, 1948, p. 1.

out forms in which they made assurances to house certain numbers of people. The people selected for Syracuse sponsorship had been chosen carefully with intent to match their occupations with those volunteering to serve as hosts. A total of nine people agreed to serve as sponsors.

Eliza Sachaklian and Missak Kalebdjian volunteered as the reception committee, often responding to telegrams allowing no time for preparations to be made in advance. They met the arrivals, attended to their immediate needs, and provided temporary housing—most often taking the weary travelers to their own homes, then sought to find a host family to receive them and help them with jobs and permanent housing.

The year had not ended when the first refugee assigned to Syracuse presented himself. He must certainly have been a surprise to the reception committee. Not only was his name absent from Sachaklian's list of names, but he was wholly atypical. Zorik Stephanian, from Soviet Armenia, was an uneducated auto mechanic. One of his first questions upon arrival was whether it is possible to come to America by land. The large numbers of automobiles evoked his admiration. He marveled that I could drive, interpreting that ability to mean that I was also a mechanic. He said that only those able to do their own repairs can drive in Armenia, because there is no one to call for help in case of breakdown. Zorik was fairly tall and well built. He was proud of his long black hair and informed us that he used to be called "Tarzan." Zorik's name appears in a 1952 AGBU directory of Syracuse Armenians, listed care of A. H. Sachaklian's address. He did not remain there long, finding a job and living quarters within a few months. Zorik died young, it is believed of a heart attack.

Over the winter of 1949–50, several more people arrived in Syracuse, as indicated by the text of a talk Eliza Sachaklian gave at an ARS Day observance in February 1950. She directed her welcoming remarks to "our newcomers," telling them, "We are all refugees. The term is the same, even though we arrived a few years earlier." She pointed out that their new country gave them the freedom to establish and develop organizations like the ARS, which helped fellow Armenians. "Now you enjoy freedom too. So, all we expect of you is to help the organizations that helped you, especially that women's organization through whose efforts you have come to this country. Unfortunately, we don't have our own building for gatherings, but we've started to work toward that goal. With your help we can reach it sooner."[467]

As newcomers continued to present themselves, the community received up-to-date news about the ANCHA program in 1951 when Zabelle Seropian,

---

467. Text of speech in Sachaklian collection.

regional director, who was also a prominent member of the ARS, spoke at the Syracuse chapter's forty-first anniversary observance.[468]

Each person who arrived was a new experience for the Syracuse community. A few young Armenian men arrived with foreign spouses—some from Russia with Russian wives and two from Greece with German wives. Rouben Markarian, a bachelor from Soviet Armenia, arrived on a rainy night in the late 1950s. I recall picking him up from the train station and taking him to the Armenian Community Center where a program was under way. He was thin and emaciated. He explained his survival saying that well-built, husky men were unable to withstand hardships during the war. They were the first to weaken and become ill. Since he had always been thin, his body was conditioned to deprivation. After finding a job, one of his first purchases was a heavy winter coat with a fur collar. He showed it off proudly. "In Russia, only the engineers have coats like this."

Although full documentation is not available, I could find no correspondence between Sachaklian's list which the Syracuse Armenians had selected for sponsorship and the fifty-three people named in a handwritten list prepared by Eliza Sachaklian from memory. From interior evidence, Eliza's list was probably prepared before 1976. Other refugees came after that date.

The last few families were especially memorable. ANCHA found its work expanding, as stateless and homeless Armenians kept turning up in Romania, Bulgaria, and other areas, totaling seventy-five hundred by the mid-1960s.[469] In 1971, Mrs. Sachaklian agreed to receive a family of eight people—husband, wife, and six children ranging in age from twelve downward—one of whom was later diagnosed as having cerebral palsy. Ohannes (John) Sahagian and his family were from Diarbekir, Turkey, where they and their children were constantly subjected to harassment. Sahagian told the Sachaklians that one day, after his son came home from school in great distress because of attacks from the Turkish boys, he consulted the local imam for advice. "I have this to tell you," was the reply. "Go where there are no minarets on the skyline." They immediately made arrangements to smuggle themselves on a wagon, under cover of night, over the border to Syria and Lebanon. The Sahagians remained for several months with the Sachaklians, while Kalebdjian solicited contributions from the community for a down payment on a house. He reasoned that it would otherwise not be feasible to find housing for such a large family. The Sahagians merged well with the Syracuse community and all regretted their

---

468.*Syracuse Post-Standard,* March 5, 1951.

469.Garo Kevorkian, *Amenoon Darekirk 1966* [*Everyone's Yearbook 1966*] (Beirut, Lebanon), p. 565.

departure (about 1980) when they decided to move to Houston, which promised better job opportunities.

The Krikor Armanian family of four also blended harmoniously into their new setting. The trustees agreed to pay their first month's rent and decided to pay Mrs. Armanian $20 a week to teach Armenian school.[470] Apparently she did not continue to teach for long, because the minutes made no further mention of the school or payments for Mrs. Armanian. The Armanians regularly attended functions at the Armenian Community Center and their daughter frequently contributed to the programs with her recitations and piano performances. Their decision to move to a larger Armenian community saddened the friends they left behind.

Syracuse's participation in the resettlement program came to a rousing conclusion with the Samuelian family experience. Nine of them arrived in April 1976: husband and wife, an adult daughter, and six other children. The Samuelians had emigrated from Lebanon to Armenia after the war, in response to the invitation extended to Armenians by Soviet authorities. Like so many others, they became disenchanted very quickly and managed to leave the country. Meanwhile, husband and wife quarrelled and separated. When the husband learned that his wife and children had received permission to resettle in the United States, he hastened to rejoin the family.

They were ungracious, rude guests in the Sachaklian home. When Mrs. Sachaklian served turkey for the second night in a row, one of them complained, "What, again? We had that last night." Mrs. Sachaklian replied, "This is what we're having. If you don't want any, you can leave the table." Frequent quarrels would erupt between the husband and his wife or daughter. When the oaths started, Mrs. Sachaklian stepped in, declaring that there would be no such talk in *her* home. All were relieved when in May they were moved into their own house (first month rent-free) with gifts of furniture and $150 worth of food supplied by funds from the Armenian Church and community center.

Within a short time, we learned that the husband had departed for New York City, where he had wanted to stay in the first place. After a few more weeks the rest of the family was gone too, without a good-bye, taking with them the gifts received in Syracuse and leaving behind the paper they were to have signed agreeing to repay ANCHA for their travel expenses.

Including the Samuelian family, no fewer than sixty-two (and possibly more) persons received an opportunity for a new life, thanks to those with ARF-ARS sympathies in the Syracuse Armenian community, and no one did more than Missak Kalebdjian and especially Eliza Sachaklian. She never dwelt

---

470. St. John the Baptist Church trustees minutes of September 13, 1961 and January 30, 1962.

on her generosity, saying simply that it was her obligation to help fellow Armenians. She had hoped to enlarge and strengthen the Armenian community in Syracuse. Unfortunately, that did not happen. Most of the newcomers stayed in Syracuse only long enough to raise travel fare to New York City or Los Angeles.

In general, those from the Soviet Union, even if from Armenia, did not integrate well with the Syracuse community. The institutions that the little Syracuse community had tried hard to maintain were totally unknown to them. Church, political parties, charitable societies were all activities that had been absent from Communist society. For the émigrés from the Soviet Union, only one thing mattered: economic advancement. Refugees from the Middle East or eastern Europe seemed to have values that more or less paralleled those of their new communities. Some of them blended well with their new community. However, those with foreign spouses tended to drift into other circles and the few families who did enter Armenian community life eventually moved away—mostly to larger cities.

Back to Church Affairs

After Archbishop Tourian's death there began a series of efforts to effect unity. All proved futile. From 1934 to 1939 the Very Rev. Mampre Calfayan governed the North American Diocese as locum tenens. During that interval, on April 8, 1936, a long-promised representative of Etchmiadzin, Archbishop Karekin Hovsepian, arrived with the mission of effecting unity and raising money for the Etchmiadzin monastery.[471] The archbishop was a noted scholar. In addition, he enjoyed the respect of ARF sympathizers because of his support of Armenian forces during the war that led to the establishment of the Armenian Republic. Their hopes began to fade, however, as they waited in vain for some positive steps to be taken toward resolving the impasse. The archbishop failed to call a new meeting of the National Representative Assembly with participation of all segments, as the Supreme Council in Etchmiadzin had ordered Archbishop Tourian to do. Instead, the delegates who had gathered at the Hotel Martinique three years earlier were reassembled. They rejected the plan for reconciliation and church unity that the archbishop proposed. As he closed the meeting, the Pontifical Legate remarked, "I notice from all your expressions that it is still too early to achieve [unity]."[472] Although he had arrived with full powers to resolve the issue, he then departed, having failed in his mission.

471.*Hairenik Amsakir,* May 1936, p. 171.
472.Ibid., January 1937, p. 172; *Documents,* pp. 46–47.

In 1937, Archbishop Karekin Hovsepian was elected primate of the diocese of the eastern United States. His confirmation was delayed and he did not take up the office until 1939.[473] Despite the failure of his earlier mission to unify the diocese, ARF sympathizers still hoped that he would initiate movement in that direction. During the battle of Sardarabad, had he not preached courage and hope, before "being captured by the Turks while holding a rifle in one hand and the Cross of God in the other."[474]

Within a few months, it became clear that no action was being taken to effect improvement in relations between the divided communities. Instead, to the indignation of the ARF press, the archbishop continued the overt deference to the Soviet Union that had so enraged the ARF populations. While in Detroit he revealed an entirely illogical novelty at the point in the liturgy when prayers are said for the Armenian nation. He gave "prayers for the safety and perpetuation of the Russian nation," which he claimed were a "historical part of every solemn mass of the Armenian Apostolic Church." In his sermon, the archbishop explained, "We pray for the preservation of Russia, not Communism."[475] At least Archbishop Tourian's prayers were for Armenia, even if a Soviet Armenia.

The archbishop made a memorable visit to Syracuse, most likely in autumn 1942. I am probably the only person still alive who was present at the event to be described here. Takouhi Kalebdjian was a member of the segment that served as hosts during the archbishop's visit. She strongly supported the church and deplored the break which not only weakened church and community, but also kept both segments from using the funds belonging to the ladies' auxiliary. The money was lying in an account bearing interest. She persuaded the archbishop to attend a small meeting in the home of her brother-in-law, Missak Kalebdjian, to discuss the matter. At Takouhi's urging, Eliza Sachaklian, my mother, was present. Takouhi had told her that this was to be a meeting to discuss the status of the women's auxiliary. Eliza dutifully obeyed Takouhi's instructions that she was to bring no men with her. I was there as her chauffeur. It is my recollection that no women other than myself, the two mentioned above, and the hostess, Virginia Kalebdjian, were present. The host, Missak Kalebdjian, was also present.

The archbishop arrived, along with a retinue of about four or five men, including a bodyguard who had accompanied him from New York City. As they came in and were seated, my mother remarked, "Had I known men were invited, we, too, had men who could have come with us."

473. *Documents*, p. 48.
474. *Hairenik Weekly*, July 3, 1952, p. 2.
475. *The Detroit Free Press*, October 20, 1941.

The conversation quickly revealed respective positions. The archbishop burst into a diatribe against the unpardonable crime that had been committed (the assassination of Archbishop Tourian). He became so heated that he sprang to his feet while speaking. My mother responded carefully, maintaining a level and respectful voice. All deplored the crime, she said, but why did half of the Armenian community have to carry the blame? When the subject of the Armenian flag was mentioned, she reminded the archbishop that during Armenia's fight for independence, he himself had encouraged the soldiers before they went into battle and had blessed the flag that was now being scorned.

The archbishop was not in the mood for further discussion. He arose from his chair and moved quickly toward the door, his companions following. As one of them, Peter Roomian, passed my mother, he sneered, "Tashnagtsagani gunig!" ("Tashnag woman [wife]!") The Armenian term *gunig* has a disparaging connotation. "If we are Communist, what are you—Nazi? Fascist?" he said derisively. My mother responded proudly, "Hai Heghapoghagan Tashnagtsagan enk, uselik me oonis?" "We are of the Armenian Revolutionary Federation. Do you have anything to say?" Roomian had been a Syracuse resident since 1913 and formerly a member of the ARF. He appears with a group of twelve young men in a picture bearing the penciled date, 1914, and marked with the Armenian letters for ARF.[476] We used to chat in happier days before the split and I had considered him a friend. I was saddened by this demonstration of the ill will that had been released in the community.

After their departure, Missak Kalebdjian assailed his sister-in-law for her interference, while she tried to understand the reason why the meeting went so poorly. She complained to my mother that she had been disrespectful. "Why?" said my mother, "What did I say?" Came the reply, "Oh, I don't know, you crossed your legs."

A few years earlier, Missak Kalebdjian had angrily rejected my suggestion that he subscribe to the *Hairenik Weekly* so his son could receive information about Armenian affairs. He called the publication "Poison!" Following the episode with the archbishop, Kalebdjian changed completely. He never joined the ARF, but he actively supported its programs and he attended the church services sponsored by those with ARF sympathies.

As for the bank account, years later the needed signatures were secured and the funds were divided equally between the opposing groups.[477]

In the last section of Part 2, it had been mentioned that the Catholicos of Etchmiadzin, while accorded primacy of honor, has an administrative equal,

---

476.Photograph in Eckhoff collection.
477.Letter, Eckhoff to Mesrobian, February 19, 1983.

the Catholicos of Cilicia, with a defined area of authority. The seat had moved from Sis, Turkey to Antelias, Lebanon after the Armenian deportations during World War I.

On May 10, 1943, Archbishop Karekin Hovsepian was elected Catholicos of Cilicia to fill the office that had been vacant since 1940. He was by now seventy-three years old. He did not assume his duties until March 1945, blaming his delay on wartime conditions. Before leaving the United States, at the general Diocesan Assembly in September 1943, the archbishop made a proposal to bring about the reunion of the divided church, but the Assembly voted against it. The primate asked the secretary to record in the minutes his observation that he did not consider this vote to be beneficial for the Armenian Church.[478]

Only three months after arriving in Lebanon, the new Catholicos traveled to Armenia to attend the conclave to elect the Catholicos of Etchmiadzin. This was the first occasion in history when a Catholicos of Cilicia had taken part in the election of the Catholicos of Etchmiadzin. After his return to Lebanon, the ARF press reported with dismay that he made frequent visits to the Soviet embassy in Lebanon. "If the Catholicos of Cilicia displays such intimacy with the Soviets, are the primates of the church to follow suit?" asked an editorial writer.[479]

Bishop Tiran Nersoyan, forty-one years old, succeeded Archbishop Karekin Hovsepian as primate of the eastern Diocese of the Armenian Church of America. He held the office from 1944 to 1953. The new primate was a cultured, well-educated person with fluency in English. He began his religious education in the Armenian seminary in Jerusalem. After holding teaching and clerical offices in several countries, he became rector of the Armenian Church in London. While in England he attended Merfield Theological Seminary and Kings College.[480]

His mission, like that of his predecessor, was to effect unity, but those with ARF sympathies were dismayed by statements expressed in his book, *A Christian Approach to Communism*, published in 1942 in England.[481] The entire work is replete with assertions such as the following:

---

478. *Documents,* p. 49.
479. *Hairenik,* 1947, day not available. Clipping in Eckhoff collection.
480. *Hairenik Weekly,* January 24, 1946, p. 6.
481. Tiran Nersoyan, *A Christian Approach to Communism: Ideological Similarities Between Dialectical Materialism and Christian Philosophy* (London: Frederick Muller, Ltd., 1942).

The Soviet regime is disliked as being a dictatorship, with all its consequent evils. Whatever the circumstances which created this dictatorship, it must be said that Soviet dictatorship is in the last resort a "benevolent dictatorship," in spite of all its incidental cruelties, and is based on the will of the majority.[482]

"Incidental cruelties," indeed! In the margin of the typewritten text available to me, Aaron H. Sachaklian has noted heatedly, "A greater lie was never uttered even by a layman, to say nothing of a would be man of God."

Another choice passage:

Christ Jesus, the Man, died for Mankind, which was epitomized in His own Person. His death was vicarious. A corporate society dies for itself in the person of an individual. This death is also vicarious. Christ's free will was his Father's will. The individual's free will is society's will. What is supremely important is that death should be suffered only for salvation in the best sense of the word.[483]

Sachaklian exploded, "In Communist society the individual does not sacrifice himself voluntarily, vicariously as Christ did. He is murdered. This is justifying murder. This is not even Christian. This is the devil incarnate."

Another:

God must have an agent in this world of temporal things to do His business transactions for Him. This again is the sound principle of Sacramentalism. Thus the form of the Communist State, which is the form of a Father-State, comes nearest to the Christian ideal. On the corresponding spiritual level stands the comparison between the Police-God of the Old Testament and the Father-God of the New Testament.[484]

Is it not the ultimate heresy to view the Godless Communist state as the temporal agent of God? Sachaklian's rebuttal seems understated: "Thus the butcher state has become the Father State." One wonders, in the process of carrying out God's will in the temporal sphere, how does this "benevolent dictatorship" in the form of a Father-State respond to the "will of the majority?"

The text is dotted with passages such as the above, pungently and pointedly refuted in Sachaklian's marginal comments. Surely, someone with a mind as

---

482. Ibid., p. 25.
483. Ibid., p. 28.
484. Ibid., 29.

flexible as this could find a reasonably suitable device to argue away the many barriers to church and community unity?

The public waited hopefully for some favorable signs, but none appeared. The primate made his first visit to Syracuse in December 1945. He made no approaches to the ARF community, nor did he mention plans or even express wishes for unity. Speaking with Nevart Apikian, a *Post-Standard* writer and daughter of Syracuse's former delegate to the church convention, the bishop declared that "difficulties in confronting religion have been removed and the church is now free in Armenia." He praised the industrial progress in Armenia that he had witnessed on his trip there in June 1945, and voiced the impression that the Soviets considered the Armenians as "wonderful people."[485]

Greeting the bishop upon his arrival at the train station were church trustees and Rev. John Adjemian, pastor of the Armenian Presbyterian mission. It is likely that the welcoming group included most of the following who became members of the parish council in 1948: Khosrov Khoubeserian, president; Vahram Aghababian, secretary; Khachig Minasian (not the man from Aramtagh), vice-president; Peter Roomian, treasurer; Sarkis Kaishian, Stephen Nalbantian, and Yeghia Der Boghosian, advisors. All were longtime members of the Syracuse community.[486]

The bishop conducted Armenian services in Grace Episcopal Church and was honored at a banquet that evening in the Hotel Syracuse. Musical selections were performed by Lucy Boyan Balakian of New York, pianist, and the violin trio of Anna (Anahid) Balakian, her husband Stephen Nalbantian, and B. A. Jackson. On the day following the banquet, the bishop spoke at a young people's meeting then returned to New York the next day.

For a time, the bishop inserted the term "Orthodox" in the title of the Armenian Church and tried to justify its use. The Armenian Church is an autocephalous national church, which cherishes the designation "Apostolic," having been founded by two apostles. While not inaccurate, the term "Orthodox" was considered by some to diminish the Armenian Church, bringing it under the shadow of the Russian Orthodox Church, a movement favored by Soviet authorities at the time. Armenians of the opposition rejected the term and even the bishop's supporters were uncomfortable with it. After several years, the term was quietly dropped from use.[487]

---

485. *Syracuse Post-Standard,* December 20, 1945, reprinted in *Hairenik Weekly,* January 24, 1946, p. 6.

486. Rev. Arden Ashjian, p. 243.

487. *Crisis in the Armenian Church,* pp.104–9; Peter Farhadian, "The Case of Archbishop Nersoyan," in *The Armenian Review,* vol. XIII, no. 2-50, Summer, July, 1960, pp. 5–7.

Choir for the Syracuse parish under Etchmiadzin, 1946. Deacon Khachadour Aghaian is seated in the center in front.

As the Cold War between the Soviet Union and the United States intensified, the tone of editorials and articles in the Armenian press became increasingly strident. The participation of the Etchmiadzin Catholicos, Kevork Cheorekjian, in the World Peace Congress held in Moscow in 1950 displayed a total subservience to Soviet directive, concluded the ARF press. "It is a full entrance into the political arena and is still another able demonstration of the political usage of the Armenian Church by the controlling Kremlin. It substantiates charges of non-Communist Armenians that the Catholicos is no longer the servant of God alone, but a tool of Soviet propaganda."[488]

It seems likely that even followers of the Etchmiadzin church became uncomfortable with the possibility of being seen as sharing the policies of the Soviet Union. At the closing session of the annual convention of the North American diocese in 1952, Archbishop Nersoyan presiding, a resolution was passed that in effect disclaimed political ties between the Armenian Church in America and the Holy See of Etchmiadzin in Soviet Armenia. The resolution expressed opposition to any doctrines or teachings that were subversive "and tend toward the destruction of the society in which we live." The resolution

---

488.*Hairenik Weekly,* December 7, 1950, p. 1.

further stated that the spiritual head of the Armenian Church "represents only the ecclesiastical authority of the church; and does not exercise political authority over his flock; and has repeatedly exhorted his people to be loyal to the respective countries in which they live."[489] This resolution of 1952 bears a remarkable similarity to that of the anti-Soviet segment, passed in its National Representative Assembly meeting in November 1934.

Archbishop Nersoyan commented, "The church does not have to be involved in economic and political problems, either national or international." It "does not have to," but is it? He also asserted that the church has the duty of "keeping our national culture alive and flourishing." "We shall try to keep alive our language, history and arts in the souls of our people," he said.[490]

During Archbishop Nersoyan's tenure as primate, the Diocese made substantial progress. Ten new churches were built in the United States, the Diocean constitution and administration were modernized, and plans were made for construction of the national cathedral complex in New York City.[491] Efforts to unify the two church segments, however, met with no success. Despite the apparent softening of the Etchmiadzin church's position, passions had not abated and it was impossible to find common ground as the basis for unity talks. Negotiations between representatives of the two groups failed to achieve positive results and church unity remained a distant prospect.[492]

Our Own Home

By 1945, estimates of the Armenian population in the United States ranged up to two hundred thousand.[493] In 1950 there were seven hundred thousand Armenians in North and South America, France, Germany and the Middle East, according to a circular letter of the ARF dated February 21, 1950. The Armenian community in Syracuse does not appear to have shared in the population growth, but at least it remained stable. A 1952 directory compiled by the AGBU gives the names and addresses of one hundred forty-nine households, including ARF sympathizers. Those listed are adult Armenian males and twenty-six women who were heads of households. Assuming that one-half of the males had spouses, the community had an approximate total population of at least two hundred ten adults.[494] Most of the names are familiar to me.

---

489. *The Hartford Courant,* October 12, 1952.
490. Ibid.
491. *The Armenian Reporter,* November 6, 1986, p. 6.
492. For a discussion of unity efforts see *Documents* and Archbishop Mesrob Ashjian, both previously cited.
493. Vratzian, p. 252.
494. The 1952 *Directory of Armenians,* compiled by the AGBU Queens Chapter.

The majority are people who had lived in Syracuse for many years, had stable businesses, and were in reasonably comfortable circumstances.

For some time both groups had felt the need to have their own church and community gathering place. In the ARF community the movement started in 1947 during a twenty-fifth anniversary party for Mr. and Mrs. K. Kyoomjian. The suggestion of a *Hai Doon* (literally "Armenian Home") was first voiced by Mianzara Eckhoff, who started the fund with a gift of $25.00. So many people opposed the proposal, saying that it could not be done, that she sought advice from Aaron H. Sachaklian. He responded, "We have tried and failed, but many times women will succeed where men have failed." Others began to contribute small amounts—even fifty-cent pieces—and the fund, once established, started to grow. It became the centerpiece of ARF community activities.[495]

Reporting on activities of the ARF in Syracuse in 1949, Betty Shahlamian wrote:

> Further plans are being made to raise funds for "Hye Doon" in Syracuse which is primarily for various functions such as Armenian School, hanteses [public programs], and also recreational center for the Armenian youth to get together. Already the ARS, AYF has contributed towards this project and the ARF Committee is planning to sponsor events to help make proceeds which will be added to this fund.[496]

Efforts intensified and the Armenian Community Center was formally incorporated in July 1953. The first board of directors was composed of Vartkas Minasian, president, Sarkis Boyadjian, Arousiag Telian, Harry Telian, Aaron H. Sachaklian, Maurice Topalian, James Abajian, Krikor Apikian, and Vartan Kyoomjian.[497]

In 1954, two donors came forward, Abraham Kevorkian and Dickran Dumanian, who offered three adjoining lots of land on West Matson Street. The gift was quickly acknowledged by a dinner on May 17, 1954, to which were invited Mayor and Mrs. Donald Mead. An enthusiastic gathering of one hundred fifty persons expressed readiness to respond to the serious fund campaign that would surely follow. An architect was hired and his preliminary sketch gave hope that the dream would indeed become a reality.[498] The first

---

495. Letter, Eckhoff to Mesrobian, February 19, 1983; Zephyr Kyoomjian Minasian.
496. *Hairenik Weekly,* October 13, 1949, p. 2.
497. Corporation record book.
498. *Hairenik Weekly,* June 3, 1954, p. 2; photographs in Vartkas and Zephyr Minasian collection.

membership list (1953–54) named ninety members paying dues at $5.00 each, including four non-Armenian spouses.[499]

Among fund-raising events that followed was a memorable evening of Armenian dancing on May 14, 1955, at the American Legion Hall, 123 South Clinton Street. The Vosbikian Band, "nationally famous Armenian and Oriental recording artists," was brought from Philadelphia for the occasion. Members of the community gave generously, both as individuals and as members of the ARF (which at this time enjoyed a junior as well as a senior committee), ARS, and AYF. The ARS alone contributed more than $2,000. By 1954–55, membership had grown to one hundred twenty-one, including six non-Armenian spouses.[500]

After many meetings, conferences, and phone calls, decisions were made and ground-breaking ceremonies were held on April 22, 1956, followed by post-Easter services at Grace Episcopal Church, Very Rev. K. Giragosian officiating.

Fund-raising efforts became intensified while construction proceeded and by autumn all were invited to inspect their new community home. An open house for members and guests on Friday evening, October 19, 1956, gave everyone an opportunity to tour the modest facility.[501] A large hall accommodates two hundred people. The sanctuary at one end of the hall may be closed when not in use. There are a stage, a kitchen, and a small coatroom.

The opening celebration continued on the following evening with a reception and banquet, followed by dancing to the popular Armenian band, the Vosbikians, brought again to Syracuse for the occasion. It was an exciting night and the modest building was jammed with a happy and enthusiastic gathering, including many from out of town.

The invocation was given by Rev. Walter N. Welsh, pastor of Grace Episcopal Church, who had made his church's facilities available to the Armenians so often over the years. Toastmaster James Abajian introduced Vartkas Minasian for the welcoming address, after which followed Harry Telian, Mrs. Zarouhi Adjemian, Sarkis Boyadjian, and guest speaker, Arthur Giragosian, the dynamic ARF leader from Providence. The next morning, Sunday, breakfast was served after which the ceremony of laying the cornerstone took place.

The commemorative program carries one hundred thirty-one names in the 1955–56 membership list. This was a time of euphoria, not analysis and introspection. No one could have envisioned that community center membership was already at its peak and that decline lay not far in the future. The first hint

---

499. List in Minute book.
500. Ibid.
501. Grand Opening booklet, 1956.

Some of the founding members of St. John the Baptist Armenian Apostolic Church and Community Center, 1960. Left to right: Frank Abajian, Missak Kalebdjian, Rev. Torkom Hagopian, the first pastor, Aaron H. Sachaklian, Minas Apikian, Hagop Telian, Krikor Apikian.

of this was revealed in the 1956–57 membership list of one hundred twenty-four names. No matter. There was much work to do and the enthusiastic community now directed efforts toward new goals.

Just a few months earlier, in June 1956, the Syracuse Armenians of the "other side," under the direction of Etchmiadzin, had purchased their own church. Although the two groups proceeded without reference to each other, there was undoubtedly a feeling of rivalry for the support of politically uncommitted Armenians living in Syracuse. To the battle for souls in the ideological war was added the competition for bodies to fill the two new community gathering places.

IV

1956 to 1998:
Two Churches, Neither Full

St. Paul's Armenian Apostolic Church

The Armenians in Syracuse remaining within the jurisdiction of Etchmiadzin, like those of the "ARF side," had longed for many years to have their own church. Their desire to organize on a stronger basis was recognized in a history of the Diocese written in 1948. The writer foresaw success for this parish of a few hundred Armenians if the Diocese could send an able worker to help.[502]

In June 1956, relying on their own efforts, the Diocesan community purchased the Geddes Street Methodist Church, after a fund-raising campaign directed by Yeghia Boghosian, Vahram Aghababian, Khachadour Aghaian, Sarkis Kaishian, Khosrov Khoubeserian, Peter Roomian, and Norhad Tufankjian.[503] A picnic on July 1 at Willow Bay in Onondaga Lake Park, under sponsorship of the "Syracuse Ladies Armenian Church Society" must have been an especially joyful occasion.[504]

For the next two years extensive renovations were carried out to prepare the church for consecration. It was especially important to redesign the sanctuary and build a new altar as well as to prepare vestments in accordance with the traditions of the Armenian Church. The small church has pews seating about one hundred persons. A narrow stairway off a vestibule entry leads to a carpeted basement area with an equipped kitchen that is used for social events. The facilities were inadequate for the crowds of the earlier years and for a time during the 1960s to mid-1970s the parishioners raised funds with the intention of building a hall to adjoin the church. As the number of parishioners dwindled, however, those plans were set quietly aside. The funds they had

---

502. Rev. Arden Ashjian, p. 243.
503. "Historical Sketch" in Twenty-fifth Anniversary booklet, 1958–83.
504. Invitation in Sachaklian collection.

St. Paul's Armenian Apostolic Church, Syracuse, NY, consecrated in June 1958.

raised were retained as the foundation for an endowment, income from which covers a substantial portion of the church's annual expenses.

The church was consecrated in June 1958 with the service performed by Archbishop Mampre Calfayan, Primate of the Eastern Diocese. He was assisted by Very Rev. Muron Gourdjikian, Vicar General; Very Rev. Vasken Tatoyan, and Rev. Mampre Kouzouian. The church adopted the name St. Paul's Armenian Apostolic Church of Syracuse. Church affairs are managed by a nine-member parish council serving staggered terms. They are elected at an annual parish assembly meeting which is open to interested observers, but only paid-up members are eligible to vote.

Visiting priests served St. Paul's parish until 1964. Through this period, neither church acknowledged the existence of the other. Over a period of many years, whenever hostilities between the two groups seemed to be softening, intransigence on one side or another would block efforts for cooperative ventures. Even (or should it be said, especially) leaders were not above provocative activity. Eliza Sachaklian's news item in the *Hairenik* reported that Very Rev. Giuregh Vartabed Kapigian, from the seminary at Jerusalem, during a visit in 1963 to Syracuse, made harsh and false accusations against the ARF. The reporter questioned whether the patriarchate at Jerusalem was aware of what the vartabed was doing.[505]

The atmosphere changed with the arrival in 1964 of the first resident pastor, Rev. Paren Avedikian. During his stay in Syracuse, Father Avedikian tried repeatedly to bring the two communities together. His greatest achievement in this regard was a joint commemoration of the fiftieth anniversary of the Armenian genocide in April 1965.

---

505. *Hairenik*, June 19, 1963.

St. Paul's founding parish council, 1958. Seated, left to right: Yeghia Boghosian, Khachadour Aghaian, Khosrov Khoubeserian. Standing, left to right: Sarkis Kaishian, Vahram Aghababian, Very Rev. Muron Gourdjikian, Norhad Tufankjian, Peter Roomian.

Father Avedikian established friendships within St. John's community and conducted Armenian language classes for adults which attracted individuals from both churches. I myself studied classical Armenian with him. At my request, he co-officiated with an Armenian priest from the Prelacy at the wedding of my daughter in Hendricks Chapel at Syracuse University. After he completed graduate work at Syracuse University, he departed in 1967 and the brief thaw came to an end.

Again the parish relied on visiting priests until 1978 when Deacon Hagop Nalbandian was ordained to the priesthood by His Eminence Archbishop Torkom Manoogian, primate, in ceremonies in the Syracuse church on September 17, 1978. Now Father Zenob, he remained as resident pastor for two years, leaving in 1980. Visiting priests served St. Paul's for the next few years.

Since the spring of 1985, Very Rev. Father Kegham Zakarian has been serving St. Paul's Armenian Church of Syracuse, St. Sarkis Armenian Church of Niagara Falls, and the mission parish in Rochester. He resides in Rochester and rotates weekly between the three parishes, whose regional union is called the Armenian Churches of Western New York. Each of the three parishes pays a quarterly assessment covering the cost of regularly scheduled services. An endowment called the Century Stewardship Fund established in 1986 provides financial support for the regional union.

Ordination of Father Zenob at St. Paul's, 1978. Left to right: Edward Tufankjian, Hasmig Nalbandian, Don Shagalian, Elizabeth Avakian, Manoog Mikaelian, Father Zenob, Archbishop Torkom Manoogian, Rev. Khajag Barsamian, Gerald Demerjian, Richard Roomian, Charles Koolakian, Vagharshag Avakian, Rev. Untzag.

Starting with a dinner dance in Rochester in 1986, the three communities come together for meetings and social affairs. In May 1995, they celebrated the tenth anniversary of Father Kegham's ministry with a special reception in Rochester at St. Thomas Episcopal Church.[506]

Over the years, St. Paul's parish has hosted the Diocesan primates on many occasions. Archbishop Mampre Calfayan and his successors officiated in Syracuse several times. The present primate, Archbishop Khajag Barsamian, who had visited Syracuse previously, made his first appearance as primate when he was the celebrant at services on November 15, 1992. In a newspaper interview he remarked on the small size of the parish—"50 or so parishioners." The archbishop stated, "It is not a large Armenian community in Syracuse, but they are very devoted people."[507] A friend who attended services that day remarked that the church was full and that there were many people she did not recognize. The Archbishop welcomed the sound of a baby, saying that it means our church is still alive.

St. Paul's success may have been at the expense of St. John's church, which had services on the same day. Rev. Khachig Megerdichian had brought two

506. *The Armenian Church,* July/August 1995, p. 15.
507. *Syracuse Herald-Journal,* November 14, 1992.

The ACYOA 1958.

deacons and four acolytes with him from Troy to assist in the services at St. John's. Anoush Minasian, the soloist, also played the organ, in the absence of the regular organist, her mother, Zephyr Minasian. Hamestouhi Golestas was the sole member of the choir. About thirty parishioners attended services.

In 1984 the community had the rare opportunity to meet the Armenian Patriarch of Istanbul, Archbishop Shnork Kaloustian. He delivered the sermon at St. Paul's services on October 14, 1984, and provided information on the condition of the diminishing Armenian population in Turkey. New laws have increased restrictions on the Armenian community, but Armenian schools remain open and Armenian language is taught, he said.[508] The elderly patriarch died not long afterwards.

For many years St. Paul's parish supplied able deacons and acolytes, as well as numerous voices for the choir. In the 1974 church bulletin, Dr. Sarkis Khanzadian, choirmaster, saw a bright future for the choir, which then numbered up to ten people. It was a severe loss for the entire community when this talented and well-liked youth, the son of Araxi Khanzadian, died in a tragic accident. Today an organist and a few singers carry on. A deacon assists in the service.

Among the first programs to receive attention in the new church were those directed toward the youth. Sunday school and the Armenian Church Youth Organization of America (ACYOA) were initiated and Armenian school was revitalized.

The ACYOA had been founded in 1946 by Archbishop Nersoyan during his term as primate.[509] In 1947 Papken Vartabed Varjapetian, who had been sent by Diocesan headquarters to conduct services in Syracuse, made an

---

508. Reference made to my notes at the time of his visit.
509. *The Armenian Reporter,* November 6, 1986, p. 6.

address to the young people in the "newly organized Syracuse branch of the ACYOA." He showed slides depicting various events in Armenian national and church history, making comments in fluent English. I had first met the young vartabed in Jerusalem in 1938, while he was a student at the Armenian Theological Seminary. His visit to Syracuse allowed me to renew our acquaintance and I took the opportunity to prepare a news report.[510]

Whereas the Armenian Youth of America (AYA), the youth group of the Progressive League, had made no headway among the Syracuse young people, the ACYOA, after a slow start, appears to have been more successful. John Hanessian, senior, was "very instrumental" in getting the organization started in Syracuse. Virginia Saxenian said that membership fluctuated between ten and twelve "or a little more." A photograph with the heading "ACYOA—1958" appearing in St. Paul's Twenty-fifth Anniversary booklet shows seventeen people. Perhaps the organization was then at its peak. The group remained active from approximately 1958 to 1967. It disappeared during the late 1960s. Among the members were Virginia Saxenian, Richard Roomian, Judy Koolakian, Manoog Mikaelian, Audrey Hamamjian. Edward Tufenkjian was local chairman.

The Syracuse youth held regional conferences with Troy and Niagara Falls and five or six people went to conventions. Virginia Saxenian was on the Central Councils from 1961 to 1964. Miss Saxenian remembered with pleasure her experiences as a delegate to seven or eight conventions and remarked that traveling around gave her the opportunity to "meet some great people." Elizabeth Markarian Avakian, on the other hand, had very little recollection of ACYOA, saying that it "did not become active."

During the bitter years of the Armenian Cold War, the ARF press closely monitored the activities and pronouncements of the anti-ARF organizations and their press, thus an editorial appearing in the October 1958 issue of *The Armenian Guardian* evoked swift response. *The Armenian Guardian* was the official organ of the ACYOA. The topic was sufficiently grave for the *Hairenik* press to issue a special booklet entitled *How They Are Educating the Younger Generation*, in which were reprinted the *Guardian* editorial and the *Hairenik*'s response, in both the Armenian original and English translation.

The Armenian Guardian bluntly attacked what was for Armenians the most sacred aspect of the Armenian Church—its national identity. Without apology or preamble, the editorial opened:

> The root cause of the present crisis in the Armenian Church being the nationalism of our people, it is only reasonable to expect that

---

510. *Hairenik Weekly,* March 6, 1947, p. 6.

the cure for her critical condition lies in the complete eradication of the nationalistic conception of the church. [511]

After further comments along these lines, the editorial reaches the conclusion that "Eradicating nationalism from our midst necessarily means also that we must henceforth cease from using the Church to preserve the Armenian language."[512]

The justification for relinquishing national identity and language is given as "to carry out the purpose of the Church, which is to save souls and glorify God." When the Armenian language becomes a hindrance to the pursuit of such a purpose, "it must be supplanted by whatever other language or languages that can truly serve that purpose. The principle of using the Armenian language to carry out the purpose of the Church must also, of course, be applied to Armenian art, culture, etc."[513]

This astounding attack on the very foundations of the Armenian Church appeared five years after Archbishop Tiran Nersoyan had left the office of primate and six years after his declaration that the church has the duty of "keeping our national culture alive and flourishing." At that time he said, "We shall try to keep alive our language, history and arts in the souls of our people." The archbishop's statements had been made on the occasion of the adoption of a resolution by the North American Diocese of the Armenian Apostolic Orthodox [sic] Church which attempted to clarify the relationship of the Armenian Church in the United States with the Holy See of Etchmiadzin in Soviet Armenia.[514]

While the ARF press reacted with horror and indignation at these assaults on Armenia's most cherished institutions, the church members to whom such messages were directed did not seem to be paying much attention. It is possible that these Communist trial balloons were released in order to observe reactions and on that basis to determine the chances for success. In any case, about fifteen years later the communities subject to Etchmiadzin were going on with their work, seemingly untouched by such heresies. The editor's note in the St. Paul's church bulletin of June 1974 (*Nshooyl*) observes that "In addition to being a religious institution, the Armenian Church has been the vanguard of preserving our tradition and ancestral traits." "The Armenian Church realizing its mission and responsibility to every Armenian in every corner of the world, continues to nourish its people instilling a spiritual and national

---

511. *How They Are Educating the Younger Generation* (Boston, Mass.: Hairenik Association, 1959).

512. Ibid.

513. Ibid.

514. *The Hartford Courant*, October 12, 1952.

The St. Paul's children in a Christmas pageant, 1959.

consciousness." And, at a reception on June 2, 1974, for five seminarians from St. Nersess Armenian Theological Seminary, Zarmair Taft, a member of the older generation, congratulated the young men and "emphasized the importance of not only realizing the religious mission of the church but also grasping its nationalistic aspect."[515]

For a fairly extended period St. Paul's appears to have maintained well-organized and active Sunday school and Armenian school programs. A 1959 photograph in the Twenty-fifth Anniversary booklet shows twenty-five young people ranging from six or eight years to mid-teens, dressed in costumes for a Christmas pageant. Six small children are shown in a Sunday school photo dated 1975. The Sunday school and Armenian school programs appear to have been especially vibrant during the mid-1970s. Carol Columbus served as superintendent of church school for many years. Among the teachers were Mary Demirjian, Angele Khanzadian, and Judy Koolakian. In 1974 there were twenty pupils in church school with an average attendance of seven to eleven.[516]

Both communities were greatly strengthened during the early 1970s with the arrival in town of Artin Boghossian, who had come from Beirut, Lebanon to study for a Ph.D. in mathematics at Syracuse University. He was the stimulus for the founding of a school that served both communities. Teachers for the program initiated in 1972–73 included another graduate student in mathematics, also from Beirut, Ara Djamboulian, as well as members of St. Paul's community Zarmair Taft, Maro Adourian, Mrs. Berjouhi Adourian, and Manas Ucarian. The year's closing program on May 19, 1973, featured songs, dances, and recitations by the students. An enthusiastic audience of more than

515.*Nshooyl,* June 1974, p. 11.
516.Ibid., pp. 12–13.

one hundred parents and friends attended the event held at the Armenian Community Center hall. Dancing and a social hour followed.[517]

Soon another newcomer to the city, Ara Jeknavorian, an American-born youth, also lent his talents to the efforts to build a community-wide school. He and Boghossian together were responsible for a program in observance of Vartanantz (St. Vartan's Day) held on February 23, 1974, at the Armenian Community Center hall. Although the printed program identifies the sponsor as "The Armenian School of Syracuse," the only school-age person participating was Sam Sahagian in a small skit with Ara Jeknavorian. The adult speakers and performers were drawn from the two parishes.[518]

The June 1974, St. Paul's bulletin reports that the Armenian school had thirty students and six faculty. Students were grouped according to age and knowledge of Armenian language. Sessions were held on Friday evenings from September to May at St. Paul's. Classes would last about one hour then refreshments were served. Special activities took place according to the season or availability of a speaker. The school year traditionally concluded with a program in which the students recited poems, sang, or performed skits. In 1975 the school had forty-four students divided into six classes.[519]

An announcement with the heading "Armenian School Cultural Night" offered a recitation contest, musical selections, and an operetta on March 22, 1975, at the Armenian Community Center.[520] This was most likely a continuation of the school program initiated by Boghossian.

The school students made several efforts to organize themselves into a social union. The purpose of "The Young Armenians of the Armenian School of Syracuse" formed in 1974 appears to have been largely social. In 1974 it had eight members between the ages of thirteen and seventeen, according to the parish publication.[521] The group, without doubt aided by their elders, sponsored a Christmas shish kebab dinner at St. Paul's hall on January 6, 1974.[522]

Inspired by the spirit of renewal that was promoted by the community-wide school, a new group calling itself "The Armenian Community Youth" took the place of the Young Armenians. The young people signalled their coming together in typical teenage fashion. They sponsored a dance that was held at St. John the Baptist church hall on June 10, 1978. The group did not

---

517.*Armenian Weekly*, June 21, 1973, p. 3.
518.Program in Sachaklian collection.
519.*Nshooyl*, February 1975, p. 27.
520.Invitation in Sachaklian collection.
521.*Nshooyl*, June 1974, p. 21.
522.Invitation in Mesrobian collection.

Armenian school staff, 1976. Seated: Ara Jeknavorian (left), Zarmair Taft (right).

remain in existence very long. After its early disappearance, the ACYOA juniors of St. Paul's community briefly appeared in March 1980.

For a time Armenian language classes for adults were offered Friday nights at St. Paul's church hall. Five people participated in the first session on March 7, 1980, but it is not known how long the program lasted or how many people made use of it.[523]

By the 1980s, interest in Armenian school had waned. At St. Paul's, Sunday school and Armenian school superintendents were still designated, but there is no evidence that classes were being held. The schedule of services for the last quarter of 1988 invited expressions of interest in having Armenian school reopened.

Through the years, the women of St. Paul's provided the continuity of service that is needed to keep an institution healthy and vigorous. The first executive committee of the Ladies Auxiliary was composed of mostly foreign-born women who had lived in the community for many years: Araxi Saxenian, president, Antaram Desteian, Shooshanig Gozigian, Sirouhi Kaish, Araxi

---

523. *Nshooyl,* May-June 1980, p. 27.

Khanzadian, Victoria Roomian, and Elise Taft. In 1974 there were forty members, seven of whom were on the Executive Board. Today's Women's Guild continues the traditions of service established by the original group. The Guild provides lunches and refreshments after church services and carries out fund-raising ventures such as an annual food sale and bazaar. For a time the skilled cooks even conducted cooking demonstrations.[524]

In 1989, the parish council decided to forego the traditional annual picnic in favor of an ambitious two-day festival to be held under a tent on church grounds. It was an inspired innovation. The event has been held successfully every summer since then, with many non-Armenians as well as Armenians from both communities attending.

By the late 1950s and early 1960s, political organizations ceased to exist in the St. Paul's community. There emerged a series of local social groups, but none established a strong presence. Church bulletins mention the Men's Club, the Armenian Fellowship Club, and the Syracuse Armenian Organization (in 1979). For a time, the Armenian Fellowship Club attempted to establish relationships with young adults from the St. John's community, but after a few social events the effort was abandoned.

Only the AGBU remained out of the many early organizations within the St. Paul's community. AGBU functions were open to the public, but members of St. John's community rarely attended. On one occasion the AGBU invited me to be their guest speaker at a Mother's Day observance at St. Paul's hall on May 14, 1972.[525] Others on the program were all members of the older generation affiliated with St. Paul's: George Arslanian, chairman, Zarmair Taft, and S. S. Kaish. My topic was the Armenian Assembly, whose inaugural meeting I had recently attended. The Armenian Assembly was the brain child of Dr. John Hanessian of Washington, D.C., a Syracuse native. His mother, a member of St. Paul's community, was still living in Syracuse. Dr. Hanessian had conceived the idea of bringing together representative leaders of the separated communities for discussion and mutual discovery in a quiet convention-center atmosphere in Airlie, Virginia. After overcoming their initial reserve, the attendants discovered hitherto unsuspected mutual values and interests. After a second meeting the following year, the group was well on its way toward becoming a force for integration, when a cruel fate determined otherwise. John Hanessian was killed in a crash of a Turkish airplane in May 1974. Thereafter, the movement was taken over by others with different ideas.

The AGBU was an old and seemingly well-established tradition in the community, but it too was defeated by age. According to Antaram Desteian,

---

524. Ibid., February 1975, p. 24.
525. Eliza Sachaklian memoir, book 3.

St. Paul's Ladies Auxiliary, 1963.

interviewed in 1992, "activities stopped about ten years ago. Roomian was treasurer. The older people dropped out and the younger people did not join." According to Elizabeth Markarian Avakian, the AGBU was "in its prime" during the 1950s and 1960s.

Since the cessation of AGBU activities, St. Paul's parishioners have focused entirely on church affairs. Like the people of St. John's community, they are responsive to major appeals on behalf of the Armenian people, but the political passions of earlier years have totally dissipated. The management of parish affairs is now in the hands of an American-born generation, whose concern is the maintenance of their church for as long as possible.

St. John the Baptist Armenian Apostolic Church, Syracuse, N.Y., consecrated in 1957.

St. John the Baptist Armenian Apostolic Church and Community Center

Two National Assembly groups had been created by the split in the 1933 church convention in New York. The segment that was no longer under the jurisdiction of Etchmiadzin had continued, governed by its own National Assembly, but without a Prelate. The few priests who since 1933 had maintained a traveling ministry to the communities not under Diocesan administration were aging and youthful replacements were not in sight.

With the opening of their brand new structure, members of the Armenian Community Center began to reflect on future prospects for the religious program. It was all very well to erect a church and community center, but what was to be done about providing new clergy, for administration of church matters, indeed for ensuring the supply of holy oil used in the sacraments? Returning to Soviet-controlled Etchmiadzin was out of the question and since 1943 the only alternative, the See of Cilicia located in Antelias, Lebanon, had been under the direction of the former primate of the Etchmiadzin churches in the eastern United States, now Catholicos Karekin Hovsepian. As primate he had shown no sympathy toward the ejected parishes and had been ineffectual in bringing about a reconciliation.

The death of Catholicos Karekin in 1952 suggested the possibility of change in the situation. The patriarchal throne of the See of Cilicia remained

vacant until February 1956, when Catholicos Zareh Payaslian, a highly popular bishop from Syria, was elected, supported by the ARF. His election was
hotly opposed by Soviet leaders who even resorted to the unprecedented act of
sending the newly installed Etchmiadzin Catholicos Vazgen Baljian to Lebanon to lobby for a candidate more acceptable to Soviet authorities. He failed
in his mission and withdrew to Egypt, where he called a meeting of bishops
and issued a demand that Catholicos Zareh acknowledge the Etchmiadzin
Catholicos as his superior. That did not happen and relations between Etchmiadzin and the See at Antelias, so cordial while Karekin was Catholicos, now
became another issue in the Armenian Cold War.[526]

With a friend now in charge at Antelias, the executive body of the abandoned parishes in America wired Catholicos Zareh on February 24, 1957,
requesting that he take them under the wing of the Cilician See. After several
months came the favorable response. The petition was granted and the ARF
press proclaimed the joyous news: "The Catholicos of Cilicia Takes the Amer-
ican-Armenian National Church Prelacy Under His Authority."[527] The communities could now enjoy an association with a governing patriarch in
confidence that they would not be subject to Soviet intrusions. Catholicos
Zareh's decision was put into immediate effect.

His Excellency, Archbishop Khoren Paroyan, Prelate of the Armenian
Church See of Lebanon and Official Nuncio of His Holiness, Zareh I,
Catholicos of the Great House of Cilicia, arrived at Boston's airport on Octo-
ber 17, 1957, to assume duties entrusted to him by his Holy Superior.[528]

The Official Nuncio had already departed for his triumphal American tour
when Catholicos Vazgen sent a wire from Etchmiadzin ordering Catholicos
Zareh to withdraw his acceptance of the appeal from the United States. Soviet
interference must certainly be blamed for this unprecedented attempt to alter
the traditional relationship of brotherhood between the two patriarchal sees.
The directive was ignored.[529] Throughout Catholicos Zareh's reign, relations
between Etchmiadzin and the Cilician See remained broken. It was not until
after Catholicos Zareh's death in 1963 and the succession of Archbishop
Khoren to the throne of the Cilician Catholicosate that cordial relations were
reestablished between the two sees.

---

526. Details may be found in Puzant Yeghiayan, *Jamanagagitz Badmoutiun Gatoghigosou-
tian Hayotz Giligyo 1914–1972* [*Modern History of the Armenian Catholicosate of Cilicia 1914–1972*], (Antelias, Lebanon: Publication of the Armenian Catholicosate of
Cilicia, 1975).

527. *Hairenik,* October 6, 1957.

528. *Hairenik Weekly,* October 17, 1957, p. 1.

529. Ibid., November 11, 1957, p. 1; December 12, 1957, p. 1.

Archbishop Khoren Paroyan, Official Nuncio of His Holiness, Zareh I, Catholicos of the Great House of Cilicia, visited Syracuse to consecrate St. John the Baptist Armenian Apostolic Church on December 15, 1957. Seated, left to right, are Maurice Topalian, Very Rev. Hrant Khachadourian, Archbishop Khoren Paroyan, Aaron H. Sachaklian.

For the Syracuse St. John's community the timing of the Nuncio's mission could not have been better. Since the opening of their building a year earlier, the sanctuary and altar had been completed and the church was ready to be consecrated as St. John the Baptist Armenian Apostolic Church. This joyful duty was added to the schedule of the seemingly tireless forty-two-year-old archbishop. Following ceremonial meetings with American religious dignitaries in New York and Washington, Vice-President Richard Nixon, and Secretary of State John Dulles, Archbishop Khoren came to Syracuse to consecrate the church in traditional ceremonies on December 15, 1957.[530]

Archbishop Khoren, accompanied by the Very Rev. Hrant Khachadourian, visited Syracuse again within a few months. This time it was his mission to solicit funds for the development of the Catholicosate of Cilicia. His last visit to Syracuse before returning to Lebanon was in autumn of 1959.

---

530. *Syracuse Herald-Journal,* November 30, 1957.

At that time, he gave the parish the glad news that they would no longer have to rely on visiting clergy. A young priest, trained at the seminary in Antelias, would soon arrive to take charge of the parish.[531]

Following the return of the Catholicosal Nuncio to Lebanon in 1959, the difficult task of the administration of a new prelacy was assigned to the youthful Bishop Khachadourian. Despite his many duties, he maintained a close interest in the Syracuse community and managed several visits. His early death in 1980 was a loss to the Armenian people.

Rev. Torkom Bozodjian (almost immediately changed to Hagopian) arrived with his wife and small family in February 1960 and received a welcoming reception.[532] The young priest's cordial manner and beautiful voice endeared him to everyone from the beginning. The community was ready with its support. In addition to Archdeacon Khachig Minasian, there was a choir of as many as ten singers, plus an organist. On September 25, 1961, Bishop Khachadourian ordained four acolytes.[533] Actually, the tiny sanctuary barely accommodated a crowd of that size. On a later visit, November 8, 1964, the bishop ordained Diran Ajemian (son of Rev. and Mrs. John Adjemian) as archdeacon.

For a time, the Syracuse church was part of a regional grouping that included Troy, Niagara Falls, and sometimes Binghamton. The new pastor's duties required him to alternate between the several parishes. After two years, Father Hagopian expressed the desire to serve a single parish and on August 26, 1962, the community tendered their priest and his family a hastily arranged goodbye dinner.[534] There was grumbling among all of the parishes at the speed of the decision, but the move to the large parish of Watertown, Massachusetts, was a fitting assignment for the able priest.

A Register of Baptisms, Weddings, and Burials, opened on September 1, 1962, by Rev. Nerses Baboorian, gives us the arrival date of the next resident pastor. Father Baboorian was a hard worker. He labored over the church notices and produced a multi-paged church bulletin called *Poorvar* (*Censer*) which ceased after five issues. He organized the school children (ten girls and twelve boys) for participation in the traditional activities of Holy Week, April 8–14, 1963. Despite his efforts, however, he was not able to satisfy the parish. His resignation in May 1964 was not contested.

---

531. *Syracuse Post-Standard,* April 4, 1958; November 23, 1959.

532. Text of Eliza Sachaklian's welcoming speech March 30, 1960, in Sachaklian collection.

533. Newspaper clipping lacking date and source in Sachaklian collection.

534. *Hairenik,* October 7, 1962.

Choir at St. John the Baptist Armenian Apostolic Church with the first pastor, Rev. Torkom Hagopian, and deacon, Khachig Minasian, 1960.

By this time, the Syracuse community had begun to realize the extent of the obligations the parish had to assume in hosting a resident pastor, and decided that the next priest could live elsewhere. Sobered by their experience, they decided to content themselves with services by Rev. Movses Shirikian, assigned to Troy and Syracuse from Worcester. The Syracuse trustees, mentioning losses by death and transfer from the city, explained that they could not assume more than one-third of the obligation of maintaining the priest. At the annual meeting on June 13, 1964, fifty-two were present out of ninety-four members.[535]

In June 1967, Rev. Zareh Maronian, the first Armenian clergyman to be ordained in the United States by Archbishop Khachadourian, was assigned to the Troy and Syracuse parishes, with Troy as his base. At this time, St. John's

---

535.List of members in minute book.

was having sixteen to eighteen services a year. Father Maronian, a pleasant young man, had a fine singing voice, as did the archdeacon, Diran Ajemian. Their love and understanding of music brought the priest and deacon together in many harmonious duets through the course of the rich Armenian services. Enhanced by choir and organ, the services were musically at their height during this period. Father Maronian withdrew from his pastorate in May 1981[536] and later left the priesthood to pursue another profession.

At the time of his accession to the patriarchal throne in 1963, Catholicos Khoren had received a warm greeting from Catholicos Vazgen, with an invitation that the two Armenian Church leaders should meet in Jerusalem. Great was the rejoicing when the two heads of the Armenian Church came to Christendom's Holy City to embrace in brotherhood. Together they performed a memorial service for Catholicos Zareh, whom Catholicos Vazgen had spurned in life. Catholicos Vazgen hailed the new Catholicos and a new era:

> I bless you as the elected and anointed Catholicos of the Holy See of Cilicia. In this reconciliation and re-establishment of brotherhood, there is neither one subdued nor a victor, but there is the perception and the understanding of the unity of the Armenian Church. . . . [537]

Apparently, the unity of the church was to be maintained by strictly circumscribing the movements and the activities of the Catholicos of Cilicia. Upon the announcement of Catholicos Khoren's intention to make a pontifical visit to the United States, the Chancellory of the Etchmiadzin Catholicosate issued an objection, claiming that

> Such visits of the occupant of the Antelias Cilician Throne without the knowledge and consent of the Catholicos of All Armenians represent a shaking of the consecrated age-old canons and orders of the Church.[538]

The primate of the diocese subject to Etchmiadzin, Archbishop Torkom Manoogian, not only spurned the invitation of the Cilician Prelate, Archbishop Hrant Khachadourian, to participate in activities of welcome, but also directed his "clergymen and church organizations not to participate in activities" of greeting and welcome.[539] Thus it was that members of St. Paul's Church were deprived of the opportunity to enjoy this historic visit of a

---

536.Minutes, June 28, 1981.
537.*Poorvar,* November 1963, p. 13.
538.*Armenian Weekly,* April 10, 1969, p. 3.
539.Ibid., April 17, 1969, p. 3.

Arrival in Syracuse of His Holiness Catholicos Khoren I of the Holy See of Cilicia on June 6, 1969. Left to right: Archbishop Hrant Khachadourian, His Holiness Catholicos Khoren I, Archbishop Sahag Ayvasian. At right are Vartkas Minasian and John Penirjian, church trustees.

Catholicos of the Armenian Church to the modest little Armenian parish in Syracuse.

For the parishioners and friends of St. John the Baptist, the pontifical visit of His Holiness Khoren I of the Holy See of Cilicia on June 6, 1969, was probably the most exciting event in the church's history. Archbishop Hrant Khachadourian and Archbishop Sahag Ayvasian of Greece accompanied the Catholicos. They had come by limousine from Troy with Rev. Zareh Maronian, local pastor, Syracuse trustee Jacob Telian, and Lawrence Doodigian, a member of the Syracuse police department.

The Catholicos was an old friend, having himself consecrated this little center of worship in 1957 while on his mission as Official Nuncio from the See of Cilicia. This was his fourth visit to Syracuse. He was welcomed with a bouquet of red roses offered by Miss Esther Tamurian, whom he had baptized at St. John's twelve years earlier. On behalf of Syracuse Mayor William F.

Walsh, Councilwoman Norma Coburn read a proclamation welcoming a "distinguished and world-renowned prince of the church." To the mayor, His Holiness presented the medal of St. Vartan, the Armenian hero-saint.

At a banquet attended by more than one hundred fifty persons at the Liverpool Country Club, it was announced that the community had raised $4,400 for the fund to build Prelacy headquarters in New York City. Among those at the banquet were Rev. Robert Grimm of the New York State Council of Churches, Rev. Michael Harmand of St. Sophia's Greek Orthodox Church, and Rev. Michael C. Shahin, pastor of St. Elias Orthodox Catholic Church.[540]

The next high churchman to visit the St. John's parish was Archbishop Karekin Sarkissian, who became Prelate in 1973. A graduate of Oxford University and a prominent dignitary in the World Council of Churches, the new Prelate elevated the stature of the position. He paid his first official visit to the Syracuse community on November 30, 1974, and was received with the ceremonies befitting his rank—a reception on arrival and a banquet and short program following church services.[541] Archbishop Karekin was elected Catholicos Coadjutor in 1977 and returned to Lebanon. Following the death of Catholicos Khoren I in 1983, he became Catholicos Karekin II of the Great House of Cilicia. In 1995 he became Karekin I, having been elected to occupy the throne of St. Gregory at Etchmiadzin.

Syracuse was not on the itinerary of His Holiness Karekin II, Catholicos of the Holy See of Cilicia, on his pontifical visit in 1983. Several carloads of Syracusans traveled to Albany for the reception and dinner hosted by the Troy community on June 22, 1983. Again, Archbishop Torkom Manoogian had issued a directive prohibiting his flock from attending activities of welcome. It was said that Archbishop Tiran Nersoyan ignored the injunction and attended the New York reception.

Archbishop Mesrob Ashjian, who became Prelate in 1977, was received with a reception and dinner at his first visit to Syracuse on January 20, 1980. At that time the Prelate, who had spent four years in Iran, assured the press that the American hostages then still held by Iran would be freed.[542] He also spoke to the parish about his recent visit to Armenia. He was on cordial terms with Catholicos Vazgen whom he visited on several occasions.

The parish's most recent regular pastor, Rev. Khachig Megerdichian, also maintained residence in Troy and served both Troy and Syracuse parishes, as did his predecessor, Rev. Maronian. He conducted ten regular services a year

---

540.*Syracuse Herald-Journal,* June 7, 1969; *Syracuse Post-Standard,* June 7, 1969.

541.Letter to parishioners, November 22, 1974, Sachaklian collection.

542.*Syracuse Post-Standard,* January 21, 1980.

in Syracuse, starting on September 19, 1982, as a newly ordained priest from the Antelias seminary. His last service in Syracuse was on December 21, 1997. Rev. Megerdichian is unusual in that he is American-born. It was his practice to deliver his sermons in both Armenian and English. Since the departure of Rev. Megerdichian, Vahan Vartabed Berberian has served as visiting pastor.

School at St. John

The dream of a church and community center was always driven by the hope that the existence of such a facility would help to maintain their Armenian identity among the growing younger generation. Already the first American-born generation had reached adulthood and now their children were coming along. How to "keep" the young people Armenian was the constant concern of the Armenian-speaking older folks. Even before the building was ready for use, Eliza Sachaklian was already evaluating prospects. Her handwritten list of names, dated 1956, identifies thirty-two children in the community at a suitable age level for a school program.[543]

With their own gathering place now available, St. John's trustees made serious plans at their meeting in autumn 1958 to institute an Armenian school. They appointed Harry Menasian, a teacher in the Syracuse high schools, to serve as superintendent. He made the following assignments: Eliza Sachaklian, kindergarten; Sirvart Berberian, grade level (beginners); Hourig Kalebdjian, high school (advanced); and Arpena Mesrobian, adult.[544]

The teachers took up their tasks with enthusiasm. Seven of the kindergarten children are pictured with their teacher before a decorated tree at the time of a Christmas performance. A photograph of the entire school taken in January 1959 shows twenty-eight children, three teachers, and the principal.[545]

Mrs. Sachaklian's instruction focused on memorization. Her collection of school materials contains large numbers of poems, songs, and scripts for short presentations. Report slips show that she graded on pronunciation, expression, and interpretation. The closing program of what was identified as Holy Redeemer School was held on June 7, 1959, and it featured songs, recitations, and a short play.[546] The children in the program included several who had arrived in recent years from Europe with their parents as part of the ANCHA program, as well as children with only one Armenian parent, and who understood very little, if any, Armenian.

---

543. Sachaklian collection.
544. Minutes of September 9, 1958.
545. *Syracuse Post-Standard,* December 22, 1958; Sachaklian collection.
546. Sachaklian collection.

Armenian school children at St. John the Baptist Armenian Apostolic Church and Community Center, 1958. Eliza Sachaklian, kindergarten teacher, is at the left and Harry Menasian, principal, is at the right. At the back are teachers Houri Kalebdjian (face turned) and Sirvart Berberian.

Mrs. Sachaklian kept a careful attendance record of the ten pupils in her class for the year starting October 29, 1960. Classes met only six times during that year. School was cancelled because of her own absence (once), the hall was rented (once), snowstorms (twice), two teachers were ill (once), and two weeks vacation at Easter time. It is a wonder that nine pupils still remained by April 1961, according to the attendance record.[547] Nevertheless, for a few years the children did dutifully come to school. Their performances at Christmas time were rewarded by having a decorated Christmas tree and $30 worth of presents, by decision of the trustees. They were also pressed into service to entertain the primate, Archbishop Hrant Khachadourian, at the time of his visit on January 20, 1963.[548]

---

547. Ibid.
548. Minutes of November 28, 1960 and December 12, 1961; *Hairenik,* 1963, clipping in Sachaklian collection.

With the help of the new pastor, Rev. Nerses Baboorian, a new school board was formed in 1962. Harry Menasian continued as principal with the assistance of his brother, Haig. There were twenty-nine pupils, and the teachers were Father Baboorian and his wife, Mrs. K. Armanian, and Krikor Apikian.[549]

Despite their enthusiasm and concern, the teachers were unable to maintain a stable teaching program. They were themselves inexperienced as educators, they lacked adequate teaching materials, had classes whose pupils were widely diverse in knowledge of Armenian language, and had difficulty in keeping the attention of the children. As for the students, they were reluctant to devote several hours of potential play time to an attempt to learn something for which they envisioned no practical use. Their resistance weakened the commitment of the parents who had the obligation of bringing them to school. The program produced results that the audiences could admire when the focus was on a play or a program, but intermittent attendance and differences in individual needs impeded learning through a progression of levels. Nothing ever came of the proposed program for adults.

During the 1963 school year, Harry Menasian resigned as school principal. Houri Kalebdjian carried on for a while, teaching on Friday evenings. It was reported that Armenian school started out very well, but attendance then dropped to the point that the school had to be closed for a week or two. The parents' cooperation was requested.[550] Now the ARS came forward, offering to assume responsibility for Armenian school.[551] At the time, the ARS chapters that maintained schools in their own communities were forgiven a certain percentage of the annual quota they were obliged to send to their central office. Mrs. Alice Hagopian volunteered to be the instructor for Sunday school.

Father Baboorian's church bulletin of December 1963 reported that Armenian school with fourteen students was continuing on Friday evenings from 7 p.m. to 9 p.m. taught by Sirvart Berberian. In the same issue, Mrs. Sachaklian urged that schools be strengthened. At Christmas time Mrs. Berberian's students put on the traditional program and received gifts.[552] But, by 1965, it was reported to the trustees that only one or two families out of a possible thirty had expressed interest in having Sunday school for their children. Nor was Armenian school any more successful, despite the deacon's offer to hold a one-hour class on Sundays if there was interest.[553] An ambitious effort was

---

549. *Hairenik,* November 25, 1962.
550. Minutes of annual membership meeting, June 20, 1963.
551. Minutes, September 25, 1963.
552. *Poorvar,* January 1964.

initiated by Rev. Zareh Maronian when he was assigned to Syracuse. At first more than twenty-three pupils gathered for classes on Friday evenings, but this attempt, too, was short-lived.[554]

A few years later, another attempt was made, this time by a newcomer to the community. In a report probably intended for the *Hairenik* on an ARS day program on April 13, 1969, Eliza Sachaklian praised the performances of the young people who had been taught by Mrs. Berjouhi Adourian, recently arrived from Beirut. She announced that "after a lull of a few years, for the past two months we have had Armenian school."[555] The Saturday school children were among those who assembled to greet Catholicos Khoren on his momentous visit to Syracuse in 1969.[556]

Thereafter, the school program again dissolved until Artin Boghossian arrived and brought together the children from St. Paul's and St. John's churches in a merged program in 1972–73. For about three years, a successful program was maintained. When Boghossian left Syracuse, no one stepped in to continue and the effort came to an end.

St. John: The Calendar

Having a home of their own accelerated the activities of all of the organizations associated with St. John the Baptist Armenian Apostolic Church and Community Center. For about two decades the calendar would be quickly filled with events sponsored by the ARF, ARS, AYF, church, school, and social groups that came into being for a short time then disappeared. For many years there was an event or a program of some kind—even Bingo parties or open house for playing cards or backgammon—almost every week on Friday or Saturday evenings or on Sunday afternoons, often following church services.

A women's auxiliary was never formed, despite Eliza Sachaklian's frequent requests. Members of the ARS and a few other volunteers always came forward to prepare refreshments and dinners in association with church activities. As the workers were, on the whole, the same individuals, there did not seem to be any need to form another organization.

The trustees took responsibility for arranging receptions and dinners on the occasion of visits from high-level clergy, on Christmas and Easter, and the annual dinner dance. The annual membership meeting, usually held in September, was also an important entry on the calendar of events.

553. Minutes, February 6, 1965.
554. *Hairenik Weekly,* November 23, 1967, p. 5.
555. Text of her report in Sachaklian collection.
556. *Hairenik,* June 28, 1969.

For about fifteen years, beginning in 1964, the new year would be launched with a New Year's Eve party, sometimes with a live band, under the sponsorship of the board of trustees. On one occasion, at the initiative of a few members, it was decided that a committee composed of members of both St. John's and St. Paul's churches would sponsor the New Year's Eve event. The venture was successful, but short-lived. The New Year's Eve party had been customarily one of the money-making ventures for the Armenian Community Center and some members objected to the loss of revenue resulting from joint sponsorship. Attendance began to drop and at the trustees meeting of November 18, 1979, it was decided to discontinue the New Year's Eve party.

During the earlier period, St. John's parish frequently observed Christmas on or near the traditional date of January 6. In recent years, however, Father Megerdichian scheduled Christmas services for the third Sunday in December. It was his custom to come to Syracuse for Palm Sunday services and to remain in Troy for Easter.

February is the month of Vartanantz, the commemoration of St. Vartan, Armenia's ancient hero who died resisting Persian efforts to forcibly convert Armenians from their Christian faith. Although Vartanantz has become an event on the religious calendar, the ARF honors it as a reminder that resistance is preferable to subjugation. There has been no public celebration of Vartanantz in Syracuse for many years.

Certain commemorative dates and activities had become so closely associated with the organizations that it was customary to reserve certain months for such activities. At one time, ARF commemoration of the February Revolution was never overlooked. This was the revolt of 1921 which briefly drove out Soviet forces from Armenia. The rebellion was provoked by Communist betrayal of the terms of surrender in the November 1920 treaty by which leaders of the Armenian Republic transferred power to Soviet forces. The incoming Bolsheviks immediately imprisoned Armenia's leaders and were beginning to kill them when the rebellion opened the gates and released the prisoners.

Year after year, the ritual programs would adhere to the customary format of speeches, songs, and fund-raising. There were always greetings from ARS and AYF representatives, which would be reciprocated by the ARF when those organizations sponsored programs. At ARF events one would inevitably hear the prediction that tyranny is not eternal and will end some day, and Armenians will again attain freedom with the Tricolor flying over Mount Ararat (the national symbol which, ironically, lies just beyond the border in Turkey). How the old-timers would have rejoiced that Armenia has indeed regained its independence, however precarious the circumstances, and that the Tricolor is again the national flag and that "Mer Hairenik" is again Armenia's national anthem.

The ARF program of February 25, 1962, adhered to the general pattern for such events. Following a dinner at which the invocation was given by Rev. Torkom Hagopian, the meeting convened. Father Hagopian and veteran ARF member (meaning that he was a long-term member) Aaron H. Sachaklian presided. Chairman Maurice Topalian made opening remarks on the significance of the February 18 revolt and asked the audience to stand for a moment of silence to honor those who were killed by the Communists in the Armenian prisons and in battle during the rebellion. Recitations were given by misses Telian, Minasian, and Armanian, after which Anna Markarian, accompanying herself, sang "Varte" ("The Rose"), an old favorite, receiving strong applause. ARS president Siranoush Minasian made a few remarks as did the pastor. Again Chairman Topalian spoke, stressing the necessity of sacrifice on behalf of the only organization to defend the Armenian cause, the ARF. Fund-raising was initiated with a $100 gift sent by the veteran member Abraham Kevorkian, one of the donors of the land on which the community center was built. He regretted that recent illness did not allow him to attend. The audience expressed appreciation with great applause. At the conclusion of fund-raising, a sum of $1,200 had been collected.[557] Customarily, ARF committees were assessed obligatory amounts to be sent to headquarters in Boston. Amounts raised in public offerings helped to satisfy those quotas.

The ARF program of March 9, 1963, in remembrance of the February Rebellion opened with singing "Mer Hairenik." The chairman and main speaker of the day, Maurice Topalian, requested the audience to stand for a moment of silence in remembrance of newly deceased Catholicos Zareh and two national literary figures, Aram Sahagian and Kourken Mekhitarian. The chairman centered his remarks on the sufferings of the Catholicos who, despite shameful and unseemly attacks made on him during his short reign by Catholicos Vazgen at Etchmiadzin, was able to reestablish the American parishes after their abandonment by Etchmiadzin. He then gave a brief summary of the events of the February rebellion, after which he remarked on the significance of the *Hairenik* Press, on behalf of which contributions were received. Entertainment and refreshments were not offered, in respect to the memory of the deceased Catholicos.[558]

The ARF sponsored a memorable program on March 30, 1974, with the reenactment of "The Trial of Solomon Tehlerian," the assassin of the chief planner of the Armenian genocide, Talaat Pasha. Ara Jeknavorian prepared and directed the performance.[559]

---

557. *Hairenik,* 1962, clipping in Sachaklian collection.

558. Reference was to Catholicos Zareh; *Hairenik,* 1963, clipping in Sachaklian collection.

The Syracuse Armenian Relief Society, 1959.

In years past, April 24, Armenian Memorial Day, was always observed with a requiem service, if church services happened to be scheduled on or near the date, followed by a commemorative program. The program was always the same: speakers, appearances by ARF, ARS, and AYF representatives, songs, recitations. On rare occasions the two communities would come together for a joint observance.

It was customary for the ARS to celebrate its anniversary with a formal program sometime in the spring. The programs rarely carried any surprises, but occasionally speakers brought from out of town provided up-to-date news on the status of Armenian communities abroad, especially those in the Middle East in which the ARS maintained special interest. Whenever possible, the members preferred to feature a woman guest speaker. Several accomplished ARS leaders visited Syracuse over the years. Mrs. K. Ganayan, wife of the military hero General Dro, was the featured speaker on March 13, 1959. Stella Sachaklian Rustigian, member of the ARS Central Executive and former Syracusan, spoke on March 5, 1961. Arpi Papazian, member of the ARS Central Executive and a driving force in the work of ANCHA, the agency that had resettled displaced Armenians, appeared on March 15, 1964.[560]

The focus of the programs remained faithfully on the mission of the ARS, which was to provide humanitarian aid to the Armenian needy without discrimination (meaning that no political favoritism would be shown), and to facilitate Armenian education. Over the years, great needs constantly opened

559.*Armenian Weekly,* May 23, 1974.
560.Invitations and text of a news report in Sachaklian collection.

up wherever Armenians lived, especially in the large communities in Lebanon and Syria. It was the ARS that rose up in support of the ANCHA refugee resettlement program and again the ARS that came to the aid of Armenians in Lebanon caught in the middle of a civil war in which they refused to take sides. The Armenians claimed a neutral position, arguing that Lebanon had given them sanctuary and they could not take up arms against any people who had befriended them. They suffered anyway, in the undiscriminating devastation that took place. In response to directives from the central executive, the Syracuse ARS chapter made an urgent appeal for funds.

The celebration of May 28, commemorating the establishment of the Armenian Republic, usually dominated the month of May, but sometimes Mother's Day programs took place earlier in the month, often on a Sunday after church services. In the earlier years, this was a suitable occasion for children to perform.

The Syracuse ARF committee observed May 28 with great ceremony, invariably inviting a guest speaker from out of town for a formal program, which also included songs, recitations, greetings from ARS and AYF representatives, ending with a buffet or, at least, refreshments and the traditional ceremony of lighting candles on the cake for fund-raising. The entire program for the ARF celebration on May 20, 1972, of Armenian Independence Day was provided by ARF members from several Canadian committees.[561]

From the 1960s to at least May 1980, a delegation would visit City Hall each year to receive the proclamations of the mayors in commemoration of the historic event and to attend the raising of the Tricolor of Independent Armenia to fly over City Hall for two days. As the years passed, Mayor Lee Alexander remarked on the declining numbers in the Armenian delegation attending the flag-raising ceremonies.[562]

A twenty-voice choir under the direction of Hagop Melkonian representing the St. John's Armenian community (described then as consisting of 150 citizens) participated in local activities in observance of Captive Nations Week in 1963. The event was dedicated to the more than one third of the world's population which "still lives under Communist despotism." [563]

Of course, summers could not be allowed to pass without the regulation picnic, usually with the men being assigned to the work of buying and cutting

---

561. Notice in Sachaklian collection.

562. An article in *Hairenik,* June 19, 1963 made reference to the raising of the flag at Syracuse City Hall on May 25 and 26; minutes of May 7, 1980; clippings from Syracuse newspapers in Sachaklian collection.

563. Captive Nations Week Observance, Syracuse, N.Y. July 14 through 21, 1963. Program in Sachaklian collection.

the meat for shish kebab, while the ladies prepared rice pilaf, salad, corn, and watermelon. As the younger people came along, their demands for hamburgers and hot dogs had to be met. Sodas and beer were generally available, but Armenians are not heavy beer-drinkers. During the early years of the Armenian Community Center, it was often the ARF that sponsored the summer picnic.

As the generations changed, certain historical events began to fade from memory. The Khanasor Expedition, such an exciting landmark for the older generation, used to be observed by the ARF during the picnic season, complete with speakers brought from out of town for the occasion and the prominent display of the Tricolor. As years went on, the event became lost in the haze of history and was dropped from the commemorative calendar.

The blessing of the grapes, a religious observance held in August, is also a tradition of the past. Picnics at St. John's Church now are simple affairs, held in the back yard of the Armenian Community Center under sponsorship of the trustees, devoid of any historical or religious significance.

It has been tradition, since the opening of the Armenian Community Center, to reserve October for the annual dinner dance. During the early years, crowds in excess of one hundred and fifty could be expected. It was possible then to hire help to cook and to serve. There was always a tug of war over the question of the band. Should it be one for American or Armenian music? Ballroom dancing or Armenian circle dancing? An Armenian band had to be brought from out of town, entailing extra expense. Sometimes a compromise was reached by having an American band with Armenian dance music played on tapes during the breaks. A Greek band was a novelty on a few occasions.[564] The matter was settled by 1987, when it became no longer economically feasible to hire a live band. Now it is necessary to use tapes for today's dancing, sometimes including line dancing as well as Armenian dance music, in order to accommodate the many non-Armenians who have attended in recent years. Volunteers do the food preparation and cooking and, if professional waitresses have not been hired, the few young people are sometimes enlisted for serving. In such cases it is not unusual for a guest occasionally to get up and go into the kitchen to refill the coffee pots and then to serve a table or two. The enthusiastic crowds of yesteryear are now memories.

In earlier years, October also used to be the month to celebrate ARF day, but in the St. John's calendar November was set aside for that event. Often ARF leaders would come from out of town to inform and invigorate the faithful and to reassure them that their cause was still just. The speakers were sometimes functionaries of the party, editors of the *Hairenik*, or field workers. As

---

564. Invitations in the Sachaklian collection provide dates and names of dance bands.

time passed, more and more civilians and prominent ARF leaders from other communities were pressed into service. The format of the observance adhered to tradition: songs, recitations, formal greetings from the ARS and AYF, and fund-raising. There was special cause to celebrate at the gathering on December 1, 1973. Four new ARF members took their oath.

The AYF made its presence known by sponsoring occasional dances and programs, and by offering congratulatory greetings at ARF and ARS events, as AYF president James Menasian did in 1963 on the ARF program observing Armenian Independence.[565] Yet, the generation that enjoyed the facilities of the Armenian Community Center never achieved the vigor of the members of the earlier era. Their activities tended to feature dances and social affairs. The Syracuse chapter announced a reorganization in 1967[566] and managed to offer a series of annual dances from 1968 through 1976, but despite enlisting nine new members in 1974, the vitality of the organization seemed to be ebbing.[567] The community responded generously to the AYF National Fund drive and donations of $1,200 were reported in 1975.[568] On January 17, 1976, the Syracuse AYF celebrated the forty-third anniversary of the organization's founding with entertainment, speakers, and buffet dinner after the program.[569] Despite these efforts, the zest of the earlier years was gone. After 1976, the Syracuse Navasard AYF chapter faded quickly from existence.

Special Events

In addition to the customary activities of the organizations associated with the Armenian Community Center, the trustees occasionally sponsored a lecture on an interesting subject or a special event.

In 1975, Dr. Yervant Terzian, astronomer at Cornell University, spoke on the possibility of life elsewhere in the universe.[570] In 1976, all were intrigued by Lila Piper's demonstration on handwriting and what it reveals about character.[571] Occasionally individuals would show slides of trips abroad and sometimes Armenian films would be brought from out of town for showing. Bingo games attracted participants of all ages for a while through the 1960s and early 1970s.

---

565. *Hairenik,* June 19, 1963.
566. *Armenian Weekly,* September 7, 1967, p. 7; October 12, 1967, p. 7.
567. Text of news report, February 2, 1974, Sachaklian collection.
568. *Armenian Weekly,* November 27, 1975, p. 5.
569. Invitation in Sachaklian collection.
570. *Armenian Weekly,* April 3, 1975, p. 7.
571. Invitation in Mesrobian collection.

On one occasion I read a student paper I had prepared on "Soviet Policy Toward the Armenian Apostolic Church." It attracted several members of St. Paul's community, including an individual with particularly strong antipathy toward the ARF. Following the talk, someone asked her what she thought. She dismissed it saying, "There was nothing we had not heard before."

It was an ambitious effort for the small St. John's community to sponsor a benefit concert featuring Eduard Gulabyan, who had moved recently to Syracuse to become principal cellist with the Syracuse Symphony Orchestra. The concert, with Calvin Custer at the piano, was held at the Carrier Theater in the Civic Center on April 27, 1980.[572] Press reviews of the performance were warmly favorable. Mr. Gulabyan and his wife both emigrated to the United States from the Soviet Union. A native of Erevan, Armenia, Gulabyan received his Ph.D. in music at the Tchaikovsky Conservatory in Moscow where he studied with Rostropovich. For fifteen years he had played as a soloist throughout the Soviet Union.

The schism that divided the Armenian people more than sixty years ago interrupted social and community interchange, but for a while a few individuals made occasional displays of good will by attending services or functions at the rival church. Among them were Eliza Sachaklian of St. John's and Araxi Khanzadian, Takouhi Kalebdjian, and Mr. and Mrs. Edward Adourian of St. Paul's. Few others followed their lead, however, and today there is practically no interchange.

The warm familial social relationships of the pre-break years were never restored, although at one time some of the older women, many of them friends from a happier era, occasionally gathered for dinners and lunches. Members of the Aintab Compatriotic Society attended a fund-raising party given by Mr. and Mrs. George Arslanian in 1972 to benefit Nor Aintab (New Aintab) in Soviet Armenia. Present were four members of the Adourian family, three Vartanian, one Sachaklian, two Arslanian. Mrs. Sachaklian was a St. John's member, but she maintained a friendly relationship with the Adourians and the Arslanians, who belonged to St. Paul's. Most of the people from that period as well as the Aintab Compatriotic Society are gone now, and similar group social events no longer take place.

From time to time an opportunity for a cooperative venture involving the two churches would present itself or a volunteer would initiate negotiations with a specific goal in view. Most often it was the observance of April 24, Armenian Memorial Day, that prompted such initiatives. It was never clear, however, on what basis this could be accomplished.

572.Concert notice in Mesrobian collection.

It had been reported at the St. John's trustees meeting of April 1, 1964, that the parish council of St. Paul's church had refused the proposal of St. John's trustees that the two parishes come together for a memorial service. However, as noted earlier, in 1965 St. Paul's pastor, Rev. Paren Avedikian, succeeded in arranging for a joint commemoration, if not a service, but only after extensive preliminaries.

The January 1965 minutes of St. John's board of trustees reported receipt of a letter from the St. Paul's pastor suggesting that the two churches meet "at a neutral location" to make plans for a joint observance of the fiftieth anniversary of the Armenian genocide. The board agreed, but suggested alternating meetings between the two churches.[573] Apparently discussions progressed amicably and agreement was reached to have a joint church service at 10 a.m. at St. Paul's and the program at 5 p.m. at the Armenian Community Center.[574] At the next meeting it was announced that joint church services were blocked by St. Paul's parish council who advised that this was not permitted by "their —."[575] The minutes do not identify. Could it have been their primate? This problem, too was resolved. During the month of April the doors of both St. John's and St. Paul's Armenian churches were draped in black in memory of the more than one million Armenian dead. On Sunday morning, April 25, requiem services were held in each church. A memorial program brought both communities together in the afternoon at the Armenian Community Center hall. There were more than two hundred persons present.[576]

The ambitious program included sixteen items. All sang the "Hair Mer" ("Lord's Prayer") and the "Star Spangled Banner" at the opening. Rev. Paren Avedikian gave the welcoming address and balance was achieved by having Rev. Movses Shirikian, St. John's pastor, give the closing address. There were songs by a choral group, solos, and recitations. John Terry, State Assemblyman from Onondaga County, issued a proclamation, and guest speakers Hrair Dekmejian, Professor of Political Science at Harpur College, Rabbi Benjamin Friedman, and Arthur Giragosian from Providence who spoke in Armenian, were heard. The local press took note of the event, with news items and photos in both newspapers. As always, Armenians prepared for fund-raising. The community raised $1,378.19 on the occasion, whose purpose has not been recorded.[577]

---

573. Minutes, January 14, 1965.
574. Ibid., February 16, 1965.
575. Ibid., March 9, 1965.
576. Syracuse newspaper April 26, 1965, clipping in Sachaklian collection.
577. Ibid.

A few years later, April 24, 1969, a newcomer to the city, Edward Adourian, a member of St. Paul's church, succeeded in arranging a united observance that took place in the Armenian Community Center. John Markarian presided, Dr. Sarkis Khanzadian sang, Zarmair Taft spoke, and Araxi Khanzadian recited.[578] None of these people were members of St. John's parish. A member of St. John's community, Samuel Hagopian, was one of the speakers at St. Paul's Memorial Day observance on April 25, 1971, although the event was not jointly sponsored by the two churches. Yet, at an ARS day program, March 17, 1974, while making brief remarks on the occasion, Rev. Zareh Maronian added that he had approached St. Paul's to propose that the two churches jointly commemorate April 24. Their parish council refused bluntly, saying that they would have nothing to do with members of the Cilician See.[579]

A new approach was chosen for the sixty-third anniversary commemoration. In addition to a memorial observance that brought together the two communities in the hall of the Armenian Community Center on Sunday afternoon, April 23, 1978, the two groups presented half a dozen books on Armenian history, culture, and cuisine to the Onondaga County Public Library. The news item does not identify the two parishes, but those acquainted with the three individuals in the accompanying photograph recognize this to be a unified gesture.[580]

Perhaps the most ambitious commemorative observance was the multi-level, week-long series of events carried out in 1975 on the occasion of the six-tieth anniversary of the genocide. Under the skillful guidance of Ara Jeknavorian, chairman, and Artin Boghossian, treasurer, two young men recently arrived from out of town, a committee of twenty-five individuals was formed. I served as secretary. Planning started in early February.

A film made by Bruce MacCurdy (the husband of an Armenian, Marian Mesrobian) called *The Invisible Genocide*, shown on Sunday morning, April 20, on WCNY, the local public broadcasting station, kicked off the week. It was followed that afternoon by a dinner at the Armenian Community Center and a lecture by Dr. Vahakn Dadrian, Professor of Sociology at State University of New York at Geneseo, a specialist on genocide. On Monday, Professor Dadrian discussed the Armenian genocide on "Extension 24" on WCNY. He spoke again that evening on the Syracuse University campus, under the sponsorship of the Armenian Club of Syracuse University. On Thursday, a public rally was held at the Soldiers' and Sailors' Monument on Clinton Square with

---

578. Eliza Sachaklian's report in Sachaklian collection.
579. Ibid.
580. *Syracuse Herald-American,* April 23, 1978.

the mayor and other officials in attendance, where Armenian representatives placed a wreath in memory of the 1915 victims of genocide. The mayor issued a proclamation commemorating the occasion.

The committee even prepared letters to school principals explaining the significance of the events of the week and requesting that Armenian school children be excused from school on Thursday in order to attend the rally and wreath-laying at Clinton Square.

The following Sunday an audience of at least two hundred people, including many from outlying areas, gathered at the Liverpool Country Club for a special commemorative program. The guest speaker, Professor Vartan Gregorian, was then Dean of the School of Arts and Sciences and head of Armenian studies at the University of Pennsylvania. He later held several positions of great distinction, among them President of Brown University.

After summarizing the historical events that were being recalled, Professor Gregorian stated that "the group was not recalling the slaughter for the sake of Armenians alone, but for all those who have died and will die because the world forgot the Armenian massacre." Another speaker, State Senator Martin S. Auer, observed that the only good thing resulting from the Armenian genocide may have been bringing "you people to these shores, giving us an opportunity to share in your great heritage."[581]

Nothing as ambitious has been attempted since the sixtieth anniversary event in 1975, but joint programs have taken place sporadically since then. The most recent observance under the sponsorship of the two churches was on April 24, 1995, at the Armenian Community Center, with their respective board chairmen, Angele Khanzadian and Arpena Mesrobian, acting as co-chairmen of the day.[582]

The program offered no surprises. A piano solo by Ara Airapetian was followed by a talk by Dr. Levon Airapetian from Armenia, postdoctoral associate at the State University of New York Health Science Center. There was a memorial ceremony by candlelight and group singing of the Lord's Prayer in Armenian, then a few closing words by Mrs. Khanzadian.

The audience was attentive, but far greater interest was shown in a guest in the audience. Suzanne Burns, a Syracuse University graduate student, had recently returned to Syracuse from a brief stay in eastern Turkey. Her articles on her experiences as an English teacher at Erzerum University had appeared in the local newspaper.[583] Miss Burns had been forced to leave the country

---

581.*Syracuse Post-Standard,* April 28, 1975; notes, copies of letters, clippings, other materials in Mesrobian collection.

582.Program in Mesrobian collection.

583.*Syracuse Herald-American,* April 2 and 3, 1995.

hurriedly because of the hostility demonstrated toward her when she was suspected of harboring sympathy for Kurds. There were so many questions for Miss Burns that following the close of the formal program she was invited to stand and talk about her experiences.

It is interesting to note that observances commemorating the genocide invariably attract Armenians with no involvement in Armenian community affairs, often Armenian women married to non-Armenians. The genocide seems to be the one observance that can bring the Armenian people together.

Through the initiative of Nevart Apikian, for several years volunteers from St. Paul's and St. John's communities came forward to lend an Armenian presence to the Festival of Nations, presented annually over a November weekend by the Syracuse Cultural Resources Council. Bringing the group together initially was not a simple process. Miss Apikian remembered that the representatives of the two communities met at least three times at a "neutral" site, the home of Missak and Virginia Kalebdjian, to battle over the question of which flag would fly over the exhibit. It was eventually agreed that the Tricolor, as the flag of the first republic, had historic relevance. Finally, it was decided to design and display flags of various periods in Armenian history.

Even though it strained their limited treasuries as well as manpower resources to the limit, the committee managed to present attractive, well-mounted exhibits, train their young people to perform Armenian dances, prepare Armenian delicacies for sale at the booth, and offer a display of Armenian books, maps, and photographs.

Their initial exhibit in 1970 featured historic Armenian costumes on life-sized manikins. The costumes had been made by Surpouhi Hamasdegh of Boston as a project for the ARS and had been brought to Syracuse for display at the festival.[584]

In 1973, the Armenian exhibit centered around handmade models of three famous Armenian architectural monuments: St. Hripsime Church, the Church of St. Gregory, and the Haghpat Bell Tower. The models, made of synthetic marble, were created by Manoog George Boyadjian of Hickory Hills, Illinois, who brought his handwork to Syracuse by car in order to spare them the hazards of shipment. A two-page handout explained the architectural significance of the structures.[585]

In 1974, the featured exhibit was a model of the monument erected in Armenia to commemorate the historic Battle of Sardarabad. Each year the usual argument over the flag display would take place. St. Paul's people objected to the Tricolor of the Armenian Republic, but the hammer and sickle

584. *Hairenik,* March 12, 1971.
585. *Syracuse Herald-American,* November 4, 1973; notes in Mesrobian collection.

was unacceptable to both groups. Finally, when the Sardarabad monument was displayed, it was agreed to show the Tricolor, because, as Nevart Apikian argued persuasively, it was the victory at Sardarabad that led to the establishment of the Armenian Republic. And it was the Republic that gave Armenia identity as a nation.[586]

While there may have been a little grumbling over the distribution of the work, the experience of working together on the successful Festival of Nations projects was generally viewed favorably by participants on both sides. Once the arguments over the flag had been thoroughly exhausted, committee members fell into their customary roles from year to year and worked together efficiently and cooperatively. The proposal to hold a joint New Year's Eve party sprang from this group. But the end was already near. The aging of some members and losses of manpower depleted the ranks, forcing the Armenians to withdraw from participation in the Festival of Nations.

The initiative of Artin Boghossian, the Syracuse University graduate student whose enterprise produced a united school for the two communities, also led in other directions. He played a part in the formation of an organization for Armenian students and faculty at Syracuse University. John Harootunian, majoring in law, and Richard Tashjian, a third-year architecture student, examined the Syracuse University directory and made a list of all names ending in "ian," which characteristically identifies an Armenian name.[587] A membership list dated March 1973 identifies an astounding number of them—forty-seven.[588] Boghossian encouraged the group and served as its cultural chairman. The club owed its vitality to its founders. When they left Syracuse, the club dissolved.

Boghossian was also the inspiration for a mini course offered at Syracuse University during the fall 1973 semester. Entitled "Selected Topics in Armenian History and Culture," the course carried one credit hour and had no language prerequisite. Dr. James Powell of the History Department served as faculty sponsor. The course was planned by myself as academic coordinator. Boghossian, as course coordinator, secured funding and handled arrangements. The series of eight lectures was open to the public, giving Syracusans an unparalleled opportunity to hear eight of the most distinguished leaders in Armenian studies from institutions of higher learning in the United States and Canada.[589] The best student paper to result from the course, in my opinion,

---

586. Notes in Mesrobian collection.
587. *Armenian Weekly*, May 3, 1973, reprinted from the Syracuse University student newspaper, *Daily Orange*.
588. Mesrobian collection.
589. *Armenian Weekly*, November 1, 1973, p. 3.

was one on Armenian literature written by a non-Armenian girl with no prior acquaintance with Armenian studies.

The Armenian Students Association has had a curious history in Syracuse. While it refuses to die, neither has it summoned the vigor to maintain continuous activity. After a brief revival in 1946–47, it again fell dormant. In 1958 it was taken under the wing of the Troy, New York branch, whose leader at the time was Toros Shamlian. Active Syracuse members were Charles Koolakian, Robert Koolakian, Richard Roomian, Zarmair Taft, Robert Chengerian. No one from St. John's community was associated with the ASA at this time. After reorganization, the Syracuse branch came briefly to life in 1962–63 and lapsed again into inactivity until another reorganization in the fall of 1982 under the leadership of Robert Koolakian, who has been a member of the Central Executive. The branch was rechartered the "Greater Syracuse and Central New York ASA" with an inaugural event attended by more than one hundred twenty-five local participants as well as by members of the Central Executive Committee.[590] For the next several years, the ASA sponsored numerous social events and lectures given by speakers brought from out of town and held at Syracuse University. No local activities have taken place under ASA sponsorship for at least six years.

No one who attended the exciting concert given in Rochester on March 8, 1968, by the renowned Armenian composer, Aram Khachadourian, will forget the occasion. The event attracted throngs of Armenians from Syracuse, Niagara Falls, Troy, and elsewhere. Barbara Hagopian, president of the Syracuse ARS, arranged for bus transportation and an enthusiastic group of more than fifty Armenians from both of the Syracuse communities formed part of an audience of three thousand for a memorable evening. At a reception after the concert, Khachadourian greeted his Armenian compatriots with warmth and affection. He thanked them and said, "Do not forget your *hairenik* (fatherland), your language, church, culture, and heritage. My music doesn't belong to me alone. It belongs to the Armenian nation. Be in peace with one another."[591]

Most members of the diasporan community, whether pro- or vigorously anti-Soviet, were greatly interested in Armenia. As the Cold War subsided, Armenians from America, among them Syracusans, were encouraged to travel to Armenia for sight-seeing or educational purposes. One of the earliest travelers, Harry Apikian, returned with enthusiastic praise for what he had seen.

---

590. Robert Koolakian, "History: Armenian Students' Association of America, Inc., Greater Syracuse & Central New York."
591. *Hairenik Weekly,* March 28, 1968, p. 5.

In 1966, Vincent (Zarmig) Taft, son of Zarmair, enrolled at the University of Erevan for a formal course of postgraduate study. It had been his intention to focus on comparative education in the United States and the Soviet Union, but after the year passed he decided to change careers. Taft recalled that he was the only Armenian student from America that year, but that others preceded and followed him. He had studied Russian in the United States in preparation for his trip. He spoke conversational Armenian, but reading and writing were difficult for him. On a visit in 1985 he found that compared to the rest of the Soviet Union, Armenians were doing well.

William S. Mesrobian, from an ARF family, was another native Syracusan who went to the Soviet Union for study. He was a doctoral student in astronomy at the University of Pittsburgh in 1970, when he was invited to visit the Byurakan Observatory in Armenia. He recalled the experience with great pleasure.

In later years, other Syracusans also made the pilgrimage to a fatherland that most of them had never before seen. Among them was Eliza Sachaklian, the grandmother of William Mesrobian, who was in her eighties when she traveled there to attend the opening of a lace factory in Nor Aintab, to which she had made her contribution as a member of the Syracuse branch of the Aintab Compatriotic Society. Her opposition to Communism did not in the least detract from her praise for the country's accomplishments.

Armenians may be quarrelsome, but they do, at least, come together in times of national need. The news of the disastrous earthquake centered in Leninakan, Armenia, on December 7, 1988, caused anxiety and concern among all Armenian communities. In Syracuse, the immediate response was the urge to help. Both St. Paul's and St. John's communities began the solicitation of funds and clothing. While television and newspaper reporters scurried to find Armenians to interview, Armenians issued announcements through the media informing the public where they could direct donations of money and clothing.

St. Paul's Church cancelled a Fun Night that had been scheduled for January 7, 1989, ordered a forty-day period of mourning, and held requiem services for the dead. The two churches came together to announce a dance sponsored by AHEPA Chapter #37, a Greek organization, to be held on February 25, 1989, at St. Sophia's Greek Orthodox Church, with all proceeds to be donated to the Armenian Earthquake Fund.

The Armenian Community Center became the collection point for huge mounds of donated clothing. Volunteers struggled for days to sort and box the articles for shipment to New York City. A trucking company provided a truck for delivery to a central warehouse in New York. The two churches collected more than six hundred fifty boxes of items.[592]

St. John's Church received contributions of about $8,000 which was immediately sent to the Prelacy office in New York and added to the general emergency fund. It proved to be much more difficult to transport the clothing. The rush of aid to Armenia apparently overtaxed the Erevan airport facilities to such an extent that long delays impeded delivery of needed supplies.

Soon Syracuse Armenians met the results of disaster, face to face. In February 1989 two Armenian children were brought to Syracuse on an Air Force jet for treatment of their injuries at Crouse Irving Memorial Hospital. They were among thirty-seven children brought to the United States under the auspices of Project Hope, a Washington-based nonprofit agency.[593] Both St. Paul's and St. John's communities provided interpreters. Members of the community took great interest in the two children during their long course of treatment.

Rosa Kazarian, six years of age, was accompanied by her father, Ardak. She had been trapped under rubble for three days and was suffering from crush injuries to her legs. It caused particular sorrow to all when they learned that she was not yet aware that her mother had died in the earthquake. Rosa had a lively spirit, however, as the interpreters quickly discovered. By April, she was called "the little spitfire who pinches the cheeks of American playmates and refuses to drink anything but Pepsi."[594] Rosa left in December 1989 to return to an uncertain future.

Ara Tadevosian, fourteen years of age at the time of his arrival, had suffered the loss of both limbs and required a series of operations and lengthy treatment. While still under care he attended Nottingham High School and proved to be a good student. He was released in March 1990 and sent back to Armenia.[595] But within a few months, the Syracuse Armenians were asked for contributions to pay for Ara's return to Syracuse for a new series of operations. He was growing taller and constant adjustments needed to be made, otherwise he would be forced to remain in a wheelchair for the rest of his life. An Armenian nurse in Syracuse, Arsho Vartanian, became his guardian and at the present time he is living with her. After receiving an associate's degree from Onondaga Community College, he acquired a degree in business from Le Moyne College in May 1996. About eighty people came to his graduation party at the Armenian Community Center to celebrate his achievements. Ara hopes to find a job and remain in the United States. He is a gentle, friendly, unassuming youth, much loved by everyone who knows him.

592.*Syracuse Herald-Journal,* December 15, 1988.
593.*Syracuse Post-Standard,* February 9, 1989.
594.*Syracuse Herald-Journal,* April 4, 1989.
595.Ibid., March 27, 1990.

Growth, Decline, Contributions

The Armenian community in Syracuse has had several periods of growth and decline. The first wave of immigration, starting just before the turn of the century, was dominated by young males. By the second decade, families that had been separated by travel were being reunited and new ones were beginning to form, creating the base for an active, youthful community.

After the end of the first World War, the number of Armenians in Syracuse was diminished briefly when there were some relocations to other cities. Soon, however, the community was renewed by an influx from abroad. Long-separated families were reunited, surviving relatives were welcomed, and with the arrival of brides from orphanages abroad new families were formed. Numerous marriages took place through the 1920s and early 1930s and children began to enrich the growing community.

By the early 1930s, the Armenians had overcome, to some degree, the traumas of the Turkish genocide and they looked forward to a peaceful future in a stable country. Even though one eye was always on their needy compatriots abroad, for whom they were constantly collecting funds, their prime concern was the retention of their children in the Armenian tradition. Rented quarters were not adequate for creating an Armenian atmosphere. It was imperative to have their own church and center, where the community could gather. It is likely that the Armenians in Syracuse may have numbered as many as three hundred adults at this time.

The division of the Armenian people into two communities, not only in Syracuse but everywhere in America, was a cataclysmic event. It interrupted the growing strength of the communities, it created an atmosphere of hate and destruction, it separated the young generations about whom so much concern was felt, and it presented a split image of the Armenian people before their American neighbors. With their diminished resources, it became so much more difficult to build churches, centers, schools.

Thereafter the two communities carried on independently, as they do to this day, except in very new communities without a memory of the split of the 1930s. Each had its own organizations which continued activities in the traditional manner, but disappeared as the old leaders faded away and the younger generation failed to take over. Young people's organizations, especially the Armenian Youth Federation movement, were immensely appealing for a time, even attracting those on the fringes of Armenian community life. But after a few years enthusiasm began to ebb, especially when World War II took away the young men. There was some renewal when the men returned, but by now they were adults. As the youth of both groups matured, marriages to non-Armenian spouses took place with increasing frequency, diminishing the degree of commitment to the traditional institutions. Some young adults began to take positions in Armenian community life, while others—even some with Armenian spouses—drifted into other circles.

The first leaders of St. Paul's Church were foreign-born, but that was not the case with St. John's. Of the nine members of the founding board of directors of the Armenian Community Center, five were young men born in this country. Yet, even as their enthusiasm converted the dream of their own *Hai Doon* (Armenian Home) into reality, the membership figures show that the shadow of the future had already appeared during the first decade of activity.

As early as the 1960s, St. John's community discovered that it lacked the resources needed to maintain a resident pastor, even on a part-time basis. Their building enjoyed frequent use at the time. There were numerous organizations and all were active, but it was essentially the same people who were involved in all of them—whether it was ARF, ARS, AYF, church, school—whenever attempted, or other activities.

As the community's manpower diminished, it became increasingly difficult to maintain the traditional organizations. The AYF was first to go. For several decades since the founding of the organization, frequent news items about Syracuse AYF activities could be found in the pages of the *Armenian Weekly*. After 1976, nothing more is to be seen about the Navasard chapter.

By the late 1970s, the ARF and ARS in Syracuse were themselves having difficulties. The community had diminished to the point that few people were available beyond the membership itself to attend the programs. The ARF formally dissolved in late 1983. I, as former secretary, sent the sad communication to the Central Executive announcing the end of the Syracuse Armen Garo Committee which had existed since 1913, together with the remittance of remaining funds in the amount of $303.33.[596] A few months later, the Syracuse chapter of the ARS also sent formal notice of its termination.[597] The only formal organization remaining within the St. John's community is the board of trustees of the church and community center.

Eliza Sachaklian kept continual watch over the size of the community and frequently expressed her concern over the downward trend. Her worries started very early. In a talk on October 1963, she expressed her joy that Catholicos Vazgen of Etchmiadzin and Catholicos Khoren of Cilicia had met and embraced in Jerusalem, thus ending a seven-year period of estrangement between the two sees. "Our community has begun to diminish. Let us come and bring our children so they will get used to being together. If not, they will

---

596. January 5, 1984, copy in Mesrobian collection.
597. August 8, 1984, copy in Mesrobian collection.

not know each other." She also worried about the future. The new generation does not speak Armenian and there is the problem of intermarriage.[598]

By the beginning of the 1970s, Eliza Sachaklian expressed her alarm over the losses through death and departure from the city. Speaking before a gathering on January 31, 1971, she expressed her concern: "One by one they are leaving us."[599] At St. John's Easter services on April 17, 1977, by my count, only forty adults were present. Even so, the small gathering produced a sum of $1,000 to send to needy Armenians in Lebanon.[600]

Toward the end of the 1970s the deaths and departure of several highly active members of St. John's community hastened the decline. The sudden death in 1982 of Harry Tamurian, a popular member of the ARF, the choir, and the building maintenance committee, was an especially severe blow.

St. John's treasurer, John Penirjian, began to warn that the center was operating at a deficit. At the annual membership meeting of April 8, 1978, he announced what was to become a familiar theme: were it not for donations in lieu of flowers on the occasions of deaths or donations for requiem services, the treasury would be empty. Membership was dropping due to deaths, departure from the city, loss of interest.[601]

Neighboring communities were experiencing similar decline. As early as 1971 the ARF and ARS of Binghamton reported a weakening community base. They had held three functions that year, but funds raised were not as great as in prior years because of losses due to deaths (three deaths were reported that year) and because most of the members and supporters were elderly and living on retirement incomes.[602] Rev. Zareh Maronian reported at St. John's annual meeting on March 15, 1980, that the Troy membership was also declining.

St. John's trustees minutes of January 20, 1980, record that sixty names were on a mailing list, but only forty-five members remained. At the services for December 30, 1984—Christmas services, assisting the priest were Syracuse's deacon, the organist, the soloist, and a choir of two. One of the two singers, Eliza Sachaklian, insisted on continuing out of a sense of duty, even though she was ninety-two at the time and so deaf that she could not sing in tune. Attending the services (by my actual count) were sixteen adults and two children. A few additional people arrived in time for the holiday lunch. By 1987, membership had diminished to thirty-eight.[603]

598. Text of talk in Sachaklian collection.
599. Text of talk in Sachaklian collection.
600. Notes in Mesrobian collection.
601. Membership minute book.
602. *Hairenik,* December 21, 1971.

St. John's thirtieth annual dinner dance on October 11, 1986, was probably one of its most successful events with more than one hundred thirty present, many of them from out of town. Most of the visitors were former Syracusans or relatives of Syracusans. Archbishop Mesrob Ashjian, the honored guest on the occasion, officiated at services and a baptism the next day. Since 1987, dinner dance attendance has dropped to eighty-three on November 23, 1991, and about sixty-five each year since then. The low point of fifty was reached in 1997. The numbers improve only when visitors from out of town and many non-Armenians are present. A non-Armenian friend, mother of the spouse of an Armenian, remarked to me with alarm, "What has happened to all your people?" By 1995, St. John's trustees made the following report to the Prelate, Archbishop Mesrob Ashjian:

> There are 21 households (i.e., individuals or married couples) who pay membership dues. Of the married couples, seven have non-Armenian or non-Apostolic spouses. One couple is living abroad at the present time, one lives permanently in Florida, two go regularly to Florida for six months of the year, two live out of the city, several are elderly and no longer attend church, 14 couples are retired. [604]

Over the years, the community has been enriched with the arrival of new talent—people who came to Syracuse for a time, made a place for themselves, and left a void when they departed, such as Hagop Melkonian, Ara Jeknavorian, Artin Boghossian, Samuel and Barbara Hagopian, Vartan and Victoria Mehrabian, as well as graduate students and professional people associated with Syracuse University and the State University of New York Health Science Center. A permanent gap was left with the departure of retirees Jacob and Arousiag Telian, who had been so instrumental in bringing about St. John's community center, and the popular Missak and Virginia Kalebdjian. Several families brought to Syracuse under the auspices of the ANCHA program entered into St. John's community life, then departed in search of better employment opportunities. Armenians attracted to Syracuse because of Syracuse University or the Syracuse hospitals sometimes seek out the local Armenian community. This was the case with the Meliksetian family, which was welcomed into St. John's community while Dickran Meliksetian was completing graduate work and again when he returned after a brief separation to take a teaching appointment at Syracuse University. St. Paul's parish, too, has been renewed from time to time by newcomers, such as Dr. and Mrs. Levon Airapetian from Armenia.

603.Minutes, April 12, 1987.
604.June 15, 1995, copy in church files.

As has been noted, almost every great event in Armenian life since the beginning of the twentieth century has made an impact on the life of the Syracuse Armenian community. Most recently, Armenian refugees from Azerbaijan have arrived in Syracuse. Driven out by ethnic pogroms, they fled to Armenia and then to Moscow, eventually arriving in Syracuse under the auspices of Catholic Charities. Most of them are Russian-speaking. A few of the older people spoke the eastern Armenian dialect which is unfamiliar to most Syracuse Armenians. With the aid of a member who speaks Russian, the St. John's parishioners made approaches to the newcomers and invited their participation. About a dozen of the new immigrants attended a brief candlelight service in observance of Armenian Memorial Day at St. John's in 1990. About six or eight of them attended St. John's picnic on August 18, 1991. By the following winter, about twenty-five had arrived in Syracuse. In an effort to welcome them and integrate them into the community, the Armenian Community Center invited all to a reception on February 16, 1992, in order to become acquainted and inquire as to their needs. About twenty attended. Most were young adults. The group included a few teenagers. The main desire they expressed was to learn English and find jobs. Most are educated and a few had been teachers. Within a few months, the young people were already able to converse in English.

A few of these newcomers made occasional early appearances at St. John's services and gatherings following the service, but none responded to Rev. Khachig Megerdichian's invitation to come forward to be baptized. They no longer attend church functions, not even the summer picnic which is generally the attraction of last resort. Some of them have attended services and functions at St. Paul's, but the future will show whether they choose to become active, contributing members of the Armenian community.

The Rochester community also welcomed several Armenian families from Azerbaijan, as reported in the August 28, 1992, newsletter of the Armenian Church of Rochester. The announcement invited information about job openings and apartments, and donations of home furnishings for the newcomers.

The immediate future of St. John's seems to indicate a precarious existence for a few more years. The decline in its supporting community has been especially striking during the past five years. The archdeacon has died, there are no subdeacons, and the choir has diminished to two, one of whom sometimes also serves as organist, when the regular organist (her mother) goes to Florida every winter. Most of the members are over the age of sixty and younger members are too few to maintain the building and continue regular church services, even on the limited schedule as at present. Whereas in the past, the AYF groomed a generation to move into positions of leadership in the community, several of today's members have children over the age of eighteen who have rarely attended any of the functions at the Community Center. Within the membership there are scarcely half a dozen children under the age of eighteen. They are seldom seen. Moreover, their ages are so disparate that even when attending they have nothing in common.

During recent years St. John's trustees have had to face repair and maintenance expenses for the aging building, forcing an extraordinary drive for funds which fell slightly short, necessitating withdrawal from the small reserve. Even the thirty-six-year-old organ could no longer be kept in tune and the organist donated her own instrument to the church. An appeal made in 1992 to former members and friends in distant cities brought some help. Members were asked to increase their annual pledges to the church. Dues provide about 50 percent of the annual budget of $10,000.

St. Paul's church is in relatively better circumstances. Their membership has slowly declined to about thirty, but recent newsletters report a slight increase in attendance. Their membership is not only greater than that of St. John's but is also more youthful. Moreover, the union with other churches in the area provides organizational breadth and strength. When the primate, Archbishop Khajag Barsamian, visited the parish on May 18, 1997, approximately eighty people, including about a dozen from Rochester and some from Binghamton, attended church services and a dinner in his honor.

St. Paul's finances are also in better shape. They have income from a reserve which can be used if needed to cover a deficit from operating expenses. Membership dues constituted 15.5 percent of receipts and 20.4 percent of disbursements in 1991. Only 15 percent of their 1992 budget relied on dues income. They have the manpower and good location for an annual bazaar and a two-day summer picnic that brings in substantial income from the neighborhood. Yet for them, too, the needs require constant sacrifice. A few years ago they conducted a successful drive for funds to renovate their aging building. They no longer maintain a resident pastor, although services are held twice a month, rather than ten times a year as at St. John's. The community's political organizations, societies, and youth groups are gone and even the AGBU disappeared fifteen or more years ago. However, a strong parish council and Women's Guild remain. In sharp contrast to St. John's, St. Paul's strives to offer a varied program of social and educational activities for adults as well as children and youth. After a hiatus, Armenian language classes were reinstated and efforts are being made to offer Sunday School instruction. A newly formed Cultural Committee plans to present programs featuring Armenian culture and traditions. The secretary of this committee is a young man from Armenia, the husband of a non-Armenian young woman from Syracuse whom he met while she was serving in the Peace Corps in Armenia. It is interesting to hear them converse in the eastern Armenian dialect.

The drop in numbers in the Syracuse Armenian community may perhaps be explained by the deaths of the foreign-born generation, the departure of those seeking large Armenian communities elsewhere, the general population drift away from New York State to the south and southwest, the disappearance of the large manufacturing centers like the General Electric Company that once employed thousands of people, and the diminished employment opportunities in Central New York.

The actual figures suggest a different interpretation, however. The 1952 AGBU directory of Syracuse Armenians listed 149 household addresses. By 1968–69, there were 187 households.[605] A listing prepared in 1973 identified 218 households.[606] In February 1975, St. Paul's newsletter reported that 216 Armenian families were found in an examination of the Syracuse telephone book. St. Paul's Twenty-fifth Anniversary booklet of 1983 listed 267 names, including non-Armenian spouses. Since then, there has been some decline, although the numbers are still better than in 1952. There were two hundred households in the combined mailing lists of St. Paul's and St. John's churches in 1993. On the basis of numbers alone, the community appears to be large enough to sustain the activities of yesteryear. What is lacking today, however, is the interest. By my count, barely one hundred families show any interest in the activities of either of the two churches. Even fewer attend regularly.

Community decline and disappearance is not a new story in Armenian life. For many centuries, the wandering Armenians have traveled the world over in search of a permanent resting place, only to uproot themselves again when driven away by hostile forces or when better opportunities beckoned. In the course of their travels, however, they invariably contributed to their environments, whether through physical structures that remained behind after their departure or through generations of productive builders and innovators.

Perhaps because their troubled history has taught adaptability, Armenians have always shown remarkable ability not only to adjust to the environments into which fate has flung them, but to make major contributions to their new worlds. A commentator on Armenian-American life has observed,

> As a people, the Armenians have achieved prominence in almost every facet of American life and the percentage of Armenians who have made their marks in the various American professions,

---

605. *1968–1969 Telephone Directory for the Armenians of Syracuse and Binghamton*, prepared by Rev. Maronian.

606. *Commemorative Telephone Directory of the Capital District, Syracuse, Binghamton, Utica, New York*, prepared by Rev. Maronian.

industries and trades is stunningly higher than the percentage . . . they represent of the total American demography.[607]

Syracuse Armenians, too, have made outstanding contributions to American life. The national ethic teaches hard work, diligence, respect for law. I am not aware of a single Syracuse Armenian over the one hundred-year history of the community who has been arrested or convicted on any charge, let alone a serious one. On the contrary, all have been good citizens and some have excelled in their chosen fields, while continuing to identify themselves with the Armenian community. Following are just a few examples: the remarkable H. B. Azadian, inventor and manufacturer; John Terzian, engineer; Aaron H. Sachaklian, one of the earliest individuals to receive certification from the State of Connecticut as a Certified Public Accountant; Arshag Sarkissian, librarian at the Library of Congress; John Enfiejian, Jr., chosen at age nineteen to accompany a Syracuse University scientific expedition to Venezuela because of his skills in taxidermy; Archie S. Ajemian, owner of a prominent beauty shop then developer of the Liverpool Golf and Public Country Club, now run by his two sons; Harry A. Sachaklian (Aaron's son), career Air Force officer who retired at the rank of Colonel and then became a successful stock broker in Washington, D.C.; Edward Kochian (grandson of Abraham Nigolian, a pioneer from Divrig), deputy county executive of Onondaga County; Eduard Gulabyan, from Soviet Armenia, principal cellist of the Syracuse Symphony Orchestra; Nevart Apikian, now semi-retired, entertainment editor of the *Syracuse Post-Standard;* Garbis Garboushian, formerly Director of Engineered Products at Carrier Corporation; Ardag Adourian, who at age seventeen became recipient of Mayor Tom Young's first Community Youth Service Award. Three of Araxi Khanzadian's children achieved prominence in their chosen careers. Sarkis, whose life was tragically cut short, was a dentist, fulfilling his father's ambition. Vahan has established himself as an opera singer, having performed at the Metropolitan Opera, and Anita made a career as an actress and director.

In addition, there are those of Armenian descent who no longer identify themselves with the Armenian community, but who have made substantial contributions to American life, such as George H. Babikian (grandson of Mihran Babikian), who was president of ARCO Products in Los Angeles, numerous doctors in Syracuse, and, from time to time, members of the Syracuse University faculty.

Whether or not a Syracuse Armenian community will exist through the next one hundred years cannot be foreseen, but it may be safe to assume that

---

607. Vahe Oshagan in *Armenian Weekly,* January 21, 1984, p. 3.

the descendants of the refugees from Turkish persecution and from inhospitable environments elsewhere who found sanctuary in upstate New York will continue to enrich the land that became their home.

The Future

Would the Syracuse Armenian community have been in a stronger position today had the schism of long ago never taken place? While conjecture on an alternate future is futile, it seems safe to assume that a united community would certainly have been better able to resist the inroads of aging, departure, and alienation.

Does the current estrangement make sense any more, if it ever did? Members of the two parishes range in intensity of commitment to the old positions from open-minded to hard-line. A few from each parish have shown willingness to attend an occasional event sponsored by the other parish, while some from both parishes may not ever have attended a function at the other church or hall, with the possible exception of an occasional mandatory funeral or a carefully negotiated memorial observance. Meanwhile, social and compatriotic ties have loosened and individual relationships are not as close as they were in earlier years.

If the community should, by some means, reunite, would this ensure a longer and stronger Armenian identity in Syracuse? Cooperation as a community—not as a church, which was prohibited by orders from the primate of the Etchmiadzin church in New York City—allowed certain ventures to be carried out from time to time, although the tension of the estrangement prevented deep roots ever from forming. Often, these activities attracted those on the fringes of Armenian community life, as well as members of the two parishes. One considers how much more could have been accomplished had cooperation been encouraged by the church leaders. Diocesan refusal to recognize the churches under the Prelacy was a constant reminder of the schism and an effective barrier to the possible quiet merger of the smaller parishes.

Unexpected and dramatic changes on the broad Armenian landscape offer new opportunities. With the collapse of the Soviet Union in 1991, Armenia has reclaimed its independence, the flag of the 1918 Republic, and its national anthem. Liberation has come at a heavy price. Friction with Azerbaijan, whose people were already enemies when they were called Tatars, exploded into war with the removal of the restraints imposed by Soviet authority. Conflict over the issue of Karabagh caused Azerbaijan to impose a blockade on landlocked Armenia, preventing the delivery of energy and supplies. Currently a halt in hostilities is in effect, while brokers attempt the seemingly impossible task of negotiating a peace acceptable to all sides.

No longer subject to Communist control, Etchmiadzin has been freed to establish new policies in accordance with its own interests. It was an immediate sign of the new order when the once-scorned Tricolor, which had provoked the split of a national community, was raised in 1991 to fly over the parking lot of St. Paul's during picnic festivities.

Even more amazing developments lay ahead. In April 1995, following the death of Catholicos Vazgen, Catholicos Karekin II of the Cilician See was elected to occupy the throne of St. Gregory at Etchmiadzin, thereby becoming His Holiness Karekin I, Catholicos of All Armenians. Three months later Archbishop Aram Keshishian was elected Catholicos of the Cilician See.

On a triumphal tour of the United States early in 1996, His Holiness Karekin was accorded a joyous welcome from old friends and new ones alike. Those seeking concrete indications that church unity was soon to be achieved had to content themselves with symbolic union. Responding to the invitation of His Eminence Archbishop Mesrob Ashjian of the eastern Prelacy, His Holiness visited St. Illuminator's Cathedral (Cilician See) while in New York City, accompanied by the Primates of the Eastern, Western, and Canadian dioceses (Etchmiadzin). During this unprecedented visit, Catholicos Karekin

> blessed the gathered faithful, specifically remembering the many times he has prayed and spoken from this altar, first as Prelate, and later as Catholicos of Cilicia. . . . He emphasized the unity of the Armenian Church and the importance of mutual love.[608]

At first it was hoped that the Catholicos, by force of his dynamic personality and thorough knowledge of the historical, psychological, and ideological background to the estrangement, would be able to bring about a miraculous dissolution of years of suspicion and mistrust. Those hoping for quiet progress behind the scenes were heartened by the decision of Archbishop Khajag Barsamian, Diocesan Primate, on May 3, 1996, to "allow clergymen serving under the jurisdiction of the Catholicosate of Cilicia to participate in liturgical functions" under certain conditions.[609]

Old antipathies have been revived, however, and the promise of a new era has faded. A dispute with the Prelacy evoked the Primate's decision not to participate or to allow his parishes to participate in the welcome accorded to Catholicos Aram of the Cilician See on his tour of the eastern United States in autumn of 1997.

The words of Eliza Sachaklian's favorite recitation, which she could still recite from memory just a few weeks before her death in 1990 at age ninety-

---

608. *Outreach,* vol. XVIII, no. 7, January 1996, p. 2.
609. *Armenian Reporter,* May 11, 1996.

eight, come to mind: "Our nation is one, our language is one, our church is one, why should not our hearts be one?"

Whether or not hearts can ever be one is questionable, people being what they are. Yet, as the inaugural and second meetings of the Armenian Assembly revealed, the American-born and/or educated generations associated with Armenian institutions in the United States are far more alike than unlike— even with the residual cultural, political, and ideological positions inherited from their elders. It is clear, also, that the Armenian communities—certainly the older ones in the northeastern part of the United States—themselves are no longer the same. There was previously a sense of immediacy—even responsibility—that seems to be much less compelling today. In earlier years, the passions and convictions as to what was best for Armenia and the Armenian people were constantly being sustained by an assortment of Armenian political parties and a press that gave voice to practically every point of view that existed. In the smaller communities today the political parties and their presses no longer play a dominant role. For example, in Syracuse, I may be the sole remaining subscriber to the ARF Armenian-language periodical, now a weekly instead of a daily.

This contraction from the world of Armenian affairs may insulate the small communities from outside conflicts, but the loss of linkage poses another danger—that of alienation. So long as the isolated community can see itself as part of the larger Armenian community, it will remain alive. It may never again feel "like one family," but at least there can be a shared concern for the family's heritage.

Appendix

The remarkable Aramtagh document which supplied much information for this study merits detailed description. The text, entirely handwritten in Armenian, is contained in a clothbound composition book with imprinted page numbers.

Occupying pages 1 and 3 through 8 is "Artsanakroutian dedrag Divrigi Ormutagh kiughi Sourp Prgcha Varzharani Ousoumnagan Miutyan usgusyal 1917 Hounvar 17-in ardagark badgamavoragan zhoghovin." Getronagan Varchoutiun, Watervliet, N.Y. ("Minute Book of Holy Redeemer School's Educational Society of Ormutagh Village, Divrig Beginning 1917 January 17 with the Special Representative Meeting." The title page bears a stamp in red ink with the legend: "Holy Redeemer School's Educational Society of Aramtagh Village, Divrig. Founded June 1, 1911, America."

Sarah Minasian has informed me (August 6, 1992) that Ormutagh and Aramtagh villages were very close to each other. They shared the same church and school. The minutes recorded sessions held in 1917 in Watervliet, New York (according to the title page) on January 17, March 29, May 22, July 4, and July 7, and are signed by the secretary, Garabed Giragosian. At that time, Giragosian, son of Minas, lived in Watervliet. Thereafter, the writing is by Khachig Minasian, who lived in Syracuse.

Odd-numbered pages 9 through 67 provide "A record of compatriots from Aramtagh village of Divrig, beginning in 1905, written by Kh. Minasian in 1955." This segment supplies brief biographical sketches of fifty male immigrants from Aramtagh. In somewhat irregular fashion, it gives the dates of their arrival in the United States, where they lived, what kind of work they did, when they married or were reunited with their wives and families, where they died and were buried.

On page 77 under the heading "Membership List" there are ten names, apparently members of the Holy Redeemer School's Education Society who lived in Watervliet.

On page 79 under the heading "List of members of the Syracuse branch" there are twenty-four names, with notations of three departures.Pages 101, 103, and 105 provide a tabulation of the population of Aramtagh by name of householder and number of people in each household. A note indicates that the list was prepared on August 27, 1916. There were 86 households and 497 people in the village in 1915.

The wealth of those 86 households is detailed on page 107, which records the number of items and value of properties such as livestock, tools, jewelry, and even firewood. Is it possible that Minasian hoped to have this information on record with the prospect of demanding reparations?

The heading on page 109 indicates that the Aramtagh society was reorganized on July 1, 1919. Members are listed by name and the amount of dues paid, totaling $890. A notation at the bottom informs us that $1,075 has been sent to aid the refugees.

Last, on pages 127 and 129, is a list of thirty-six Aramtagh "pilgrims" who had died since 1908, with date and place of death. The record ends in 1959.

Index